THE LIFE AND DEATH OF
MARY, QUEEN OF SCOTS

THE LIFE AND DEATH OF
MARY, QUEEN OF SCOTS

JAN-MARIE KNIGHTS

AMBERLEY

First published 2024

Amberley Publishing
The Hill, Stroud
Gloucestershire, GL5 4EP

www.amberley-books.com

British Library Cataloguing in Publication Data.
A catalogue record for this book is available from the British Library.

ISBN 978 1 3981 1765 5 (hardback)
ISBN 978 1 3981 1766 2 (ebook)

1 2 3 4 5 6 7 8 9 10

Typesetting by SJmagic DESIGN SERVICES, India.
Printed in the UK.

Contents

Introduction

Although she died more than four centuries ago, the tumultuous life of Mary Stuart, Queen of Scots (1542–1587), as viewed through contemporary letters, diaries and accounts, continues to fascinate: Queen of Scotland at six days old; Queen of France at sixteen; widowed three days before her eighteenth birthday. Grieving, she wrote of her husband Francis II: 'His image comes to me, The sweet smile on his face ...True love cannot pretend, And though we are apart, Grows no less in my heart.'

In the summer of 1561, a year after her husband's death, Mary sailed to Scotland. During the next few years she dealt with recalcitrant nobles and clergy, presided over the trial of a dead earl in a coffin and fell passionately in love with the English nineteen-year-old Henry, Lord Darnley, whom she married. A year later, her husband plotted to kill her favourite minister in her presence while she was six months pregnant; a cocked pistol held against her swollen body. Months later, an explosion rocked Edinburgh in the middle of the night. Darnley's residence had been razed to its foundations. Citizens searched the ruins for his body, puzzled to find him lying dead in the orchard without a mark upon him.

Placards sprouted in the city accusing the Earl of Bothwell of murdering the king. Tried, he was found innocent. But after he had supposedly abducted and raped her, Mary scandalised her lords by marrying Bothwell and her subjects accused her of being an adulteress and murderess. In a confrontation with her nobles at Carberry Hill in 1567, she surrendered to them and was subsequently imprisoned at Lochleven Castle. She signed an abdication document and miscarried twins while, to great celebrations, her one-year-old son was crowned James VI at Stirling.

Helped to escape by a lovelorn admirer in 1568, Mary raised an army, only for it to be defeated by her regent half-brother, James Stewart, Earl of Moray. She fled into England, never to return: the result of various intrigues around and by her in the belief she was rightfully Queen of England. In 1586 Mary consented to ascend the English throne once Queen Elizabeth was assassinated; this projected death brought about her own. Aged only forty-four years, she was executed at Fotheringhay Castle on 8 February 1587.

'Ladies fair and goodly men arrayed'

1503–1542

Delighted citizens were charmed as their handsome king, James IV, rode through Edinburgh's tapestried streets with his new queen, pretty thirteen-year-old Margaret Tudor, eldest daughter of King Henry VII and Queen Elysabeth, riding pillion behind him. The causeway, doorways and windows were crammed with cheering people watching the pair ride past: the king wore a cloth-of-gold jacket edged with black fur and a violet satin waistcoat over a shirt sparkling with jewels and pearls; his bride in a lustrous cloth-of-gold gown trimmed with black velvet. Before them, Adam Hepburn, Earl of Bothwell, bore the Sword of State, scabbarded in purple velvet; the words 'God my defende' picked out in pearls along its length.

They paused to watch the pageants: Mercury giving the golden apple to Paris, who gave it to Venus; the Archangel Gabriel saluting the Virgin Mary and the Four Virtues wreathed in thistle flowers and red roses. A fountain at the Mercat Cross dispensed free wine. They dismounted to pray at Holyrood Abbey and when they left the abbey the king, to the crowd's shouted approval, held a protective arm around his bride. Later that day, James Hamilton was created Earl of Arran for bringing about the marriage.

Next day, 8 August 1503, the Sword of State borne before him, the king entered the abbey wearing a robe of 'white damask figured with gold over his scarlet hose, a jacket with slashes of crimson satin' and cuffs of black velvet, a gold waistcoat above a shirt embroidered with gold thread and his own sword scabbarded at his side. His black velvet bonnet was looped by a great ruby glowing in the sunlight. Queen Margaret entered wearing a magnificent crown, her strawberry-blonde hair flowing down the back of her 'robe of white and gold damask bordered with crimson velvet'. Trumpets blew, and the king doffed his hat and led his queen to the High Altar. After she had been anointed by Robert Blackadder, Archbishop of Glasgow, assisted by Thomas Savage, Archbishop of York, James himself handed her the sceptre.

At the banquet afterwards, with the pair seated under a single cloth of estate, James commanded his queen be served first: to trumpets in came a gilt boar's head, a fair piece of brawn with mustard and a ham accompanied with twelve dainty dishes. When later the hall was cleared for dancing, the royal couple danced together before dancing with other lords and ladies.

On Saint Lawrence's Day, after mass, James knighted forty-one men to be his wife's own knights who jousted in her honour in the Basse Court-turned-tiltyard before the windows of the castle. An English spectator wrote of 'robust highland men ... with targets and two-handed swords to the music of their bagpipes, fighting as in a true battle to the admiration of English and French who had never seen men so ambitious of wounds...'

Thus began Margaret Tudor's life in Scotland with a king who did all to please his wife. The court poet, William Dunbar, welcomed her as 'the flower of our delight' and his poems reveal the jousts and water pageants and other gaieties of James' court. King James was a cultured man who encouraged international trade. Craftsmen flocked to Scotland from all over Europe as his interests ranged from science and architecture to printing and shipbuilding. In July 1506, James sailed in his newly built ship, named *Margaret* in honour of his wife, which weighed around 600–700 tons, cost around £8,000 and was painted with red Tudor roses. Treasury accounts also reveal he wore an iron chain around his waist as a self-imposed penance for those of his actions which had caused his father's death.

Queen Margaret gave birth to a prince, named James, at Holyrood on 21 February 1507. His father, 'grieved sore' that his wife was 'brought near the last agony of death', set off on foot (though three horses carried his necessities) on 10 March to make a pilgrimage to the shrine of St Ninian at Whithorn to pray for her recovery. Although he also returned on foot, having his shoes resoled on the way at a cost of 16*d*, his Italian minstrels proved less hardy and returned on hired horses. Finding Margaret convalescent on his return on 23 March, he prepared to host a celebratory joust. James' tournaments were famous throughout Europe, as was his military prowess, spread by visiting nobles. One such was the Frenchman Antoine d'Arces, Sieur de la Bastie, who jousted as the White Knight in honour of his queen. He had participated in the coronation tournaments and at another held in January 1507 when James awarded him 400 crowns and wine with which to ease his horse's feet.

News of the prince's birth and James' challenge as the Black Knight were sent out together, set for mid-June in Edinburgh Castle's 'Garden of Patience' wherein on the Tree of Hope, with its 216 leaves of Pleasure, flowers of Nobleness and fruit of Honour, hung five shields, each bearing the name of a knight and his lady.

Jean Damian, the king's alchemist, boasted to Scottish envoys leaving for France that he would reach Paris long before them. He buckled on a pair of wings and launched himself from the battlements of Stirling Castle – and immediately plummeted. When rescuers found him, they were amazed to find him alive. As they carried him into the palace, having broken his thigh, he assured them he should never have used hen feathers.

Historians have speculated whether the Black Knight's Black Lady was Ellen or Margaret More, both of whom were African ladies-in-waiting, but the accounts show the Black Lady wore black gauze around her shoulders and arms and black chamois gloves. On the day, wearing a gown of Flanders damask ornamented with gold flowers and edged with yellow and green taffeta, she arrived in a red-flowered taffeta-covered chariot 'pulled by a unicorn'. Accompanying her were two lady attendants wearing green taffeta gowns edged with yellow along with two squires, William Ogilvy and Alexander Elphinstone, wearing white damask half-coats. James was well known for his romantic streak so perhaps the Black Lady was Alexander's betrothed, Elizabeth Barley. They married in August that year. For her marriage gift, Queen Margaret gave Elizabeth a velvet and satin gown, a featherbed, Holland sheets, blankets and a bedcover.

Little Prince James died on 21 February 1508 at Stirling Castle. The queen being pregnant, James arranged another great jousting in May to raise her spirits. Bernard Stewart, Lord d'Aubigny (of the Darnley Stewarts and kin of the Earl of Lennox) arrived at court. Margaret knew him as the famous warrior who had commanded her father's French troops at Bosworth Field; he was honoured by being seated at the king's own table. This time the Black Lady, wearing a green dress, was carried in a chair by fourteen men from the castle to the tiltyard. The Black Knight and his horse entered completely attired half-and-half in black and gold, including his sword belt, scabbard and shield. At the last banquet at Holyrood, the evening ended when a cloud descended from the hall ceiling and whisked the Black Lady away to be 'seen no more', a special effect created by Andrew Forman, then Bishop of Moray, called by Robert Lindsay an 'ingramanciar' who 'caused men to see things appear which was not'.

More sorrow followed: on 15 July, the queen gave birth to a baby daughter who died a few days after her christening, and in April the following year she lost her father. Her brother ascended the English throne and was crowned King Henry VIII. At Holyrood, on 20 October 1509, she gave birth to a prince who was christened Arthur but only survived nine months. Her solicitous husband took her on progress to Aberdeen in spring 1511. Before they arrived, citizens in a flurry exiled all the pigs from the town and hung the high street with arras, birch boughs and holly, covering the ground with herbs and leaves. To cannon-shot and minstrels 'blowing to the sky', richly dressed burghers greeted Margaret while four young men in velvet gowns bore a canopy of crimson velvet over her head. And 'great was the press of people and pleasant pageants played prettily' while the commons shouted their welcome to her, full of 'mirth and joy, for at their cross abundantly ran wine...' In October, James journeyed to Newhaven Dock to see the launch of his newest ship, a carrack called the *Great Michael*, the largest warship of its time, with four masts. It weighed around 1,000 tons and had twenty-four bronze cannon, three basilisks and thirty smaller guns.

On Easter Eve, 10 April 1512, Margaret gave birth to a son at Linlithgow. James wrote joyfully to his cousin King John of Denmark that his son was christened James on the 'Feast of the Lord's Resurrection' and gave 'promise of health and of succeeding after us'.

In August, Henry VIII joined the Pope's Holy League against France and, calling himself the Pope's soldier, displayed increasing hostility towards Scotland, despite James' complaints to the Pope. Convinced Henry would try to invade Scotland if he was successful in France, James welcomed the French ambassador aboard the *Great Michael* at Blackness three months later. The Auld Alliance between Scotland and France was renewed; King Henry, meanwhile, procured papal permission for James to be excommunicated for supporting France.

Henry VIII sailed to Calais at the end of June 1513. Appointing the sixty-nine-year-old Earl of Surrey Lord Lieutenant of the North, he left him orders to assemble a northern army. Meanwhile, James by 27 July had ordered a fleet of twenty ships to sail to provide aid to the French. Pandering to James' 'romantic notion of honour', Queen Anne, the wife of Louis XII, sent him a 'love-letter' imploring him to be her 'true knight' and strike a blow for her on English soil, even if just a foot over the border. She sent him a token from her own finger, a gold and turquoise ring, along with 14,000 crowns. James sent out a call to arms to all Scots liable for military service, which was taken up with enthusiasm. His wife, upset at his responding to the French queen's appeal, tearfully beseeched him to desist, asking, 'Why do you prefer the Queen of France over my tears and your son?'

Tears rolling down her cheeks, Margaret watched her husband leave for Edinburgh from a tower window. The army left Edinburgh on 19 August. Three days later it had crossed the River Tweed near Coldstream. In atrocious weather, with a great cold wind and continuous rain, James strategically captured the castles of Wark, Norham, Chillingham, Etal and Ford, creating a clear 8-mile supply line. The Earl of Surrey sent Rouge Croix Pursuivant to Ford Castle on Sunday 4 September with a challenge for the armies to meet in battle on Millfield Plain. James replied through his own herald the next day: it would be to his 'joy and comfort to give battle'. He demolished Ford Castle and moved his army across the river. On 7 September the English army arrived at Wooler Haghe, where they had sight of the Scots encamped upon Flodden Hill with trenches and gun-pits on three sides 'so there was no passage nor entrance unto him but one way where was laid marvellous and great ordnance of guns'. Rouge Croix was sent with a new message: though James had said he was ready to fight, he had unchivalrously withdrawn to ground more like a fortress. Refused entrance to the camp, the herald was given a response: 'It was not for an earl to dictate to a king.'

The next day, Surrey took the English army in array from the west bank of the River Till, which led up to Millfield, and crossed to the east side, encamping for the night at Barmoor Wood, 2 miles north of Barmoor Castle; this gave him a short supply line to Berwick. Lord Lindsay of the Byres, elected as spokesman for the Scottish nobles who had held council, told James they considered he had fulfilled his part and should withdraw with his forces. James countered they could leave but, if he had to, he would fight the English alone. Asked to watch the fighting from a distance, he refused. When told he was being rash, he responded by arranging his force in battle array and appointed 'ten shadows' to impersonate him.

Next morning, the English continued wending north. Around eleven o'clock they passed over Twizel Bridge and turned southwards to march down the west bank of the river. The Lord Admiral, Surrey's son Lord Thomas Howard, led the vanguard and artillery; the Earl of Surrey followed in the rearward. At this point the English were between the Scots and the border; equally the English army was enclosed between the Rivers Tweed and Till. Nearing Branxton, they were surprised to find the Scots nearer than they expected for, silent and unseen, they had moved forward onto Branxton Hill, 2 miles north of Flodden Hill. Lord Thomas, 'seeing the great power of the Scots', despatched an urgent message to his father to bring up the rearward without delay. As the distance closed, the Scottish 'shot sharply their guns' while the English artillery, trying to advance and shoot uphill, was unable to return successful fire.

Accounts relate that in complete silence the Scots descended the hill to meet with the English army. Robert Lindsay wrote: 'The vanguards joined together, to wit Earl of Huntley, Lord Home with the borderers and countrymen ... and on the other side the Lords Percy and Westmorland with the English borderers ... and fought cruelly ... the Earl of Huntley's Highland men with their bows and two-handed swords defeated the Englishmen ...' Meanwhile, the two great battles 'led by Lord Howard and the Earl of Surrey came furiously upon the king's battle, streams of blood ran on either side so abundantly that all the fields and waters were made red.'

Night fell. Fighting faltered and stopped. 'The Earl of Surrey and his son retired a little from the field but stood on their feet that night until morn and found they had won the field. They searched the field for noblemen, and more especially, the king, finding many who looked like him clad in his coat armour', including two of his guard, and James' favourite, Alexander Elphinstone. William Drummond intimated in his own account that Lord Elphinstone's body was mistaken for the king's, 'having heaps of slaughtered bodies environing his'. Whatever the truth, the corpse was riddled with arrows, the neck gashed by a bill-stroke and the left hand almost sundered from the body. Identified as the body of the king, it was taken to Berwick; however, men noted that 'it wore not the iron belt'.

The tragic news reached Edinburgh the day after the battle and spread quickly through Scotland. In every town, village and hamlet women bewailed the deaths of their husbands, fathers, sons and brothers. In Edinburgh, the Provost created a guard of twenty-four men, ordered fortifications and issued proclamations: men were to assemble in military array to defend the city if the common bell tolled; women who filled the streets weeping were 'to repair to their work and be not seen upon the street clamouring and crying', and women of the better sort were to repair to church and pray. There was immense relief when the Earl of Surrey disbanded his army, although English incursions continued, laying waste to border villages and towns and destroying crops and stores.

Seventeen-month-old James was crowned in the chapel royal at Stirling on 21 September. Margaret was appointed regent provided she remained unmarried. Her council included James Beaton,

Archbishop of Glasgow (who in 1522 became Archbishop of St Andrews after the death of Andrew Forman) and earls Huntly and Angus. She appointed the poet Gavin Douglas as her personal adviser. (In his *The Palace of Honour* he had described Margaret thus: 'Borne within a golden chair, over-fret with pearls ... drawn by hackneys all milk white, was set a queen as lily sweetly fair, in purple robe hemmed with gold ... a diadem ... sat on the tresses of her golden hair.' She gifted him the prayer book her father had given her.) That autumn, sixty-four-year-old Archibald Douglas, 5th Earl of Angus, nicknamed 'Bell the Cat', died and was succeeded by his twenty-three-year-old grandson Archibald, described by his uncle Gavin as a 'young witless fool'. He was a widower, although many thought he had secretly married Janet Stewart of Traquair.

In England the Earl of Surrey was created Duke of Norfolk, his son taking the earldom. In a calculated heraldic insult, the Howard arms were augmented with the Lion of Scotland pierced through the mouth by an arrow. Across the Channel, thirty-eight-year-old Queen Anne died from kidney disease at Blois Palace. Peace with England was negotiated.

At Stirling Castle on 30 April 1514, Margaret gave birth to a son who was christened Alexander. Then, rashly, bewitched by a handsome face and courtly manner, Margaret fell madly in love and secretly married Archibald Douglas on 6 August. When he realised his wife would lose the regency as a result of their marriage, he ceased to show her any affection, loyalty or respect. Her brother, gleefully receiving her many letters of complaint, beguiled her with a glittering vision of the comfort and riches awaiting her in England and proposed himself as Governor of Scotland. Other heads thought differently: many favoured the king's nearest male relative, John Stewart, Duke of Albany, who had lived in France all of his life, but he and James IV had corresponded regularly; younger nobility favoured the already present James Hamilton, Earl of Arran. Both were grandsons of James II and Queen Mary of Guelders but the former had the better claim.

Duke Albany's response to Scottish overtures was lukewarm and he stayed in France. In January 1515 he attended the coronation of King Francis I, at which he wore an outfit of white satin brocaded with silver, adorned with silver birdwings which fluttered as he moved, and a white-plumed bonnet of white velvet. He reluctantly left France, landing at Dumbarton on 26 May. Queen Margaret received him with due honour. But Parliament directed the princes should be placed under his charge aided by four guardian lords.

When those lords arrived at Edinburgh Castle, crowds were thronging the streets, agog to see what Margaret would do. The young, pregnant queen stood within the iron gates holding her eldest son's hand. Alexander was in his nurse's arms behind her. As the lords came within yards of the gates, she bade them halt. They demanded she deliver her boys to them. Her husband standing to one side bleated for her to obey them. Instead, at her signal, the portcullis slammed down. The crowds cheered as defiantly she told the lords, 'Edinburgh Castle is ours, given to us by our sons' father.' A few days later, with Archibald having already abandoned her for his own castle of Tantallon, Margaret fled with her boys to Stirling Castle, leaving behind a message: if the duke came with an armed force she would set King James upon the walls, crowned and sceptred, so all could see how he made war upon his king. When the duke arrived on 4 August with 7,000 men and artillery, he found Margaret and her son waiting at the gates with the keys. Everyone else had fled. The duke left the princes at Stirling with the Earl Marischal and Lords Fleming and Borthwick and proposed to escort Margaret to Edinburgh Castle. She loudly declaimed to the populace that she feared her princes might disappear like Edward IV's children.

Nearer her lying-in, the queen was granted permission to enter seclusion at Linlithgow. She, with Angus, slipped out one night, journeying to Tantallon Castle to await Lord Home bringing her sons. Instead, he was caught by Albany and Margaret and Archibald fled to the border leaving behind, to her distress, all her jewels and clothes. Margaret fell ill but recovered when Lord Dacre arrived post-haste at Coldstream Priory with a safe-conduct to escort them to his family residence, Morpeth Castle. Margaret's baby had other plans. Going into labour, Margaret was rushed to Harbottle Castle on 5 October. Dacre insisting no Scot would be allowed in – man or woman – meant Margaret endured a painful forty-eight-hour labour without women attendants while borderers made hourly assaults on the castle. On 10 October she sent a letter to Albany, informing him of baby Margaret's arrival and blaming him for putting her in fear of her life and causing her to flee Scotland. Two letters arrived: one from the Privy Council; the other from Albany. Both offered to allow her to remain her boys' guardian if she promised not to remove them out of Scotland. She refused.

In November, Margaret recovered enough to move to Morpeth Castle before having a relapse. So ill was she that some feared the worst. Archibald chose this moment to return to Scotland to make peace with Albany and live with his mistress (or wife). Margaret would never forgive him. When Lord Dacre gathered the courage to inform her Alexander had died at Stirling Castle on 18 December, she fell into a fever, ranting Albany was 'another Richard III'. When she finally recovered, she travelled on to London. All summer long she complained about Albany, who continued to send her fine clothes, jewels and all her rents. She was able to attend in splendour the grand tournament, rich pageants and other entertainments her brother put on in her honour. She stayed until the following May when news came Albany was travelling to France to visit his sick wife. Arriving in Scotland in June, she found Albany had instructed his council she could only visit her son under supervision.

In January 1518 Albany was still in France, first overseeing the moonlit marriage of his sister-in-law Madeleine to Lorenzo de' Medici at Amboise, and a few months later attending the christening of Dauphin Francis, with decorations designed by Leonardo da Vinci. Later, in the summer of 1520, he travelled to Rome where the Pope confirmed him as Protector of Scotland and James V. During this time, King Henry continually pressed his sister to reconcile with Archibald. She not only refused, saying her husband was using her money to live openly in one of her dower castles with Janet Stewart, but insisted she intended to divorce him. An outraged Henry sent a priest to threaten her with hell's fires. In defiance, she wrote to Albany asking him to help her cause with the Pope. Henry, trying to stop the action, wrote to the Pope that the duke intended to marry his sister to the destruction of his nephew.

Albany's absence from Scotland left a power vacuum and increasing hostility between the Earls of Angus and Arran. In April 1520, Arran and his adherents assembled near the archbishop's palace on Cowgate intending to kill Angus. Gavin Douglas, now Bishop of Dunkeld, went to Archbishop Beaton, asking him to use his influence to calm the situation. The archbishop said, striking his breast, 'There is no remedy. Upon my conscience I cannot help it.' A faint clink revealed he was wearing armour. Gavin replied, 'How now, my lord, methinks your conscience clatters.' When Archibald entered the city, he was assailed by citizens offering him their weapons. Directing they barricade all the wynds ending in the High Street, he took a band of men to wait opposite Blackfriars Wynd, thus enticing Hamilton's men to rush at him in a narrow space. The first few were easily struck down, driving the rest into retreat. The Earl of Arran, with his son James, fought their way across the High Street, escaping across the North Loch causeway into open countryside. The archbishop escaped to Linlithgow, saved from death by Gavin, who had stopped soldiers dragging him out from behind the altar of Blackfriars Church. Arran's party being swept from the streets, the skirmish, which saw seventy men killed, was named 'Cleanse-the-Causeway'.

The Duke of Albany unwillingly returned to Scotland. At the state entry into Edinburgh on 3 December 1521, Queen Margaret delivered the castle keys to him, signifying government was returned into his hands. Angus stirred up trouble by telling King Henry his sister was 'overtender' with the duke. The king sent Clarenceux King of Arms to accuse the duke in the February Parliament of inciting Margaret to divorce her lawful husband 'for what corrupt intent God knows' but presumably to marry her, kill her son and usurp the crown. The duke was known as a good-natured man but in Scotland he was frequently seen snatching off his cap to fling it into the fire to release pent-up exasperation. At the dinner that night, the duke told the herald not only was he happily married but marvelled King Henry should think so ill of his sister. Angus disappeared for a while into exile and his uncle Gavin died of plague in London.

In August 1522, King Henry ordered the Earl of Shrewsbury to enter Scotland with a large force, which was repelled, as was the fleet of English ships in the Firth of Forth. Albany began preparing for war, and Margaret secretly revealed his plans to her brother. Finding the Scots preferred to defend than attack, Queen Margaret negotiated a truce in September although incursions carried on in the borders. Appointing a Council of Regency, Albany sailed back to France on 24 October upon hearing his wife was again ill. While visiting her son, Margaret described to him the delights of the English court and the adventures of escaping. One day, he was so agitated that he stabbed one of his guards in the arm attempting to 'break his captivity'.

In August 1523, Margaret wrote to the Earl of Surrey to march on Edinburgh to help her son assume full power. While burning Jedburgh, Surrey was surprised at news Albany had landed in Scotland with a fleet of 87 vessels, 4,000 men-at-arms, 1,000 arquebusiers, 600 horse and artillery. In the parliament convened immediately, Albany boldly proclaimed that the Scots should 'revenge all the hurts done to us'. He won the day. The army marched out of Glasgow on 22 October. The weather turned bitter with hail and snow. Artillery got bogged down in the mud. Scotsmen decided they had no desire to invade England. On 4 November Albany was forced to withdraw and make peace. Recriminations began being whispered against him. Hearing his beloved wife was ill once more, the duke returned to France in May, spending his last day talking quietly with the king.

On 22 August 1524, James, now twelve years old, rode through cheering Edinburgh crowds to the Tolbooth to open parliament. Wearing his crown, with the support of Arran, he formally took hold of full royal authority. He named his mother his chief councillor. Her brother wrote to insist she reconcile with Archibald, who secretly came from France into Scotland. She refused. Rumour was rife she was madly in love with the Master of the Royal Artillery, Henry Stewart, the twenty-nine-year-old son of Lord Evandale.

During the early hours of 23 November, Edinburgh citizens were rudely awoken by the loud tramp of marching feet as hundreds of armed men, led by Angus, converged on the Mercat Cross. A panicked queen ordered the cannon to be fired upon them. As Angus withdrew, Margaret and James rushed from Holyrood by torchlight to the security of the castle. Angus retreated to Dalkeith Castle and, using funds from King Henry, secretly began gathering support by which Margaret was pressured into admitting him to the Regency Council in February 1525. Insisting James was removed from his mother and restored to the quarterly guardianship of four earls, he arranged to take the first – and only – rotation and made James and his mother virtual prisoners, spreading a rumour Margaret was no longer seen in public because she was pregnant by her lover. Throughout the next few years there were several unsuccessful attempts to liberate James. In one endeavour, to James' great grief, the Earl of Lennox was killed in cold blood. His ten-year-old heir, Mathew, and his younger brothers were sent by their mother into the care of their great-uncle Robert, Lord d'Aubigny in France.

In December 1527 Margaret found the Pope had nine months earlier granted her a divorce. On 3 March 1528 she secretly married Henry Stewart at Stirling Castle. As soon as Angus knew of it, he imprisoned her new husband and removed his twelve-year-old daughter Margaret from her mother's care. Ironically, Henry VIII castigated his sister for making her daughter 'base-born'.

At the end of May, James, now sixteen, stole into the stables of Falkland Palace at dusk disguised as a guardsman. Leaving unseen, he galloped all night to reach Stirling Castle, arriving before sunrise. There, he slept with the castle keys under his pillow. Next day he outlawed all of the House of Douglas, excepting his half-sister, and bestowed upon the freed Henry Stewart the title Lord Methven.

James spent the next few years eradicating lawlessness, removing from baronial courts the 'jurisdiction of life and limb' and power of sentencing to '[drowning] pits and gallows' by creating a separate Supreme Court of Justice. In October 1532 Angus led an English force into Scotland causing James to create four divisions of fighting men to defend the marches in rotation.

The following year, James invited papal envoy Silvester Darionis on a hunting trip to Atholl where Earl John had built an enormous glass-windowed castle made 'of green timber and birches' in a meadow. A drawbridge over a deep, 30-foot-wide moat led the party through a great gateway with two round towers. Inside the castle, rooms were brightly lit, the walls colourful with tapestries and glossy silk arras, and green turf and flowers made the carpet. For three days the company stayed, drinking ale and fine red and white wines and eating dainty dishes with fine napery: 'almond bread, gingerbread, beef, mutton, lamb, rabbit, heron, swan, wild goose, partridges and plover, duck and peacock, wildfowl and salmon, trout, perch, pike and eels' and sweet confections for desserts. James wore his favourite Highland dress for the hunting, in which 600 animals – deer, wolf, foxes and wild cats – were slain. When the party departed, the castle was set on fire; James told Silvester that Scottish custom was to burn places built to sleep in.

Meanwhile, Albany wrote to inform James he was at Nice, awaiting the arrival of his niece Catherine de' Medici, to convey her (and her embroideries, jewels, rich clothes, velvet bedcurtains and magnificent pearls) to Marseilles for her marriage to Henri, second son of King Francis. The betrothed teenagers, both fourteen years old, were married by her cousin Pope Clement VII on 28 October 1533. Catherine, sparkling and witty, wore a brocade gown decorated with pearls and diamonds, her headdress flowers entwined in her hair. The bridegroom, sullen at marrying a mere duchess (or already in love with the widowed Dianne de Poitiers), was already known for his proficiency in tilting, fencing and tennis. Albany began negotiating a marriage for James with the French king's daughter, Magdalene. However, King Francis said his daughter, showing signs of consumption, was too frail. He suggested Marie de Bourbon, daughter of the Duke of Vendome. Portraits were exchanged.

By now, James had enjoyed the charms of many mistresses and had many natural children: Lord James by Elizabeth Shaw was five years old; James by Margaret Erskine (married to Sir Robert Douglas of Lochleven) was three, as was Lord John by Elizabeth Carmichael; Robert by Euphemia Elphinstone was one, as was Lady Jean Stewart (who later married Archibald, Earl of Argyll).

Sad that Albany had died before seeing the marriage he had arranged come to fruition, James sailed to Dieppe on 1 September 1536, where he borrowed clothes to look like one of his servitors and travelled with them covertly to St Quentin, to the Duke of Vendome's court. The princess recognised him – it was said by his red hair – and introduced him to her father, who entertained him with dancing and masques. He dined under a gold state canopy set with precious stones. Invited to Amboise by the royal family, he fell in love, and it was ardently returned. Early October, supposing he was incognito, he went to Paris where he bought clothes and jewels including a diamond wedding ring worth 1,100 crowns. French newsmongers soon discerned James and Magdalene were to marry, she ignoring her father's protestations. They were 'handfasted' at Blois on 25 November.

On New Year's Day 1537 they were married at Notre-Dame in the presence of all the royalty and nobility of France and Navarre. The bride wore a white damask gown, embroidered with gold. On her light brown hair, she wore a cap of pearls and diamonds. A string of large pearls fell below her jewelled belt. The bridegroom wore a sable-furred, dark-blue velvet mantle over white satin hose. At the magnificent wedding banquet, King James sent in a dessert course: covered cups containing 'fruits' from Scotland. Lids were lifted to reveal pieces of gold from the Scottish gold mines. After supper there were games, dances and masques, followed by days of banquets, feasts and plays, music and 'flying dragons in the air shooting fire at both their ends' as well as feats of magic by conjurers. The French king's wedding gifts to his son-in-law were two ships – the *Salamander* and the *Morischer* – and great horses from his stable with overgilt enamelled harness; to his daughter as much jewellery and gold, velvet, damask and satin cloth as she pleased.

To great excitement the young couple arrived at Leith on 19 May 1537. Fifty days later Magdalene died on 7 July in her husband's arms at Holyrood. The country plunged into mourning. She was buried in Holyrood Abbey. Her funeral pall cost £85 13s 9d.

During that summer, Queen Margaret was horrified to find her husband was living on her money in one of her castles with a new mistress – also called Janet Stewart – who was the daughter of the Earl of Atholl. She began divorce proceedings. Her son stopped them. Immediately she wrote to her brother to complain that her son was ill-treating her.

James asked King Francis for the hand of the recently widowed twenty-two-year-old Marie, Duchesse de Longueville, daughter of Claude de Lorraine and Antoinette de Bourbon, Duc and Duchesse de Guise. He had a rival in the recently widowed Henry VIII. The auburn-haired, hazel-eyed Marie protested she had no wish to remarry, still mourning her beloved husband Louis and a son who had died shortly after his father. And their other son, Francoys, was too young to leave; he would not be two until October.

Claude pressed Marie to marry Henry; Marie accepted James' proposal. Their proxy marriage took place at Chateaudun on 10 January 1538, with Lord James Maxwell placing the diamond ring on her finger. She wore a gown of white silk brocaded with gold. Six months later, Queen Marie embarked from Le Havre and arrived in Scotland on 16 June, formally received by the king at St Andrews the next day and welcomed by her subjects with pageants and plays. They were married in person on the following day. Celebrations ensued for forty days and afterwards James took his wife on a honeymoon tour of the Highlands, where they hunted and hawked, coming back for a tournament in September. Her state entry to Edinburgh took place in November. The royal couple enjoyed spending time at Stirling, Linlithgow and Falkland; at the latter James had a tennis court built. The king also enjoyed playing the lute and could read music. Those who heard him sing said his voice was 'rawky and harske'.

Marie's coronation was held on 22 February 1540 at Holyrood Abbey. The January household accounts show she received a black velvet gown, a crimson kirtle bordered with goldsmith work, and purple velvet for her robe royal. A gold crown with a sapphire was made for her, along with a sceptre of silver gilt, and her chairs were covered in purple velvet and fringed with purple ribbon. James had his gold crown remodelled, adding to it twenty diamonds, sixty-eight pearls, three large garnets and a great emerald. For the celebrations he personally devised a firework display with his master gunner.

Their first son, James, Duke of Rothesay, was born at St Andrews on 22 May 1540. Their second son was born and baptised Robert, Duke of Albany on 12 April 1541. He died nine days later; his brother followed at St Andrews the same day, 'only six hours between their deaths'. They were buried in the abbey next to Queen Magdalene.

Dowager Queen Margaret, after a stroke, died at Methven Castle on 18 October, a month short of her fifty-third birthday, leaving all her personal possessions to her daughter. She was buried in the Charterhouse in Perth in the royal vault alongside Queen Joan Beaufort, wife of King James I.

Although Scotland was tranquil, James quietly purchased armour, weapons and artillery alongside a personal outlay for a silver clamshell to house his tooth powder at a cost of £3 2s. In January 1542 James paid £400 to Sir David Murray for lands to create a new park beside Holyrood. In May, Queen Marie paid £6 10s for Venetian crimson damask for a gown, and purchased a yellow velvet kirtle. In June the king treated himself to twenty-four gold buttons and four rings: one with a diamond, one a ruby, one with three emeralds and a diamond, and a fourth with a large sapphire. In the same month Marie received a letter from her mother, Antoinette, advising her she should either wash her hair once a month or cut it short – greasy hair making it easier to catch colds – and if she was pregnant, she should allow herself to be bled.

To stop an escalation of warfare when serious fighting again broke out on the borders, James quickly sent envoys to London and York. King Henry asked for a meeting. James agreed but requested it be deferred while his wife was pregnant. On 24 August, Robert Bowes and Archibald Douglas crossed with an army into Scotland but, to their surprise, an army of Scots, led by the Earl of Huntly, was waiting for them at daybreak in full battle array at Haddon-Rigg about three miles east of Kelso. About 1500 English men were killed and 600 taken prisoner but Angus evaded capture.

In October, King Henry despatched Thomas, Duke of Norfolk to invade Scotland 'as far and as fiercely as possible'. He crossed the Tweed, burning Roxburgh, Kelso and several villages and hamlets, but by 28 October a lack of victuals and only puddle water to drink forced him to turn homewards. By 31 October James had assembled an army on Fala Moor, but once the nobles saw the English had recrossed the Tweed they refused to follow. James was forced to disband while Henry continued to order Sir Thomas Wharton, Sir Ralph Eure and Sir William Bulmer to burn Scottish towns, villages and abbeys, despoil the country, steal goods and take prisoners 'without respect of person'.

Raising a new force, James allowed rumours abroad that the army was going to enter England on 23 November on two fronts: one host via the West Marches, another on the East. A spy informed Sir Thomas it was a feint: the Scots intended to bring their whole power into the West Marches via Lanrigg. Wharton laid an ambush and engaged the betrayed Scottish army near Solway Moss. Intense fighting followed, with the Scots penned between the River Esk and the Solway bogs. Unable to flee, they were forced to surrender and many were taken prisoner, the most noble being sent to London.

News of the defeat reached Edinburgh while James was in council investigating the unlawful killing of Somerset Herald. He spent the first few days of December at Linlithgow Palace with his wife but was back in Edinburgh on 6 December, then left for Falkland, where he fell ill. Vomiting much and having 'a great lax', James died on 14 December aged thirty. As he would have passed Linlithgow en route to Falkland, he may just have seen his tiny baby daughter who, on the day of his death, was six days old. Now Queen of Scotland, she was baptised Mary.

'Like not this wooing'

Scotland, 1542–1548

On the day James V died, Cardinal David Beaton produced a notarised document, dated to five o'clock that morning, written in the presence of the king and eleven witnesses stating that James, 'afflicted only in body, but sound of mind and reason', appointed the cardinal, James Stewart, Earl of Moray (natural son of James IV by Janet Kennedy), twenty-eight-year-old George Gordon, 4th Earl of Huntley, and thirty-five-year-old Archibald 'the Red' Campbell, 4th Earl of Argyll as governors of his daughter and lawful protectors of the realm during her minority. All were pro-French and pro-Catholic, hence the exclusion of James Hamilton, 2nd Earl of Arran, deemed pro-English and pro-Reformist.

On 19 December John Dudley, Viscount Lisle wrote from the Borders to King Henry VIII that he felt it was not to the king's honour to continue to 'make war upon a dead body, or a widow, or a suckling his daughter'. At first Henry was not disposed to cease hostilities. On further reflection, he turned indulgent gaoler, releasing his noble Scottish prisoners from the Tower and lodging them with English gentlefolk. They were feasted and feted at court. To gain safe-conduct back to Scotland they gave oath to King Henry they would strive to orchestrate a marriage between their queen and Henry's son Edward and arrange for her to be brought up in England, while he ruled Scotland as governor on behalf of his great-niece.

21 December 1542: Lying in State

At Falkland the king's body was embalmed, leaded and placed in a wooden coffin. This was covered with black velvet with a white satin cross, fringed with black silk and placed in the chapel. The crowned effigy of the king dressed in his royal robes and regalia was placed on top. The carver completed the image by setting a lion above the crown. Several images of the red lion of Scotland against its golden field shone brightly in the candlelight against the chapel's black wall-hangings.

3 January 1543: Sole Regent

The Privy Council overturned the governorship proclaimed in December and appointed twenty-three-year-old James Hamilton, Earl of Arran, being heir-presumptive, sole governor. The new regent is married to Margaret Douglas, daughter of James, 3rd Earl of Morton, who is ten years older than her husband: a fraught marriage for Margaret has short periods of mental instability.

8 January 1543: Burial

The king's body, having been conveyed by ferry from Falkland Palace to Edinburgh, was received and attended by the Earls of Arran, Argyll, Marischal and Rothes. Preceding them, Cardinal Beaton followed by a long train of nobility and gentry wearing deep mourning carried lit torches. The long cortege passed through throngs of silent, tearful people lining each side of the causeway, paying respects to their beloved King James as he was carried to Holyrood Abbey. After the funeral mass, the king's body was placed in the vault alongside Queen Magdalene and his two baby sons.

20 February 1543: 'High advancement'

Charles, Duke of Suffolk, Lord Lieutenant on the Borders since January, wrote to Queen Marie he was pleased that she 'like a good and virtuous lady' had shown approval of a marriage between her daughter and Prince Edward, not only to the 'high advancement' of her daughter but 'thereby shall cease much trouble and effusion of blood'.

12–19 March 1543: Parliament

Wearing a cap of state, attired in French brown lined with white taffeta, girded by a purple belt, James, Earl of Arran opened Parliament in Edinburgh. The Three Estates of clergy, nobility and the burghs agreed to negotiate a treaty of marriage between Queen Mary and Prince Edward, with provisos: that Queen Mary be brought up in her own realm until her perfect age; that when she married and lived in England, Scotland would retain its name, liberties, privileges, freedoms, laws and college of justice; that government remained in the hands of the lord governor until lawful succession; and that perpetual peace be declared between the two realms.

Governor Arran also had an Act proclaimed at the Mercat Cross which allows all men and women to read the Scriptures in the 'vulgar tongue'.

22 March 1543: 'Heart too high'

At Linlithgow, the English ambassador, Sir Ralph Sadler, was given audience with Queen Marie. Shown her baby daughter, he remarked she was 'as goodly a child' as he had ever seen. He then asked whether the rumour was true that Marie was going to marry Mathew Stewart, Earl of Lennox. She told him having been a king's wife, her 'heart was too high to look any lower' and explained King Francis was sending him as his envoy; that talk of her marriage was as untrue as her father the Duc de Guise coming to Scotland with an army. The murmurs have not stopped. Twenty-six-year-old Lennox is deemed the handsomest and most distinguished of the gallants gracing the French court. And as lieutenant of the elite Scots Guard and captain of 100 lancers, he has seen heroic service in the French wars.

Sir Ralph, talking with Scottish noblemen, has found them unwilling for Queen Mary to be delivered into King Henry's hands; they say he will take Scotland for his own and they would rather suffer any extremity than be subject to England.

5 April 1543: French Aid

The Earl of Lennox, who had arrived at his own castle of Dumbarton on 30 March from France with two ships and a small company, was granted audience with Queen Marie today at Linlithgow. He declared to her that if King Henry invaded, King Francis would aid her with men, money and munitions.

18 April 1543: Warning

Inviting the Earls of Cassilis and Glencairn to dine with him at his lodgings, Sir Ralph offered news that Lennox was assembling a force of men and believed they should warn Arran to remove Queen Mary to the security of Edinburgh Castle so no one, not Lennox nor the cardinal, could seize her. They countered that not only was she well guarded but Arran was well aware Edinburgh was too near England, the English also desirous of abducting her.

20 May 1543: 'Avoid paying homage'

At Glasgow, in audience with Governor Arran, Sir Ralph was informed by him he had just returned from Dumbarton Castle hoping to see Lennox but was informed the earl had gone into the Highlands, 'hiding in rocks and mountains', to avoid paying homage to Arran as 'second person of the realm'.

2 July 1543: Proposal

Archibald, Earl of Angus sent word to Sir Ralph that Mathew, Earl of Lennox had requested to marry his daughter, Lady Margaret. Seeing she is also King Henry's niece, and living at his court, he has asked the ambassador to refer such marriage 'wholly to the king'.

26 July 1543: Safety

For months Queen Marie, scared for her daughter's safety, has sought permission to remove from Linlithgow to Stirling Castle. Now well furnished with ordnance and artillery for their safety, today Cardinal Beaton with the Earls of Huntly, Argyll, Lennox and Bothwell escorted them to the castle. They, with the Earls of Sunderland and Menteith and many lords and bishops, have sent a Bond to Governor Arran decrying his keeping Queen Mary and her mother imprisoned at Linlithgow and leaving them open to being abducted and transported to England. They demanded guardians be set about the queen, naming Lords Erskine, Graham, Lindsay and Livingston. They desire Arran in future to rule Scotland with a council of barons, excluding the Earl of Angus to stop him meddling in affairs.

The little queen is teething. The bonny baby looks set to take after her mother in stature.

25 August 1543: Ratification

On behalf of Queen Mary, Governor Arran ratified the Peace Treaties of Greenwich in the Abbey of Holyrood in the presence of most of the nobility. This will be sent to King Henry to ratify in his turn.

3 September 1543: Absolution

Today, in front of earls and lords, Governor Arran made a solemn oath to Cardinal Beaton that he embraced the Catholic faith and renounced his alliance to England. He was given absolution and received the sacrament. His eldest son, six-year-old James, has been sent to St Andrews to be tutored by the cardinal.

9–20 September 1543: Coronation

At ten o'clock on the morning of 9 September, Queen Mary, dressed in a miniature jewelled gown and crimson velvet mantle trimmed with ermine, was carried into the chapel royal at Stirling. All her nobles in attendance in procession, she was carried to the altar. Before her, the Earl of Arran held the crown, the Earl of Lennox the sceptre and the Earl of Argyll the sword.

When the cardinal opened her robes to anoint her with Holy Oil, the little queen began to cry. Her hand was gently moulded around the sceptre and her crown was held above her head. The queen continued to scream and cry while those present pledged their allegiance to her. Afterwards, the queen's nurse, Janet Sinclair, the wife of John Kempt, tucked the little queen back in her warm cradle while lords and ladies banqueted and danced in the great hall of the castle. It was noted some of the lords who favour England did not attend including the Earls of Angus, Glencairn and Cassilis and Lords Maxwell, Somerville, Ogilvy and Grey. Neither did Sir Ralph, too scared to leave Edinburgh after an attempt on his life.

Tournaments and masques followed the coronation with much 'dancing, singing, playing and merriness in court'. Much amusement ensued as Mathew, Earl of Lennox vied with thirty-one-year-old Patrick Hepburn, Earl of Bothwell, being both 'young, lusty gentlemen, fair and pleasant in sight', to woo Queen Marie. Every day they tried to outdo each other in fabulous clothes, 'showing off in dancing, shooting, singing, jousting and running of great horse at the lists and other games for the queen's pleasure'. Lennox, better practised in war than Bothwell, is 'a strong, handsome man, well formed in legs and arms' and much favoured by the ladies; the queen mother merely gives them both fair words.

The Earl of Glencairn, after giving Sadler a love letter from Lennox for Lady Margaret, revealed to him that Lennox believes he is next in line to the Scottish crown after Queen Mary and not third, for he says Arran's father's divorce and second marriage was invalid, which makes Arran illegitimate and a usurper to the title which is properly his; moreover, that Lennox would change his allegiance to King Henry if he was aided in gaining his proper position.

6–15 October 1543: Duped

A fleet of seven ships arrived at Dumbarton on 6 October, bringing with them the papal legate Marco Grimani, and two ambassadors from King Francis – Jacques, Seigneur de la Brosse and Jacques Menage. Before travelling to Stirling, they rested for a few days while overseeing the safe bestowal of the cargoes of money and munitions for safekeeping in the castle. Ambassadors and legate arrived at Glasgow on 11 October. Warned the Earl of Angus was on his way to stop their journey, they set off in the early hours in the morning in disguise, taking only a single servant and leaving the rest of their retinue to follow later.

Reaching Stirling on 15 October, the ambassadors were told Lennox had joined the 'English party and was betrothed to King Henry's niece'; and the money and munitions they brought were 'lost'. They said they could not credit the earl would so dishonour himself and not only lose his property in France but the favour of the French king. Queen Marie said it was purely for indignation at her receiving Governor Arran into friendship; the legate muttered, 'Thus goes the world!'

24 October 1543: Sad Conclusion

Invited by Queen Marie to court, the Earl of Lennox said in the presence of all that he would rather be dead than fail in his service to King Francis. Yet when asked to release the money and munitions he staunchly refused, saying they were safe in his hands. In an attempt to sway him in supporting the Franco-Scottish alliance, the queen mother even offered her daughter in marriage to him, which was refused. The ambassadors have sadly concluded that Lennox had come to Scotland merely to deprive Arran of the governorship if he could, and will inform King Francis the earl will do anything to become governor himself and be declared heir presumptive.

5 December 1543: Violation

News was brought into Parliament, which opened two days previously, that King Henry not only refused to ratify the peace treaties but had openly broken the peace: by his orders, five or six Scottish ships sailing to France had been seized and at Rye the Scottish ship *Boneaventure*, laden with the goods of Edinburgh merchants, had been impounded. Outraged at such wanton violation, the Estates agreed, to overwhelming acclaim, the marriage contract was nullified and the Auld Alliance should be renewed with France.

16 December 1543: War

The herald sent by King Henry declared in Parliament he intended to make war on Scotland unless they immediately fulfilled the terms of the treaties.

12 January 1544: Agreement

At Greenside chapel, the Earls of Angus and Lennox promised Governor Arran that they would, in all time coming, remain true and faithful to Queen Mary and that they would assist him in defending the realm and holy kirk.

7–26 March 1544: Bad Faith

The Earl of Lennox has complained by letter to Queen Marie that he is accused in murmurs of being the author of division in the realm and her greatest enemy. He asked for an 'unsuspect place where my innocence may be tried'. Yet almost immediately after, as if to prove the rumours true, he raised a force of 10,000 men intending to battle the cardinal and governor at Leith. After mediation he agreed to return to Glasgow but garrisoned the bishop's castle with his own men before secretly journeying to Dumbarton. Arran also proceeded to ignore the mediation and collected a force at Stirling. On 16 March, he, Cardinal Beaton, the Earls of Argyll and Bothwell and other lords marched on Glasgow. The town offered no resistance. The castle was battered with brass guns for the next ten days. Promised safe conduct, the garrison surrendered. As soon as they opened the gates many were shot, and eighteen men were taken captive, condemned to be publicly hanged on 1 April.

23 April 1544: Sack and Burn

Intelligence arrived from Newcastle that Edward Seymour, Earl of Hertford has received instructions dated 10 April from King Henry VIII to 'burn Edinburgh, beat down the castle and sack Holyrood House … sack and burn Leith and all the towns and villages round, putting man, woman and child to fire and sword where resistance is made'. Regarding St Andrews he is to 'leave no stone or stick stand by another ... sparing no creature alive', thereafter to burn and destroy Jedburgh. For their safety, the queen mother and infant queen will be removing to Dunkeld Palace, nearer to the Highlands.

4–18 May 1544: The Great Burning

The English army landed 2 miles west of Leith on 4 May. Marching towards the port in three battles with small artillery, they were intercepted in a valley near it by 5,000 to 6,000 Scottish horse and infantry. After exchanges of artillery, the Scots broke ranks and rode towards Edinburgh, while the English continued into Leith and commenced to build a strongly fortified camp bound by trenches. Next day, 200 sails swept into the haven and soldiers captured the fine ships in the harbour, including the *Unicorn*, built by the late king, and the *Salamander*, given to him by King Francis. Two days later the English army marched on Edinburgh. At a morning parley, Hertford told Adam Otterburn, provost of the city, that because the Scots often broke their promises he came not to treat but to take vengeance and commanded every man, woman and child should issue into the fields or be put to the sword. Otterburn replied that they would 'stand to their defence'.

That evening, English soldiers began their assault at Netherbow Port. Gaining entrance, they fired heavy artillery down the causeway to the castle, but they 'were answered with smart, well-directed fire'. Unable to reach the castle, they set fire to as many houses as they could, hackbutters and archers shooting fleeing people. Over the next three days, English horse and foot continued to burn the town, leaving not one house unburnt, including the palace and abbey of Holyrood.

On 8 May, while Arran was still in the west parts gathering a force to fight Lennox, English soldiers passed to Craigmillar, burning the castle and villages round it, laying waste to the country in a 7-mile arc around the capital. They left 'neither pile, village, nor house unburnt, nor stacks of corn' and seized goods and cattle Edinburgh citizens had conveyed out of town for safety.

Before the English fleet left Leith, they burnt the pier and harbour. Admiral Viscount Lisle then proceeded to burn every ship or boat he came across and every village, town or house found on either side of the Firth between Stirling and the sea. On 15 May every house in Leith was burned to the ground before the English army marched out, flames at their backs. They encamped for the night at Lord Seton's house and the following morning 'destroyed his orchards and gardens, the fairest in the country'. During the next two days both Haddington and Dunbar were burnt; the latter not until townsfolk had gone to bed, when 'their first sleeps closed in with fire; men, women and children were suffocated and burnt'.

Lords Seton, Home and Buccleuch, having amassed a great power, thought to stop the army at the Pease on 17 May but, betrayed by spies, they were forced to fade into the morning mist and were unable to stop the English reaching Berwick the next day.

12 June 1544: Death

At his castle of Darnaway, James, Earl of Moray, the wise diplomat and half-brother of King James V, having been long 'vexed with the gravel', died aged forty-four. People have never stopped marvelling at the banquet he gave for Peter the Patriarch in his house at Edinburgh when, to display the resplendence of Scotland, he showed off a cupboard filled with the finest crystal glasses. He arranged for a servant to, as if by accident, catch the cloth on which they stood, making them crash to the floor. The patriarch, mourning the loss of such lovely glassware, was surprised when the earl merely smiled. He ordered more glassware to be brought in, better and more numerous than was displayed before. The patriarch declared he had never seen better in Venice where he himself had been born. The earl leaves behind a daughter, Mary, by Lady Elizabeth Campbell, daughter of Colin, Earl of Argyll.

21 June 1544: Unkind War

The English continue to war on the borders, taking cattle and captives or killing any they please, burning hamlets and villages.

Today, a letter was sent from Stirling in Queen Mary's name to King Henry decrying his unkind war upon her since her father's death despite terms of peace having been sought.

June–August 1544: News

At St James's Palace in London, Mathew Stewart, Earl of Lennox married Lady Margaret Douglas on 29 June in the presence of King Henry and Queen Kateryn Parr. Prince Edward and his sisters attended. Princess Mary gave Margaret a generous wedding gift of jewellery: several gold brooches with sapphires, emeralds, rubies, diamonds and pendant pearls showing Biblical stories. The king threw a banquet with five courses and a void. All the royal family attended along with many lords and ladies.

Lennox having become an English subject, the king settled on him and his niece lands and manors in Yorkshire and made him his Lieutenant of North England and Southern Scotland. With the promise he will be made Governor of Scotland, the earl 'ceded to the king his title' to the Scottish crown.

In August, acting for the king, Lennox arrived with a fleet of eighteen English ships at Dumbarton Castle where its keeper, his own man, not only resisted him but attempted to capture him.

As Lennox continued burning villages and fortresses along the coast, Governor Arran outlawed him and took Dumbarton into royal possession. When Lennox's pressganged Scots defected, he earned their undying hatred after he ordered the slaughter of their children, whom he held as hostages.

19 November 1544: Proclamation

Landed men, substantial yeomen and their households are to meet in Edinburgh on 26 November with eleven days' victual to go to the Borders to resist enemies of Scotland and expel those who have been burning and slaughtering, sparing neither wife nor bairn.

29 December 1544: Rumour

Rumour is the French ambassador goes to France to request money, munitions and men to aid Scotland and that King Francis desires the young queen to marry the son of the dauphin.

27 February 1545: Ancrum Moor

A 4,000-strong force of English, led by Sir Ralph Eure and Sir Brian Layton, invaded Teviotdale to sack and burn the abbeys of Melrose and Jedburgh. As the English came in sight, a small party of Scots led by Governor Arran 'showed their backs'. Over Palace Hill prey and predators raced, into the waiting Scottish army on the far side, arrayed under the Earls of Angus, Bothwell and Glencairn. Battle was joined just as the sun began to shine in English eyes. A charge by pikemen drove the invaders back and their long reach 'had them all riven down'. Then Scottish borderers, compelled to fight with the English force, tore off their red crosses and started killing those who had lately been their enforced comrades. At the end of the fighting, both leaders of the English force with 800 of their men lay dead on the field, and a thousand prisoners were taken. The Earl of Arran, when the body of Sir Ralph was identified, said, 'God have mercy on him for he was a fell cruel man, over-cruel which many a man and fatherless bairn might rue.' Shedding tears, he lamented 'that ever such slaughter and bloodshed should be amongst Christian men'. When the Earl of Angus came up, Arran took him 'about the neck and kissed him twenty times', saying he had 'done a great good day's work' for Scotland. Celebrations were had afterwards at Hume Castle.

14 March 1545: Proclamation

Governor Arran has issued a proclamation for all between sixteen and sixty to be ready to go the borders with fifteen days' victuals upon twenty-four hours' warning, after vessels arrived from France bringing artillery, gunpowder and money.

22 March 1545: String

The queen mother joyfully received a letter from her son Francoys, who is now nine years old. In it he had sent her 'a piece of string so she would see how tall he has grown'.

4 June 1545: Reinforcements

The captain of the French force, Jacques de Montgomery de Lorges, was today received by both the queen mother and governor at Edinburgh. He had arrived four days ago at Dumbarton, bringing with him 2,000 gunners, 500 horse, 500 footmen with pikes and 200 archers of the guard, great provisions of food and wine, and enough money to pay wages for twelve months. While he was speaking, two large culverins were being dragged in torrential rain by thirteen horses up the steep slope to the castle.

August–September 1545: Deaths

While, during August, Scotsmen and Frenchmen encamped on the Tweed and rode across the river to burn and ravage English villages and fields, in the burghs the 'pest was great' and many people died for the great scarcity and 'want of victuals'.

Mid-September English soldiers crossed the border at Coldingham burning Scottish towns and villages and as many crop-fields as they could.

The queen mother and her daughter, with the cardinal, went into 'concealment in the mountains beyond reach of attack'.

1 March 1546: Burning

Found guilty of being an obstinate heretic, George Wishart was sentenced to burning at the stake at St Andrews. Cardinal Beaton had carpeting laid on the battlements and soft velvet cushions placed in the window recesses so he and others could watch the burning in comfort. When the preacher emerged from his prison, he was dressed in a buckram coat with pockets and sleeves packed with pokes of gunpowder. While the flames crackled about him, George Wishart stared defiantly at the cardinal. In January, at Perth, the cardinal had four men hanged and two women drowned for heresy.

May 1546: Borders

Having 2,000 men in wages all summer, Scots brag that the Earl of Angus intends to attack English borderers. Most Scottish border-men have moved inland, leaving behind widows and orphans to 'travail as they may to manure the ground and to sow corn'. If their hovels are burnt, they just make a new one the day after, so wretchedly do they live while the English steal what few cattle are left.

5 June 1546: Rotation

George, Earl of Huntly was appointed Lord Chancellor of the realm in place of Cardinal Beaton after his brutal murder at St Andrews at daybreak a week ago, the killing blow struck by Wishart's close friend James Melville with his stag-sword. Arran has been told he is to govern in all matters with the aid of his Privy Council, certain lords remaining with him monthly in rotation, except Lords Erskine and Livingston as keepers of the queen's person.

2 July 1546: Portrait

With his letter, Duc Francoys has sent a portrait of himself to his mother, commenting he thinks the 'artist has improved upon his model'.

3 August 1546: Peace

The Privy Council appointed William, Lord Ruthven Keeper of the Great Seal. Scotland was included in the peace between France and England, although none believe the English king has any intention to abide by it.

22 August 1546: Primate

John Hamilton, thirty-four-year-old half-brother to Governor Arran, was today consecrated Archbishop of St Andrews and Primate of Scotland in place of Cardinal Beaton, and appointed Treasurer of Scotland. Like his predecessor he has illegitimate children: six by his mistress Grizzel Sempill. Cardinal Beaton had two more, having had eight children by his mistress Marion Ogilvy, though some called her his wife, believing they had married in 1520 before the cardinal had taken holy orders.

14 November 1546: Growing Tall

In his latest letter to his mother, Duc Francoys wrote that when King Francis visited he was nice and told him to grow 'big to do him service'. He says he wants very much to do this and has grown taller but wishes much more he could see his mother.

December 1546: French Court

Aware the English army intends to invade the realm next February, the Privy Council sent ambassadors to France to ask King Francis to provide men to help them defend the realm and send cunning men expert in the making and taking of fortifications. The French king has suggested to them a neutral way to calm matters might be to negotiate a marriage between Queen Mary and the Prince of Denmark; King Francis has asked Denmark's king to enter a defensive league with France and Scotland.

31 January 1547: Death of King Henry

News has seeped from the English court that King Henry VIII died during the early morning hours of 28 January, although the usual ceremony of bearing the royal dishes to the sound of trumpets continues as if he was still alive. Those in the know say Edward Seymour, Earl of Hertford (soon to be Duke of Somerset), as the senior of King Edward VI's two uncles, will be created Protector of the realm.

31 March 1547: Death of King Francis

When fifty-two-year-old King Francis first fell ill with a serious cold in February, he joked that he would soon be well but that 'if the

King of England had summoned him to follow, it would be another matter'. Although at first recovered, bouts of fever and languor kept returning which medicine did nothing to alleviate. On the king's better days, he tried to exorcise his affliction with hawking and exercise. Out hunting near Rambouillet, pain from his stomach abscess grew so bad he was forced to lodge at the castle. Fever returned and worsened until he fell into delirium. He died early in the morning on the twenty-eighth birthday of his son, who succeeds as King Henri II.

4 May 1547: Irony

It is reported that Protector Somerset said if King Henri II wanted to make war upon England, he would find them ready but hoped the king would not 'make war upon a child by which no honour nor profit could be gained'.

25 May 1547: Beacons

Having strengthened border defences and arranged people to be trained in weapons and military strategy, Governor Arran has ordered a line of beacons upon the hills from St Abb's Head to Linlithgow and mounted sentinel stations so news of any English invasion can be conveyed night or day.

29 July 1547: Grand Chamberlain

Duc Francoys has written to his mother explaining that he fulfilled his role as grand chamberlain at Henry II's coronation at Reims Cathedral and participated in all the tournaments.

Mid-August 1547: Crann Tara

The Fiery Cross was sent to all corners of the kingdom by Governor Arran to summon all men between sixteen and sixty to assemble at Fala Moor on Wednesday 31 August, ready to defend Scotland from invasion.

2–7 September 1547: Waiting

Scouts watched the 19,000-strong English army, which had entered Scotland on 2 September, advance along the coast shadowed by its navy of sixty-five ships – thirty-four of them warships, several boasting as many as fifty guns.

By 4 September the Scottish army, boasting around 22,000 men, assembled near Musselburgh placing cannon port side. Then between Musselburgh and Inveresk, blocking access to Edinburgh, they encamped on the steep west side of the River Esk on Edmonston Ridge, protected by the hills and marshland behind. On the sea side two large field pieces were placed and hackbutters secreted under a turf wall. With the bridge so guarded, the English would be forced to ford the Esk under fire and advance up the slope to engage. Three days later, the English fleet anchored in Musselburgh Bay and the enemy army crossed Linton Bridge. Governor Arran sent out parties of light horsemen to keep watch from the hills overlooking the English lines.

September 1547: True Love

As English troops moved along the coast, the queen's guardian, John Erskine, moved Mary with her four friends, all named Mary and close to her majesty's age, to the safety of Inchmahome Priory on a little isle in the Lake of Menteith, overlooked by Ben Lomond. In the autumnal sunset the waters of the lake burn gold, edged by trees turning gold, while the peaks have coronas of crimson.

In the church, the girls discovered the romantic effigy of Walter 'the Freckled' Stewart, Earl of Menteith lying with his wife Mary, both dead nearly 250 years. She has her arm around his neck and he lies on his side, his arm around her waist, as they gaze into each other's eyes.

9–10 September 1547: 'Nowhere any safety'

Early morning of Friday, 9 September, Lord George Home took a skirmishing party of 1,500 cavalry along the high ridges at the west end of Fawside Brae, overlooking the English encampment. Shouting and waving pikes, they provoked Somerset into sending a large body of light horse and heavier demi-lancers to chase them away. Lord Home's plan was to lead them into the 500 pikemen waiting in ambush, but he miscalculated the speed at which the demi-lancers could move – so fast that, being almost 'at their elbows', his party was forced into a hasty retreat, fighting a running battle with sword and lance in a chase that lasted almost 3 miles with dead and broken bodies littered behind them. Meanwhile, the English moved camp to set up a small guard post on Fawside Brae, a scant half-mile south-east of the Scottish camp, while scouts reconnoitred around the church, marking sites for setting up artillery on the hill.

Seeing how badly the reduced cavalry was cut up, Lord Home out of action with a broken collarbone and his son taken prisoner, Governor Arran decided the best strategy was to take the offensive and strike first using pike columns, for if they reached Inveresk church before the English they would gain the advantage of the slope. Next morning, although Somerset had his army on the move before eight o'clock, Arran had already crossed the River Esk, with his three columns of pikemen reaching the church before the English had climbed halfway to it.

Arran commanded the centre, Angus the right wing (though he had argued against the move), the Earl of Huntly commanded the left wing and with him were the Earl of Argyll's contingent of Highland archers. To English surprise, they advanced at speed, 'more akin to cavalry than infantry'. At first they were clear of the English naval guns, but as soon as Huntly's rearward was exposed and in range ships' guns opened fire, catching the Highlanders, who broke and fled. Cannonballs crashed into pikemen, killing many and tearing great holes in their ranks. Huntly, checking his advance, attempted to move his men out of range by shifting inwards but his men coursed into Arran's battle, which momentarily disordered them, yet they still managed to advance, with Angus' column coming up on Arran's right flank. At the same time the Scots began to freely shoot ordnance off towards the English soldiers.

Somerset ordered in his heavy cavalry – heavily armoured men with lances, maces and swords – but they were given no time to bard their horses. Between the English and the Scots was a wide ditch. Many of the horses leapt but missed the bank and stumbled, blocking the way for those galloping behind them, and were then slowed as they attempted to negotiate the deep furrows of the field. Old hands at defending against cavalry, the Scots stood firm, shoulder to shoulder, the front rank kneeling with long pikes outward, their fellows behind holding theirs point-forward in both hands, 'the whole ward so thick that as easily shall a bare finger pierce through the skin of an angry hedgehog'. Don Pedro de Gamboa's Spanish carabineers and mounted hackbutters came to the edge of the ditch and discharged their weapons into Scottish faces. English archers sent a hail of arrows. The Scots held but their advance had halted fleetingly, giving the English time to get ordnance above them on the hills to shoot into the Scottish ranks at a devastatingly short range.

The fighting waxed hot on both sides with terrible thundering of guns from the hills and the sea. The day, already very cloudy, darkened with smoke of shot and closer at hand 'bullets, pellets and arrows flying' so thickly that 'nowhere was any safety'. The Scottish pike formations wavered, faltered and broke. Seeing Scotsmen fleeing, Lord Grey of Wilton, bleeding badly from a pike thrust through his mouth and throat, swept down with his cavalry from Fawside Brae, inflicting massive casualties as Scots fled across the Esk, some south-west through marshland and others towards the bridge to head for the coast. Among the 7,000 slain were Lord Fleming, masters of Graham, Livingston, Erskine, Ogilvy, Ross, Sinclair, Buchan and many other heirs of distinction. About 2,000 were injured and maimed, many pretending to be dead so they could escape in the night. But the dead bodies were a pitiful sight, some without legs, 'others arms cut off, necks half asunder, many heads cloven, the brains of sundry dashed out, some others their heads quite off'.

Nearly 2,000 prisoners were taken including the Earl of Huntly who, sitting on a blasted tree stump in his dented armour caked in mud amid dead and dying, was asked by a gloating Englishman how he felt about Mary marrying Edward seeing God had shown his favour for it. Huntly sighed, 'I would it should go forth and hold well with the marriage, but I like not this wooing.'

9–13 September 1547: Western Assault

Setting off from Carlisle on Friday 9 September, the Earl of Lennox, with Sir Thomas Wharton, marched across the border with 2,000 foot and 500 horse. They arrived at Castlemilk on Saturday. On sight of Lennox's glove, castellan James Stewart gave up the castle and they lodged there that night, placing an English garrison in it before they left on Sunday to march on Anand. At eight the next morning, despite brutal hand-to-hand fighting, an undermining operation began at the nearby church and by Tuesday morning they had 'cut and razed down the church walls and steeple and burnt the town, not leaving anything therein unburnt which was the best town in Annandale'. Failing to gain Scotsmen to join them, they returned to Carlisle with eighty prisoners and twelve hostages, plus ordnance and ammunition.

17–24 September 1547: Conquered

Before Protector Somerset departed from Leith on 17 September, he set fire to the town and ships. In the intervening period between the killing field and his departure, he burnt Kinghorn and other fishing towns, garrisoned the island of Inchcolm in the Firth of Forth and spoiled Holyrood Abbey by tearing off its lead roof. Garrisons of English were placed in the castles of Hume, Roxburgh, Moffat, Ferniehirst and Eyemouth. He ordered the fleet to assault all the towns and castles on the coast and build 'forts to make their own strength'. On 24 September the admiral gained possession of Broughty Castle, thus commanding passage into the River Tay, with Dundee next in his sights. The entire country is plundered; England has conquered Scotland as never before.

12 January 1548: Brother Protector

In his letter to his sister Queen Mary, Duc Francoys wrote in answer to her desire he should come to help her that he 'practises wearing armour every day, and tilting at the ring, so he can help and serve her against all her enemies'.

22–23 February 1548: Haddington

Lord Grey of Wilton marched into Haddington with a large force of English soldiers and Italian mercenaries and took the town, then burnt Dalkeith, Musselburgh and all outlying villages. After strategically placing large artillery, he left Haddington with a garrison of 2,000 soldiers well provisioned with live oxen, bacon, cereal, peas and three types of wine.

February–March 1548: New Gowns

Queen Mary was removed to Dumbarton Castle in February. Around Valentine's Day she fell severely ill with measles but was recovered by 23 March. Her recuperation was sweetened by her mother having ordered new gowns: cloth-of-gold and crimson silk; cloth-of-gold and violet silk; half-velvet and silver in the new fashion; two fronts in cloth of gold and black silk and cloth-of-silver and green silk for a front with matching sleeves.

April–May 1548: Entrenched

Lord Grey and Thomas Palmer, after viewing Haddington, cleared much ground to build ramparts to enclose all the houses of the town with bastions at each corner. The tollbooth, a tall and solid stone structure, has been filled with earth to form a gun platform.

July 1548: Siege

Six thousand French soldiers arrived at Leith on 1 July, commanded by Andrew de Montelembert, Sieur d'Esse. Assisted by an equal number of Scots under Henry, Lord Methven, entrenchment work was immediately undertaken around the outside of Haddington up to the ramparts and the tollbooth gun platform was demolished. Powerful artillery augmented those that Methven had seized and brought from the siege of Broughty Castle. Despite their work, a band of mounted Spanish carabineers, commanded by Captain Pedro de Negro, charged through the Franco-Scottish line carrying bags of gunpowder to buttress English provisions.

Of far more importance to the starving townsfolk, the French had brought food with them.

7 July 1548: Haddington Parliament

The regalia brought from Edinburgh saw Parliament convene at Haddington Abbey. The Three Estates unanimously accepted King Henri II's proposal for Queen Mary to marry Dauphin Francis and for her to be brought up at the French court. Four French galleys, commanded by Nicolas de Villegaignon, left Leith Harbour within a cluster of ships. They passed English ships lying around St Abb's Head as they struck out for France. Out of sight, they turned north, sighting seals and porpoises as they braved the fast and dangerous waters around Pentland Firth. Turning south, they travelled down the west coast to the Clyde, collecting pilots to help them with the intricate navigation which would bring them to Dumbarton Castle.

9 July 1548: Fright

The queen dowager, coming to view the siege at Haddington, had too close a shave when a cannon shot landed so close to her it injured some of her companions. She frightened everyone when she collapsed; fortunately, she had merely fainted.

29 July 1548: Embarkation

Five-year-old Queen Mary, after a last tearful hug from her mother, who had intended to sail with her as far as Whithorn but which press of business had prevented, boarded the royal galley, having been given into the charge of. M. de Breze. Sailing with her are her governess and half-aunt, the widowed Lady Janet Fleming, her nurse Janet Sinclair and her four Marys (Fleming, Livingston, Beaton and Seton). Also sailing with her are her guardians, Lords Erskine and Livingstone, her three natural brothers, Robert, John and James, along with Governor Arran's second son and second daughter, John and Jane; their elder siblings, James and Barbara, sailed a few months earlier.

'One of the happiest girls in the world'
France, 1548–1561

When King Henri ascended the throne, he ignored all his father's deathbed counsels and immediately appointed his longtime friend Anne de Montmorency, who had been exiled by Francis, as chief of his Privy Council and restored to him the office of Constable of France. The Privy Council included two of Queen Mary's uncles: Francois de Lorraine, Duc d'Aumale, who was the same age as the king and nicknamed '*Le Balafre*' (Scarface as a result of a terrible injury from a lance in 1545), and his younger brother Charles, Cardinal de Guise and Archbishop of Reims.

Henri was crowned on 26 July 1547, the day beginning at six in the morning when the ducs de Guise and d'Aumale, sporting gemmed coronets, knee-length 'tunics of gold damask … mantles of scarlet and purple' and round ermine-trimmed capes, went with others to the king's chamber. There they dressed him in a fine Holland chemise and crimson satin camisole, both with slits front and back, over which he wore a long robe of cloth-of-silver.

Constable Montmorency led the procession to the cathedral, bearing the unsheathed sword of state, followed by the king. As hereditary grand chamberlain, young Francoys, Duc de Longueville walked at his right. Henri knelt at the high altar to pray and was seated in a gold-covered chair. Once Henri pronounced his coronation oath, Francoys knelt to place buskins on his feet; the

King of Navarre placed the spurs. During prayers the king held the sword Joyeuse then laid it on the altar before being anointed and garbed in his coronation robes. Seated on his throne he received the diamond ring, sceptre and Hand of Justice. The Crown of Charlemagne was held over his head as the cathedral resounded to the shouts of *Vivat Rex in eternum*. The *Te Deum* was followed by mass and the holy sacrament.

A month of fetes followed, after which the court moved to Fontainebleau for the rest of the year. On 12 November Queen Catherine gave birth to a second daughter, who was christened Claude. The stay at Fontainebleau extended into the first few months of 1548 save for a few hunting trips. In April 1548, the king set off to Piedmont intending to assert his claim to Italy. In mid-August, as Queen Mary was setting off from Scotland, he was in Turin being feted by its governor and citizens. On 23 and 24 September, he and Queen Catherine made their separate triumphal entries into Lyons, welcomed initially by a group of nymphs in an exotic artificial forest. On 8 October 1547, while still at Lyons, King Henri gave his mistress Dianne de Poitiers the title Duchesse de Valentinois; she was granted the right to walk directly behind the Princesses of the Blood, making her one of the chief ladies-in-waiting to Queen Catherine who, to the chagrin of many, always treated her rival with exquisite courtesy.

The triumvirate of Catherine, Dianne and Henri busied themselves with arrangements for Mary's arrival, deciding she and three-year-old Princesse Elisabeth (nicknamed Ysabel) would share an apartment in the hopes they would become as sisters, although Mary would take precedence, being an anointed queen and betrothed of the dauphin. Lastly, they appointed Jean d'Humieres and his wife, Francoise, to be the governors of all the royal children, which included Mary's half-brother Francoys.

15 August 1548: Safe Landing

The voyage, begun at Dumbarton in fair weather, lasted more than a fortnight before Queen Mary and her companions disembarked safely at Roscoff. High winds had tossed the galleys unmercifully although Queen Mary had revelled in the large waves, teasing her four Marys for being seasick. Twice they had set off and been forced to return to safe anchorage. Eventually the wind favoured them, but as they passed the Cape of Cornwall one night the sea was so wild and roiling that the rudder broke, although it was skilfully replaced almost at once by the sailors despite the heavy seas. Mary's governess, Lady Fleming, was so ill and weary that she begged Captain Villegaignon to allow her and the children to go ashore for respite from the surging waves. The irritated captain told her she should 'either go to France or drown by the way'.

September–November 1548: Travelling

After a few days spent resting at Morlaix the party travelled to Nantes in easy stages and then by barge up the River Loire to Tours, where Mary met her grandmother Antoinette de Bourbon, Duchesse de Guise. She was delighted with her pretty grandchild, who resembled her mother in the colour of her hair and eyes, had white skin with a clear complexion and was intelligent and graceful.

While Mary was taken to Orleans before meeting the royal children residing then at the Chateau of St Carrieres, King Henri and Queen Catherine attended the marriage on 20 October at Moulins of Antoine de Bourbon to Jeanne d'Albret, daughter of Henri's aunt Marguerite, Queen of Navarre.

Mary, with the rest of the children, moved to the Palais de St-Germain-en-Laye in November where, on the ninth, she and King Henri met for the first time. He was charmed by her, having already been told that she and the dauphin 'got on as well together from the first day of their meeting as if they had known each other for a long time'.

4–31 December 1548: Wedding

In the presence of the king and queen, Queen Mary's twenty-eight-year-old uncle Francois, Duc d'Aumale married seventeen-year-old Anna d'Este at St-Germain. King Henri was delighted when he saw Queen Mary dancing with Dauphin Francis at the wedding banquet and declared she was 'the most perfect child' he had ever seen. Marriage and Christmas festivities merged into one and all at court deemed Queen Mary amiable and intelligent. Antoinette wrote to her daughter that Mary and Elisabeth, being frequently with Queen Catherine, 'see much company'. And despite Lord Livingston complaining Mary did not have separate quarters, she believed Mary and Ysabel sharing would benefit both girls.

3 February 1549: Royal Birth

At four o'clock in the morning Queen Catherine gave birth to a boy at Fontainebleau. He was named Louis and entitled Duc d'Orleans as second son.

8 February 1549: Ennoblement

Regent James Hamilton was today created Duke of Chatellerault and a Knight of the Order of St Michael by King Henri, with appropriate estates in France to uphold the title. His eldest son, James, takes the title of 3rd Earl of Arran.

30 March 1549: Made for Each Other

Constable Montmorency commented how careful and loving the dauphin is to Queen Mary as though she were 'already his lady and wife' and that 'it is easy to see that God made them for each other'.

10 April 1549: Court Gossip

In a gossipy letter from St Germain to Mary's mother, M. de Breze was delighted he could tell her a number of things: the 'little queen' grows in beauty and grace; all her teachers say she is clever; she dances galliards as well as anyone at court; the bruit is 'the king loves her as much as his own children'; the dauphin had recovered from his illness and enjoys anecdotes of horses, hunting and weapons; Henri and Catherine worry about his health for the doctors say that, because he does not blow his nose, humours accumulate inside his body.

10 June 1549: Coronation

The day began at dawn for Queen Catherine when her ladies dressed her in a blue velvet robe embroidered with gold *fleurs-de-lis* and a surcoat and royal mantle edged with ermine. Her bodice and head ornament glimmered with great diamonds, rubies, emeralds and pearls.

At eleven o'clock the procession set off for the Abbey of St-Denis, Constable Montmorency preceding the queen holding his gold grandmaster baton. Her long train was carried by the younger and older duchesses de Montpensier and the Princesse de la Roche-sur-Yon. The king's sister Marguerite walked alone after the queen, followed by duchesses and comtesses, all richly dressed in jewel-encrusted gowns, their diadems signalling rank. Trumpets sounded as the queen arrived at the abbey. She walked to the large platform that had been built in the heart of the church in front of the high altar, its barriers draped with gold and silver cloth glowing against the crimson velvet that covered the steps and floor. The two steps up to her velvet-covered throne were hung with cloth-of-gold frieze. When the queen went to kneel at the altar, young Duc Francoys placed a pillow there for her. Kissing a reliquary, she moved to sit on her throne. Nearby was a little cloth-of-gold stool to seat her lady of honour, Dianne's daughter Francoise de la Marck.

After prayers, the queen left her seat to kneel at the altar for her anointing. The ceremony was performed by Cardinal de Bourbon, who, taking the Holy Oil onto his finger, anointed her on her forehead and chest before putting the bridal ring on her finger. In one hand he placed her sceptre; in the other the Hand of Justice. Finally, the great crown, which had to be supported, was placed on her head briefly, replaced quickly by her lighter crown encrusted in diamonds, rubies and pearls.

18 June 1549: State Entry

As King Henri had done two days before at his own state entry into Paris, Queen Catherine mounted the platform at the Priory of St Lazare. She wore her ermine mantle and jewelled crown, her bodice covered with matching jewels so she glittered as she seated herself on her throne. She was attended by her lady of honour while the other colourfully dressed ladies were seated below her in two rows. In an arc behind them all stood the Princes of the Blood and other noblemen, all gay in coloured silks, cloth-of-gold or -silver embellished with frilled gold, gems or gold buttons.

The procession began: the clergy first, then officers of the city trades, ambassadors, and Guard members with Parlement and Treasury officials. Fifes, drummers and heralds passed next. Then the Lord Chancellor, in a robe of patterned cloth-of-gold over crimson, atop a mule caparisoned in crimson and gold and joined the procession. One of the queen's esquires, dressed in white and green velvet, rode a Spanish horse alongside two bareheaded pages who, with their horses, were attired in cloth-of-silver. Once the 200 gentlemen of the king's household had walked by in pairs, each carrying an axe in their hands, Queen Catherine joined the procession, riding in an open litter covered inside and out with cloth-of-silver. She entered the city around three o'clock in the afternoon to the sound of loud artillery, the princesses and noble ladies following, all mounted on white hackneys caparisoned in silver.

On the River Seine seven ships and thirty-three galleys fired artillery while their mariners set to besieging a well-defended port that had been built on one of the islands. At Notre-Dame Cathedral the queen was received by the clergy. After prayers, she was escorted to the palace to be served supper in the great hall, seated at a marble table under a velvet canopy decorated with gold *fleurs-de-lis*.

Near the Bastille, a street was cleared of its paving stones for the two-week tournament starting on 23 June, at which Mary's half-brother Francoys is to proudly lead ten men-at-arms.

19 June 1549: Invitation

Preparing to leave after hearing mass at Notre-Dame Cathedral, several children of the city, with merchants, aldermen and councillors, begged Queen Catherine to favour them by dining in the house of Cardinal Jean du Bellay. They led her to a cathedral door where some pretty stairs rose like a bridge over the Seine to the cardinal's door. She and her ladies were welcomed into a room with paintings of landscapes and statues of gods and goddesses in the spaces between.

The Moorish parquet floor had gold rosettes in the middle and four corners, all festooned with rich green ivy. Washing her hands, she sat down at the table and was served with exquisite delicacies while gentle music played. After dinner a ball was held and, to her great pleasure, the king entered and danced with her.

4 July 1549: Burning

Watching heretics burn on the Rue St-Antoine today, a shaken King Henri vowed he would never again watch such a horrific sight. He was there because, having questioned a tailor about his beliefs, he had been enraged when the tailor insolently told Dianne, 'Madame, rest satisfied with having corrupted France, and do not mingle your filth with a thing so sacred as the Truth of God.' He told the tailor he would personally watch him burn. He had kept his vow, watching from a window as the faggots were lit beneath the tailor and three others. None of them made a sound as the flames rose up around them. The tailor stared at the king until he lost consciousness.

12 April 1550: Death

Mary's maternal grandfather, fifty-three-year-old Claude de Lorraine, Duc de Guise, died at Joinville after a two-month illness. He received his ducal title after distinguishing himself at Marignano in 1515, when he received twenty-one major wounds. King Francis' physician had healed him so well that he was able to repair home to see his new-born daughter, Marie. Claude's son Francois succeeds to the dukedom, passing his title of Duc d'Aumale to his brother Claude, Marquis of Mayenne, son-in-law of Duchesse Dianne; Rene becomes Marquis d'Elboeuf.

18 May 1550: Death

Jean, Cardinal de Lorraine, brother of Duc Claude, died at Neuvy-sur-Loire after suffering a stroke while he was travelling home from Rome. Charles, Cardinal de Guise now assumes the title Cardinal de Lorraine.

3 June 1550: Joyful Tidings

From St-Germain Queen Mary wrote 'joyful tidings' to her grandmother that her mother had 'promised to come over soon to see you and me', which she described as 'the greatest happiness that I could desire in this world'. She promises to study to become very wise to satisfy them both.

27 June 1550: Royal Birth

Queen Catherine gave birth to her fifth child, a son, at St-Germain between three and five in the morning. He is to be baptised Charles Maximilian and entitled Duc d'Angouleme.

July 1550: Death

Jean d'Humieres died suddenly after a short illness at St-Germain. King Henri has retained his wife as the children's governess and appointed Claude d'Urse in the position of governor.

30 August–10 September 1550: Queen Mary Ill

There has been worry in the court for the little Scottish queen has been dangerously ill of the flux for many days. Only in the last two days has she begun to improve.

25–27 September 1550: State Welcome

Queen Mary was delighted at her mother's arrival at Rouen on 25 September, though not so pleased to be told Scottish gentlemen were 'squabbling great among themselves about their lodgings'. Two days later, by the 'good pleasure' of King Henri, Dowager Queen Marie was privileged to receive a state entry into Rouen, attended by Dauphin Francis and her son Duc Francoys. Received by all the estates of the city, princes and princesses of the blood, lords and ladies of the court, and princes and ambassadors of foreign nations, she arrived at the Priory of Bonnes Nouvelles in the suburbs beyond Rouen Bridge. There, the king and queen warmly welcomed her, revealing they had brought her daughter with them so mother and daughter could witness together all the public entertainments to ensue.

2 October 1550: Queen's Entry

Wearing a gold-embroidered robe of light silver enriched with pearls and precious stones and a ducal cap sporting white feathers and covered in gems, Queen Catherine watched the procession from the loggia set in the meadow of the Priory of Sainte-Catherine de Grandmont. First came the clergy, merchants, soldier bands and worthy Rouen citizens, all of whom had cleverly changed their plumes, collars and ribbons to the queen's colours of white and green from the king's black and white as had been displayed the day before. Next came triumphal chariots: the *Char de Renommee*, battle scenes on its sides, drawn by four winged horses with two soldiers lying dead at the feet of a skeletal Death, chained at his neck to Fame sounding a trumpet. Two unicorns led by men in Turkish attire drew the *Char de Religion* with winged Vesta holding a church. Six elephants preceded Flora, whose band of musical nymphs scattered flowers before the *Char d'Heureuse Fortune* carrying an actor depicting King Henri, around whose feet sat four children with a lookalike dauphin riding on horseback behind.

Now, Queen Catherine, riding on a white hackney covered with embroidered silver cloth with fringes and tassels of gold and silver, entered the procession with two silver-attired pages carrying her train. They were followed by her ladies, all in rich jewelled robes, each holding a perfectly white plume. At the city gate they entered a Brazilian Forest of red-barked trees with parrots, marmosets and squirrels flitting among the leaves. Naked Brazilian men and women went about their lives: some swinging in hammocks, others chopping wood or loading goods into skiffs on the river. Suddenly loud cries announced an enemy tribe and a battle was fought and won.

At the entrance to the Seine bridge stood an enormous rock 'enriched with the arch of a rainbow', the queen's emblem. In a grotto Orpheus played a harp harmonising with the Nine Muses to his left; Hercules at his right chopped heads off a hydra. Mid-bridge, Catherine was welcomed by Thetis and her nereids, all wearing whale-skin scaled in silver and blue.

On the day before King Henri had been greeted by Neptune and his Tritons. Queen Catherine, watching from a mock fortress, had been so enthralled at their dives, gyrations and antics in the river she forgot to eat the fruits and sweetmeats provided for her. This time it was Thetis and her sea nymphs who dived one after the other into the river, swimming with Arion and a great silver-scaled whale with five baby whales, all blowing waterspouts and carrying musicians on their backs. To a blare of music, Neptune appeared in a chariot pulled by hippopotamuses accompanied by Aeolus and the Four Winds. A great thundering startled the ladies as a fight began between two ships, one with white crosses for France and the other with red crosses representing Portugal; the latter ended up in flames while red-painted men dived into the water.

Moving on, four men dressed in satin robes met the queen at the city gate, where an arch had been erected with a pageant entitled The Golden Age, and presented her with a gift of silver-fringed green silk and silver cloth. As she came towards the cathedral, hundreds of people on platforms and galleries, leaning out of windows or standing on roofs and steeples waited to see her; so crowded were the tapestried streets that it was like a 'single mass of human bodies'. Outside Notre-Dame Cathedral, by the statue of Hector, a winged horse sprang out of a large flaming globe which shut and reopened to reveal a picture of King Henri holding a flowering sword in his right hand. The queen was still smiling as she moved through the Elysian Fields full of shrubs, fruit trees and flowers, before being received by the clergy and led into the cathedral where she listened to an oration, which she said delighted her, as much because of the well-honed pronunciation as the accomplished words.

24 October 1550: Death

Twenty-month-old Louis, Duc d'Orleans, died at Mantes from smallpox, causing much heaviness at court.

April 1551: Governess

Mary's governess, Lady Fleming, was sent away from court in disgrace after she boasted of giving birth to the king's natural son, whom she named Henry. Francoise d'Estamville, Dame de Parroys replaced her as Mary's new governess.

21 May 1551: Silver Cast

A likeness of the Princesse Elisabeth has been cast in silver ready to be taken to England and presented to King Edward VI.

The dauphin wrote today thanking Duc Francois for his gift of armour, promising to keep the suit in his wardrobe to look at it every day to ensure it is well maintained. At their first fight he hopes to wear Mary's favour and put the duke's armour in such a state that the armourers will find it hard work to repair. While he waits 'for that hour, I exercise myself as often as I can, like a gentle knight'.

17–20 June 1551: Order of the Garter

Late in the afternoon of Friday 17 June, the Marquis of Northampton was met half a mile outside of Chateaubriand to be brought, still booted and spurred, into the presence chamber of King Henri, who embraced every man, even the meanest. After supper, the marquis and some of his young lords were invited to pass time shooting at the butts with the king. Afterwards, until bedtime, they were entertained in Queen Catherine's chamber by the ladies dancing, including eight-year-old Mary with her mother.

On Saturday, after dinner, the English party were invited to watch the king play tennis, and after supper to watch – or engage in – wrestling with Bretons. Again, dancing took place in the evening until King Henry invited the English commissioners into his bedchamber to hear his musicians sing.

Before mass the following morning, the marquis went to the king's privy chamber to dress him in the robes and garter of St George. That evening, the weather being hot and humid, King

Henri invited the marquis and his gentlemen, with all of the court, to sup under the trees in the park and after to join in the deer coursing, stands being set up for the ladies.

19 September 1551: Birth

At twenty past midnight at Chateau de Fontainebleau, Queen Catherine gave birth to her fourth son. The baby was named Alexandre-Edouard.

22 September 1551: Death

At Amiens, Francoys, Duc de Longueville died in his mother's arms a month short of his sixteenth birthday.

October–November 1551: Departure

Dowager Queen Marie embarked at Dieppe on 19 October. News came that tempests had driven her into Portsmouth three days later, and King Edward VI graciously invited her to Hampton Court. On 2 November she was taken by the king's state barge into London. Two days later, seated in a chariot with Margaret Douglas, Countess of Lennox, Frances Grey, Duchess of Suffolk and her daughter Lady Jane, she was taken to dine with the king at Westminster. Before resuming her journey to Scotland on 6 November, she spent a few days sightseeing around London.

28 November 1551: Nursery Gossip

Over the last year, King Henri has supplied Queen Mary with lengths of purple, crimson and yellow velvet, fine Holland cloth, white Venetian satin and blue, crimson, violet and black-and-white taffeta, all to make her dresses, headdresses, caps, collars, robes, fronts, skirts, bodices and sleeves. She has had more than sixteen dresses, some taffeta-lined, and among them are a dress of gold damask edged with gold braid with upper sleeves banded with crimson satin, one of silver edged with green satin and silver braid, another of black damask with sleeves edged with silver, and a coat and sleeves of white satin speckled with 120 diamonds and rubies. For outside wear she has marten fur and wolf skins. Accessories have included gold, silver and silk ribbons, gloves, pins, combs and brushes and dozens of buttons, some made in crescents and trefoils. Her rosaries are decorated with jasper and pearls. She has so many jewels they have to be kept in three brass chests. Most of this is intended for her ceremonial attire when she attends events and dances, but on a day-to-day basis she dresses simply. The little queen loves music and plays the lute, cittern and harpsichord and enjoys singing with the others the hymns of Marot. She can speak Spanish and Italian and understands Latin better than she speaks it. She enjoys needlework and embroidery and sets apart two hours every day for study and reading, especially poetry, to the joy of court poets.

The children have many pets including caged birds, twenty-two small lapdogs and four large (well-muzzled) mastiffs, besides ponies and horses for litters and chariots. They also receive gifts such as two bears given to the dauphin (looked after by a squire called Florimond), a hind which he particularly loves and hackneys from King Edward of England. For hunting, they have their own falcons, gyrfalcons and hawks. Dauphin Francis and Mary often walk or hunt together. The dauphin has three favourite horses called Fontaine, Enghien and *Chastillon*. Queen Mary has two hackneys called *Bravane* and *Madame la Reale*. They both like to gallop in the shade of the forests. They also read the Romances of the Round Table together, and other heroic tales full of adventurous knights rescuing beautiful prisoners, which all the children and pages of the household join in to play, the queen being the princess and the dauphin the knight errant. When nomadic actors, acrobats, clowns or musicians pass by, their governor asks them to enter and entertain them.

A typical day for the food in the royal children's household includes two calves, sixteen sheep, five pigs and seven geese plus beef, chickens, pigeons, hares, larks, partridges, pheasant and seventy-two-dozen loaves.

12 February 1552: Regency

King Henri announced to the Paris Parlement that Queen Catherine would rule as regent of France while he was away in Italy campaigning against Emperor Charles V; he insists she is to be obeyed as he would be.

March 1552: Scarlet Fever

Queen Catherine fell dangerously ill with scarlet fever at Joinville-en-Champagne and was nursed diligently by Duchesse Dianne. As soon as the queen is fully recovered, she plans to travel to Laon where she can more readily receive news of the king and his campaign.

26 October 1552: Charm

While at Amboise with the dauphin and the other royal children, Claude d'Urse wrote to Queen Marie that her daughter so 'grows in charm' it makes her daily more suited for the place her mother desires her to occupy. The household moves soon to Blois, where the king is expected to arrive around 11 November.

November–December 1552: Hero of Metz

Emperor Charles, with a huge force, came to besiege Metz, the citizens having put themselves under the protection of King Henri, who took the young Duc de Lorraine into his household for safety. The defence was led by Queen Mary's uncle Francois, with 6,000 men and a handful of guns. Willing citizens demolished their own houses and churches to help fortify the city, Francois gaining their affection by labouring with a shovel alongside them.

On 13 November a breach in the walls was opened but the advance was stopped by defenders fighting them in the moat. The emperor arrived six days later, welcomed by artillery salvoes, and rode through his lines mounted on a white horse (though he had been carried thither in a litter). He looked pale and wasted, his hair and beard white. His unexpected visit meant his lodging was a hastily constructed wooden hut, but he told the Duke of Alva he would consider it 'a beautiful palace' when the keys of the town were in his hands.

By 26 November, Imperial engineers had made a further three breaches despite heavy bombardment from the defenders. Two days later the whole wall collapsed with a tremendous crash, leaving a huge gap. The loud cheering of the emperor's soldiers ceased abruptly as they saw behind the fallen wall a strong, 8-foot-high earthwork bristling with small cannon. Bombardment continued elsewhere until another earthwork was revealed behind a breach. And in lulls, defenders would suddenly emerge to harry the enemy who would 'come out of their tents and huts as thick as ants when you uncover the ant-hills'. In one of these forays Claude, Duc d'Aumale was wounded and captured.

If November had been cold and wet, December came in worse. In the emperor's camp, dysentery and typhus broke out. On 31 December, the emperor and the remnant of his army departed. On New Year's Day, when the defenders emerged, even rough soldiers cried upon seeing how dying and dead men had been left heaped up together; the wounded and feverish stretched out on gory, muddy earth; others sunken into the mud unable to move, frozen to their knees, plaintively asking for the mercy of death. That day the Duc de Guise sent out surgeons to save all whose lives could be saved; the dying and suffering receiving every care and attention that could be bestowed. And his garrison of soldiers followed his example and gave their enemies kindness instead of brutality. Tales of such errantry have made Queen Mary very proud of her uncle.

February 1553: Independence

The cardinal has written to Mary's mother that King Henri 'takes great pleasure' in conversing with the little queen, and does so for an hour or more, discussing sensible topics with her as though she was twenty-five years of age. Anticipating Mary will soon have her own household, he has sent Queen Marie a list of people her daughter will need and the expected cost, saying, 'I think in the list as it stands there is nothing superfluous or mean (meanness is the thing she hates most in the world). Her spirit, I assure you Madam, is already so high and noble that she lets her annoyance be very plainly seen because she is thus unworthily treated. She wants to be out of tutelage and to exercise her independent authority ... I must not omit to tell you that Madame de Parroys is doing her duty as well as possible and you may be sure that God is well served according to the ancient way.'

14 May 1553: Royal Birth

Queen Catherine gave birth to a third daughter, named Marguerite after her aunt.

July 1553: News from England

King Edward VI died at Greenwich Palace on 6 July. Four days later Queen Jane, grandniece of King Henry VIII, was proclaimed Queen of England but, by popular acclaim, was deemed without right to the throne and Queen Mary Tudor, King Harry's daughter, was proclaimed Queen of England on 19 July.

1 January 1554: Perfect Age

Having now reached eleven years of age, Queen Mary was decreed by the Parlement of Paris to be of perfect age to reside with her own household at court. By way of celebration, she invited the cardinal to a New Year supper. Having her own presence chamber in which to hold audiences, her household now comprises – besides her officers – eight ladies (excluding her four Marys), squires, ushers and pages, a tailor and a maître de dance; the king has loaned her an Italian gentleman to take care of her stable.

20 February 1554: Toothache

The little Queen of Scots arrived today in Paris, recovered from the toothache that had left her with a swollen face and forced her to remain at Fontainebleau when the court moved.

March 1554: *'Holding herself straight'*

Francoise de Parroys wrote in her latest news report to Mary's mother that her charge's household has been reduced to the writer, a nurse and two maids (but with 'no one to dress her hair' since Mlle de Curel left, although the writer does her best). The only gentleman with them is Mr Erskine, who has been ill for a long while. The other servants and her ladies have left complaining they have had no pay. Mary had an illness but it was gone after one day, the doctors having prescribed a little rhubarb. As to her studies, 'she is quick, nothing is impossible to her, she works hard', but they quarrel sometimes about her 'holding herself straight'. And she is kind-hearted, for when the dauphin and Princesse Elisabeth both had fevers and moved to other rooms, Mary insisted on staying at Blois to cheer them.

As for court gossip, it centred on the 'sweet and accomplished ... poor young Queen Jane', executed on 12 February, upon which telling Duchesse Dianne could not restrain herself from crying.

26 March–18 April 1554: *Christening*

On 27 March, Queen Mary arrived at beautiful Meudon, her favourite chateau, located between Paris and Versailles, missing by a day the birth of her aunt Anna's second son. The Duchesse de Guise has named him Charles after his uncle the cardinal. He and the Duke of Ferrara will be his godfathers. Writing to his sister of the happy event, the cardinal told her that, contrary to reports, her daughter was not sickly, though he admitted that 'sometimes she is not well when she has eaten too much; because of her hearty appetite she might often eat too much but he will be more careful than ever about her diet'.

On 10 April, the little queen waited excitedly to welcome King Henri and Queen Catherine, along with the court including her grandmother and Duchesse Dianne, who is to be godmother.

While still at Meudon, news came from Scotland that on 12 April James, Duke of Chatellerault had resigned the regency, presenting the royal regalia to Queen Marie. During the banquet that followed, Edinburgh citizens had celebrated outside with bonfires and festivities. Queen Mary has sent a letter to congratulate her mother, saying she is informed that 'all the lords of my kingdom are quite willing to obey you and to do both for you and me whatever you may be pleased to command'.

The court moves on 18 April to go to Dianne's Chateau d'Anet with its lovely gardens, galleries and aviaries.

11–31 May 1554: Family Letters

Duchesse Antoinette writes frequently to her daughter and on 11 May informed her that her brother Claude had been ransomed and she was leaving court to attend him for he had been badly treated. She explains that 'his wounds do not show except on his hand', where he has lost at least two fingers, 'but fortunately, it is his left hand … but with war imminent again she is sad to see him go back into danger' and dreads Marie's 'new neighbour' for news has come that Queen Mary Tudor intends to marry Prince Philip of Spain.

Francois wrote to his sister on 27 May that all the family were proud of her daughter, who grows in 'beauty and virtue'. He informed her he expects by 15 June to set out to meet the army and lodge under canvas. Already, everyone has 'begun to bid farewell to their ladies hoping not to return until they have frustrated the plans of the enemy'.

On 31 May, Mary's governor wrote to Mary's mother that her stable had only five hackneys, three mules and a muleteer, three pages, one groom and his helper but they need three baggage mules to carry her bed and baggage to stop things being spoiled when carried on village carts. They also require a horse for the plate, another for a page, plus two further carts, one for the kitchen and one for the pantry, but the chairmaker had insisted on being paid first so they had been unable to obtain what they needed.

12 July 1554: Reims

Queen Catherine, having moved to Reims, has taken Queen Mary with her so she can daily visit St Pierre Convent to see her aunts Renee and Antoinette, her mother's younger sisters, who have been overjoyed to see her. While there, news arrived that King Henri is encamped at Dinan, intending to march on Namur, where Emperor Charles is in person.

12 August 1554: Battle

Commanded by Duc Francois, who had a horse killed under him, French soldiers forced the emperor's advance guard to flee in four hours of fierce fighting at Renty. 600 prisoners were taken, from whom it was discovered the emperor had promised his army 'the sack of Paris'. King Henri said that he would be content with what he has gained if the rain does not cease, providing Charles accepts peace conditions.

September–October 1554: Growing Pains

To show her mother how strong and tall she is growing, Queen Mary sat for her portrait at Chateau de Villers-Cotterets, on the edge of Retz Forest. Thus occupied, Madame de Parroys wrote at length requesting instructions from Mary's mother regarding alms and plate and explaining how pleased Mary was 'when she can give orders and will ensure she uses her power well when she is allowed, for she does not lack wit ... and pleases all who see her and everyone praises her'. With the letter, Mary's governor sent the accounts with mention of the problems he faced. Specifically, over the last nine months the household has cost 18,000 livres with another 1,600 livres on the stable, which latter is projected to increase with draught horses needed for the constant travelling. With King Henri refusing to provide any more money (his treasurer will not advance even one eu), the governor thinks Mary's household will require at least 53,000 francs next year while merchants demand payment in cash because they say they would find it too hard to extract payment from Scotland if Mary were to die. Similarly, the servants who have only their wages insist on being paid quarterly.

In more cheerful news, an invitation arrived on 24 October for the queen to attend the wedding of her cousin Nicolas Comte de Vaudemont and twenty-three-year-old Princess Joanna de Savoy-Nemours, to be held in Paris on 24 February. The governess has added to her letter that Mary is keen to be as well dressed at the ceremony as the king's daughters Claude and Elisabeth; they had cloth-of-gold and cloth-of-silver gowns for the wedding of M. d'Urse; ordinarily they 'wear fronts of cloth of gold which are dear' and receive two outfits a year. She suggests making Mary a gown to look as impressive as they do, not so much for the value of the outfits but to show her rank, and could get material for 40 ecus the ell; however, if she waits until nearer the wedding it will be cheaper if paid for in cash. The little queen is persistent in asking for 'ciphers for her dresses like everyone else' but has been told she must wait to see what her mother advises. Madame wishes to purchase two diamonds to lengthen Mary's 'touret' (a kind of headband); otherwise, her ruby necklace with the best pearls set between will do.

1 January 1555: Latin Oration

In the great hall of the Louvre, before King Henri and Queen Catherine and the court, Queen Mary delivered a Latin oration decrying those who thought women should not be taught Latin and in defence extolled fifteen learned women.

27–28 February 1555: Right Glad

Fontainebleau received English ambassadors who greatly admired the outer court, 600-foot gallery and the garden with its great pond, cypress-shadowed walkways and natural rock grotto where the royal family are wont to repair in hot weather. They were also shown the privy garden and the great fountain, for which the chateau is named, with its five spouts which shoot water out of the natural rock. The chateau is surrounded by forest full of deer, wolves and bears. One of the secretaries later boasted, 'I saw a real live ostrich, and plucked a white feather out of it.'

Receiving them at five o'clock in the evening, King Henry embraced them and then had them escorted to Queen Catherine's presence chamber to be introduced to her, Queen Mary and the princesses.

The following day some Scottish gentlemen in the retinue made it known they would like it if they could see their own queen and hear her speak. Hearing of their request, Queen Mary had them brought to her presence chamber, even those whose rank did not entitle them, and told them she was 'richt blythe tae see ye'.

18 March 1555: Royal Birth

At Fontainebleau, Queen Catherine gave birth to a prince; he was named Hercule-Francois, Duc d'Alencon.

June 1555: Scottish News

Attempting to stop murders and mutilations between feuding clans, Mary's mother on 20 June decreed her nobles should limit the number of feudal retainers they bring with them into the capital. Mary's step-grandfather Archibald, Earl of Angus arrived in Edinburgh with 1,000 horsemen. At Queen Marie's reproof, he replied, 'The knaves follow me; gladly would I be rid of them for they devour all my beef and my bread; and I would be beholden to you if you could tell me how to get quit of them.' Thereupon he was ordered to ward in the castle, but when he handed the warrant to the constable he was told, 'I am here enjoined to receive your Lordship only with three or four to wait upon you.'

'So I told my lads,' answered the earl, 'but they replied that they durst not, and would not, go home to my wife Meg without me.' Sending word to the queen that he had been refused admittance, he rode home.

April 1556: Virtuous

Since the beginning of the year, when Mme de Parroys and Queen Mary had a huge argument, the governess has been absent, said to be ill with dropsy in Paris. Despite being alone for four months, the queen mother has been informed her daughter is good and virtuous and behaves as well 'as if she had a dozen governesses'.

The rift between them occurred after the governess found Mary giving away her childish dresses, some to churches and others to relatives. Believing the dresses to be her prerogative Madame de

Parroys exclaimed angrily, 'I see you are afraid of my enriching myself in your service, it is plain you intend to keep me poor!' and threatened she would write to her mother that Mary had deprived her of control of the wardrobe and showed little discretion in disposing of her possessions.

Stung by the unjust accusation, Mary wrote to assure her mother that her governess had never allowed her 'the credit of giving away so much as a pin, and thus I have acquired the reputation of being stingy ... I will send you an inventory of all the clothes I have had since I came to France, that you may see the control she has exercised.'

24 June 1556: Twins

Queen Catherine nearly died giving birth to twin girls. Surgeons saved her life by breaking the legs of the stillborn baby Jeanne so she could be removed from her womb. The second baby survived and has been christened Victoire. The king has been advised the queen should have no more children.

17 August 1556: Death

To the queen's great sorrow, Princess Victoire died. She is to be buried at St-Denis next to her sister.

August–October 1556: Fevers

Late summer and early autumn being remarkably hot, the court moved to Fontainebleau. Through eating too much melon, Queen Mary suffered indigestion, but then fell ill with fever, having persistent attacks. Bloodletting was ceased by her physicians when the attacks continued. Through all Mary's illness, night or day, Queen Catherine hardly left her side despite being in recovery herself after her difficult delivery and the deaths of her children. It is a strange malady for the fever dies away for a short while, then returns 'in the form of little shiverings'. Many have been afflicted with it this year, including the dauphin, lodged at the Palais des Tournelles. After being sent to convalesce at Meudon, Queen Mary was moved in October to the Hotel de Guise in Paris, where she was visited by the king and queen.

January 1557: Scottish News

The French king asked Cardinal Charles to write to his sister requesting that Scotland prepare to declare war on England, suspecting Queen Mary will send English troops into France in support of her husband, King Philip. Queen Marie has replied she believes Scotland too badly prepared for war, having few soldiers, and fears the nobles would flatly refuse, for all her 'undertakings are thwarted; the great lords are little desirous of justice'; when she attempts to improve the situation, they instantly say she 'wants to change their laws ... God knows what a life I lead ... I can say that for twenty years past I have not had one year of rest and I think that if I were to say not one month I should not be far wrong.'

Archibald, Earl of Angus died in great pain on 22 January, aged sixty-eight years. He leaves his daughter Margaret, Countess of Lennox as his only surviving heir. He was buried with his ancestors at Abernethy.

July 1557: Smallpox

Queen Mary has been ill with smallpox but the king's physician, Jean Fernel, has protected her face from the usual scarring with a lotion of his own making.

29 August 1557: St Quentin Fallen

Panic took hold in Paris when news came St-Quentin had fallen to King Philip and the way open all the way to Paris. King Henri commanded all the people who could to leave and for all precious items and sacred relics in the capital to be removed to prevent them being looted. In the midst of the chaos, Francois, Duc de Guise arrived from Italy and was embraced many times by the king, who immediately created him lieutenant-general of the kingdom.

1–9 January 1558: French Calais

Surprised that King Philip decided to return to Brussels for the winter and not capitalise on his victory in August, Duc Francois made secret preparations to surprise the Spanish forces. All through midwinter, he assembled an army of 30,000 infantry and cavalry and launched a swift surprise attack on Calais. At six in the morning on 7 January, the supposedly impregnable town surrendered. The French agreed to spare the lives of those within, and those willing to take oath to the King of France would keep their houses and property. Those who did not were taken prisoner.

In the evening dusk of 9 January, news of the victory came to the Palais des Tournelles while the king was dancing at a wedding. At court, it is said the Duc de Nemours only went on campaign to escape being killed by the King of Navarre for courting his cousin Francoise de Rohan, getting her pregnant and reneging on his promise to marry her, and that Duc Francois brought him along so that he could not try his amorous antics on Francois' own wife.

20 January 1558: Eastern Joust

In the light of forty-eight flaming torches, King Henry and Dauphin Francis with several princes and lords left the Palais des Tournelles mounted on small horses, wearing loose robes made of white silk like Turks. On their left shoulders were quivers full of arrows and one hand held a shield while the other held a hollow clay ball. Preceding them were the king's musicians: twelve men, also dressed like Turks, mounted on donkeys and mules playing trumpets and kettledrums. As they entered the lists on the Rue St-Antoine they were challenged by another band dressed like Moors who had ridden out of the Hotel de Montmorency. Combat ensued: balls were thrown and arrows loosed, all to 'a strange music'. In a finale, riders arranged their horses into a circle and made them dance in rhythm, while they screamed terrible hoots and boos.

4 April 1558: Closet Meeting

In a strictly private meeting with the king, Queen Mary signed three documents using her royal signature 'Marie R': one stipulated if she died childless the Kingdom of Scotland and all her rights to the crown of England would pass to Henri II and his heirs; another pledged to him 1 million crowns from Scottish revenues to reimburse him for the monies he had expended on her education and defence of her realm; the third voided all future demands prejudicial to them.

15–19 April 1558: Marriage Contract

At Fontainebleau, nine Scottish commissioners, including Mary's brother Lord James, now twenty-six years old, had arrived to complete details of the marriage contract. To them, Queen Mary promised to maintain Scottish laws and liberties, writing a letter of confirmation to her Estates faithfully promising 'on our word as a queen to observe and protect the laws, liberties and privileges of our realm of Scotland for, all and singly, our subjects … for all time to come, just as they have up till now observed', and attached her great seal. Four days later the marriage contract was signed. Francis was entitled King of Scotland and offered the crown matrimonial. If he died, Mary would receive a dower of 60,000 livres and the choice of living in France or Scotland, but she could only remarry with joint consent of France and Scotland. If she died without issue, the Scottish heir presumptive would succeed her in Scotland.

Francis' betrothal gift to Mary was a gold ring set with diamonds, rubies and pearls surrounding a small figure of Cupid trying to catch a mouse.

24 April 1558: 'Gold, Silver and Jewels'

Even before dawn, the streets and bridges of Paris were brimming with excited people crowding into every nook and cranny between the bishop's palace and Notre-Dame Cathedral. On the square in front of the cathedral, a 12-foot-high walkway lined one side, embowered with a trellised arcade of vine leaves from the palace culminating in an enormous, blue-carpeted stage in front of the cathedral doors. A canopy overhead, decorated with *fleurs-de-lys* and with tapestries falling either side, formed a wedding pavilion that allowed the people to see the wedding of fourteen-year-old Dauphin Francis to fifteen-year-old Mary, Queen of Scots.

A stir ran through the crowd when, between ten and eleven o'clock, the Swiss Guard, some holding halberds and others tambourines and fifes, heralded the arrival of the bride's uncle Duc Francois. Ascending to the stage, he gave reverence to Eustache du Bellay, Bishop of Paris, who stood waiting, with lords and gentlemen, for the dauphin to arrive. The crowds cheered when the hero of Metz and Calais, realising that some in the bishop's party were blocking the citizens' view, asked them to move.

Musicians dressed in red and yellow, playing trumpets, oboes, violins, zithers and guitars, alerted the crowds to the procession: first, 100 of the king's gentlemen, then abbots, bishops, archbishops and cardinals and the papal legate of France, Cardinal Trivulzio. Louder cheers and shouted blessings presaged the approach of the king-dauphin and his brothers, Charles and Henri, with Antoine, King of Navarre.

King Henri, resplendent in a gold-embroidered red velvet robe, escorted Queen-Dauphine Mary wearing a gown 'whiter than the lily' decorated with white embroidery, contrasting with her rich chestnut hair. Her mantle and 12-yard train, of bluish-grey cut velvet, was richly embroidered with white silk and pearls, and both covered in precious stones. Her crown, commissioned by the king, was of the finest gold and had a large central pendant ruby with diamonds, pearls, rubies and emeralds set around it. She was followed by Queen Catherine, escorted by Louis, Prince de Conde and Queen Jeanne of Navarre. Princesse Marguerite, princesses, ladies and damsels followed so that 'one could see only gold, silver and jewels'.

At the cathedral doors, King Henri drew from his finger a ring to be used in the nuptials and gave it to the Cardinal de Bourbon, Archbishop of Rouen, who was to conduct the ceremony. As he spoke the words of the marriage ceremony, the cheers of the crowd grew even louder, resounding and echoing along the Rue Neuve de

Notre-Dame and from all the windows and doors of the houses in the Place du Pave. During the oration by the Bishop of Paris, heralds threw handfuls of gold and silver coins into the crowd, who begged them to stop when there came screams from those who had fallen or fainted in the resulting crush. Many that day not only lost their hats or cloaks but some their clothes. At ceremony end, the Scottish commissioners paid homage to Mary's husband and left when the royal party entered the cathedral for the nuptial mass, the raised walkway continuing along the nave to the chancel and a gold-cushioned pavilion at the high altar.

Before the wedding party departed the cathedral for the palace, Henri was informed that many people had been unable to see the couple and, to the great delight of the commons, he asked them to walk all around the outside of the stage. In the early evening the company moved to the Palais de Louvre, impeded by crowds waiting to see the ladies and gentlemen ride by on magnificent horses and the queens and princesses pass in their open cloth-of-silver-covered litters.

In the great hall, with its massive pillars and statues of previous kings, the royal party sat at the marble 'Table of the Bride'. Duc Francois, wearing a robe of frosted cloth-of-gold covered in precious stones that vied with the colours from the stained-glass windows, signalled the courses. These were carried in by twelve servers to trumpets and drums playing a march, which echoed into the azure double-vaulted oak ceiling, and to which the bareheaded officers timed their steps. Dancing followed the removal of the tables, and Mary's long train was carried after her by gentlemen trailing the figures of the women dancing. The whole company then moved into the golden chamber to watch a celebration parade: first, winged Mercury came in, wearing white satin with a gold girdle, with Mars in armour and Venus dressed as a goddess, while the other four planets marched along the length of the hall singing. Drawn by gentlemen pulling their reins, the royal princes and younger Guise children entered riding wicker horses richly caparisoned in gold and silver cloth. Each horse drew a carriage filled with singers, glittering with gems, who sang praises to the bride and groom. Two lute players preceded a gentleman leading two white hackneys by silver cords. They drew a chariot with harpists and guitarists followed by twelve unicorns leading a chariot carrying the Nine Muses singing. Everyone watching had been 'charmed into silence' before the dancing began.

To end the evening, six beautiful gold and crimson ships with silver tinsel sails, looking as if they were blowing in a breeze, came from the chamber of requests. On the deck of each vessel sat a masked prince in Turkish costume next to an exquisite unoccupied chair. They 'sailed' around the hall, rocking as if on a sea, a floorcloth moving gently to resemble waves. At the marble table, they stopped and little ladders descended. Each prince came forth to make a capture: King Henri captured his son's bride; King-Dauphin Francis captured his mother; the young Duc de Lorraine his betrothed, Princesse Claude; the King of Navarre his own wife to much merriment and the Prince of Conde caught Anne d'Este, the wife of the Duc de Guise. After the ships 'performed a dance', all sailed safely 'into port' and everyone retired. As people left, they 'could not say whether the torches and lanterns, or the jewelled rings, precious stones, gold and silver were brightest'.

During the day Queen Mary snatched a moment to scribble a note to her mother, telling her she was doing well with her Scots and had been given great honour by the king and queen 'receiving me as their beautiful daughter ... I consider myself one of the happiest girls in the world' for having a husband who 'esteems me so much'. As a gift for the commissioners and others she had designed a jewelled gold locket set with a wreath of pearls, and when it was opened it revealed miniatures of herself and Francis; when closed, her face rests on his chest.

April–September 1558: Scottish News

On the day Queen Mary married Dauphin Francis, there were bonfires, pageants and celebrations all over Scotland. In Edinburgh, 'Mons Meg was raised forth from her lair, and opened her huge mouth in honour' and her 330 lb shot was found on moorland 2 miles away and brought back to the castle to be stored for a future occasion; at a cost of 10s 8d.

Four days later, Walter Milne, a married and lapsed priest, was ordered by James Beaton, Archbishop of Glasgow, to be burnt at the stake. The infirm eighty-two-year-old man had been apprehended at Dysart while teaching a poor woman and her children the commandments. People were so horrified they refused to bring wood or rope, and reformist preachers were vehement in their denunciation of the event.

In July the Earls of Argyll, Glencairn and Morton and Lords Lorne and John Erskine, calling themselves Lords of the Congregation, informed the regent that in the previous year they had made a covenant to reform the Scottish church along Calvinist lines. And so quickly had the movement grown, they requested freedom to listen to their own preachers and, for themselves, liberty to read and discuss the Scriptures and have certain ceremonies and prayers conducted in Scots.

On St Giles Day, a riot broke out in Edinburgh when the saint's image was carried in procession through the streets, seized, thrown into the North Loch, fished out and burnt.

19 November 1558: Queen Elizabeth

News came today Queen Mary had died on 17 November. And the people of England had acclaimed Elizabeth Tudor, daughter of Queen Anne Boleyn and King Henry VIII, for their queen. Mary Stuart, deemed in Catholic eyes England's rightful queen, was immediately proclaimed in Paris by King Henri as Queen of England, Scotland and Ireland; she and Francis have assumed the arms of England.

22–23 January 1559: Marriage

At Notre-Dame Cathedral, Charles, Duc de Lorraine and Princesse Claude were married on Sunday 22 January. The day after, Duc Charles headed a grand joust performed at the back of the Guise Palace with a band of twelve jousters, which included King Henri and the Duc de Guise, all wearing embroidered cloth of gold and silver. The opposing band was headed by the king-dauphin equally richly dressed. For the evening there was a grand masquerade.

March 1559: Scottish News

On 23 March, Regent Marie denounced attacks on priests, disruption of church services and unauthorised persons preaching or administering the sacrament. In response, reformers preached publicly and churchmen were attacked, churches vandalised and their images and ornaments despoiled. Having fallen ill while at Stirling, the regent has asked leave to sail to France.

18 April 1559: Peace

Royal heralds all over France proclaimed peace by trumpet. Bonfires have been lit in villages and towns to demonstrate universal joy at the news. Two marriage alliances were brokered to shore up the peace treaty: pretty fourteen-year-old Princesse Elisabeth is to marry the recently widowed King Philip II, who was charmed by her picture; Emmanuel Philibert, Duke of Savoy and Prince of Piedmont agreed to take Henri's sister Marguerite as his bride, admiring her lively intellect.

May 1559: Scottish News

John Knox preached so vehemently at Perth on 11 May that 'God commands the destruction of the monuments of idolatry' that before the afternoon became evening nothing was left of the cathedral but bare walls. Two days of destruction followed in which churches and monasteries and their gardens were destroyed. At Charterhouse the tombs of James I, Margaret Tudor and Jane Beaufort were desecrated. John Knox sent out a letter threatening with death any priest who celebrated the mass.

Gathering an army led by the Duke of Chatellerault, the regent called a halt at Auchterarder on 24 May to send the Earl of Argyll and Lord James to parley. Meanwhile, the Earl of Glencairn and Andrew Stewart, Lord Ochiltree with 1,200 horse and 1,300 foot marched into Perth to join the Lords of the Congregation. An amnesty was agreed on condition the queen-dowager allowed 'their faith to go forward' and left no French garrisoned in Perth. Both armies disbanded, but when Queen Marie departed the town she left behind Scottish soldiers. Now revealing they had converted and joined the Lords of the Congregation, Lord James and the Earl of Argyll accused her of violating the treaty, saying the soldiers she left had been in French service.

28 May 1559: Ratification

At Notre-Dame, in the presence of all the princes, nobles and ambassadors, King Henri gave the oath to ratify the peace treaty between France and England. During the afternoon, a special courier arrived from England asking for the oath to be administered to Queen Mary and King-Dauphin Francis, which they took in a chapel near the court at evensong, before joining the dancing during the evening.

Meanwhile, preparations continued for celebratory wedding jousts, masquerades and balls, while the Cardinal de Lorraine is busy arranging a comedy. Dressmakers are being kept busy with all the gowns and attire for marvellous display of colours and silks. For his sister's trousseau, the king has given her a huge number of tapestries, linens, various silks, bed trimmings and domestic furniture to go with her to her new abode.

10 June 1559: Mercuriale

Giving no notice of their coming, King Henri, Constable Montmorency and Cardinal de Lorraine, with other nobles, came to attend the quarterly examination of members of the judiciary. The king signalled he wished to speak first, saying that now the country was at peace heretics must be brought to trial and punished according to the law. Motioning for them to proceed, he was astonished to hear Anne du Bourg fervently declaim against burning men whose only crime is that the light of the Scriptures reveals the corruption of the Church of Rome. Furious, the king ordered the arrest of du Bourg and four other councillors as soon as the meeting was over. Further, he issued a decree that judges are bound to sentence all Lutherans to death and not mitigate sentences as they had done in times past.

20–21 June 1559: Wedding

In the great hall of the Louvre, the Duke of Alva stood in as proxy for King Philip II to formally betroth Princesse Elisabeth. Rings were exchanged, followed by a banquet and ball. At Notre-Dame Cathedral the following day, the proxy wedding took place. Elisabeth wore a magnificent dress adorned with many jewels and an imperial crown. The formal wedding ceremony will take place when the new queen arrives at Guadalajara in Spain.

21 June 1559: Protest

The newly arrived English ambassador, Sir Nicholas Throckmorton, protested strongly in audience with Constable Montmorency at Mary and Francis quartering their arms with those of England. Presenting coloured drawings, he insisted they not be displayed, for the College of Heralds adjudged the arms being thus borne were prejudicial to Queen Elizabeth, her state and dignity; that no foreign prince, 'what marriage soever he has made with England, cannot quarter, bear or use the arms of England otherwise than *in pale* as in token of marriage'. And although James IV married a daughter of Henry VII, the Scottish queen, being collateral, 'cannot, nor ought not, to bear any escutcheon of the arms of England'; nor can her husband in right of her, 'it being contrary to all law and order of arms'. The constable's nonchalant reply was that Queen Elizabeth bears the arms of France; therefore, it was similarly 'lawful for the Queen of Scots being of the house of England and so near the crown'.

28–30 June 1559: Celebrations

The Duke of Savoy made his entrance on 28 June with sixty gentlemen dressed in cloaks of black velvet with gold lace worn over red satin doublets and crimson shoes. Celebratory wedding tournaments began the following day. Dauphin Francis and his band opened the joust, preceded by two heralds showing the arms of England embroidered on their breasts, backs and sleeves.

On the third day, to honour his daughter Queen Elisabeth of Spain, the forty-year-old King Henri, wearing his customary black and white, mounted his favourite horse, Le Malheureux, and entered the lists. Loud cheers went up when he defeated both the ducs de Guise (wearing red and white in honour of an unnamed lady) and de Nemours (wearing yellow and black to symbolise joy and fidelity). As the tournament neared its completion, King Henri suddenly decided to break a lance with Gabriel, Comte de Montgomery, the young captain of his Scottish Guard. When Gabriel attempted to refuse, the irritated king commanded him to compete. When Queen Catherine asked her husband to desist, he replied he intended to break one more lance in her honour. The crowd's indrawn breath revealed their surprise at King Henri being nearly knocked from his saddle on the first round. The king insisted on tilting again. Montgomery's lance struck the king's visor. The lance shattered and splinters pierced Henri's right eye. Blood pouring down his face, the king fell from his horse. In shocked silence, he laid 'as one amazed' before being carried into the Palais des Tournelles.

June 1559: Scottish Devastation

Information arrived that on 3 June Queen Mary's half-brother Lord James, Prior of St Andrews, with the Earls of Argyll and Menteith, burnt books and manuscripts and despoiled every church in St Andrews of their ornaments. Kelso, Montrose and Dunfermline abbeys had been destroyed and the tomb of Robert the Bruce, housed in the latter, smashed. Queen Marie had assembled a Franco-Scottish force at Cupar Muir. Finding herself outnumbered, she asked to parley and pleaded with the rebel lords to stop destroying abbeys and churches, offering them remission for all crimes past. They replied that 'they would not suffer idolatry'. A truce of eight days was agreed in which neither side would 'invade, trouble or disquiet' the other, although during it the monastery of Lindores was attacked.

Towards the end of June, the Lords of the Congregation proclaimed they only sought 'liberty of conscience' and marched on Edinburgh, forcing Queen Marie to flee to Dunbar Castle from where she wrote to her daughter that Lord James was using religion as a pretext to overthrow her and become ruler of Scotland, egged on by John Knox, who had written *The First Blast of the Trumpet against the monstrous Regiment of Women*, which begins with the statement that it is repugnant to nature and God for 'a woman to bear rule, superiority, dominion or empire above any realm, nation or city'. The palace and abbey of Scone has been sacked; in Stirling, all the monasteries and nunneries have been torn down and their gardens and orchards destroyed; in Edinburgh, Holyrood was sacked and the mint seized.

9 July 1559: Tearful Marriage

Around midnight, at King Henri's insistence, the Duke of Savoy married Princesse Marguerite in the small church of St Paul's by the Tournelles Palace in a subdued ceremony, the bride and groom both in tears. The Duke of Savoy has sent for King Philip's personal physician.

10 July 1559: Death

Despite the skilful removal of five pieces of wood from the king's brain by his surgeon, Ambroise Pare, the king's pain and fever only worsened. After days of extreme agony, King Henri II died on 10 July. Queen Catherine had stayed constantly by his bedside, not wanting to lose one moment with him.

11 July–21 August 1559: Broken Lance

Moving into the Louvre on 11 July, Queen Catherine, dressed all in black apart from an ermine collar, gave orders for black silk to cover the bed, walls and floors of her apartments, allowing only two candles to give light on a black-covered altar. Observers said she was in such anguish that she barely acknowledged foreign dignitaries paying their respects, and many said they were moved to tears at the sight of her utter desolation. She was attended constantly by Queen Mary and Marguerite, the king's sister.

On 12 July, a day on which an exceptional six-day heatwave began, the embalmed king's corpse was carried into Notre-Dame to lie in state for forty days. At the palace, his effigy was presented every morning and evening with the usual table service as if he was still alive, the food and drink later distributed to the poor. His funeral was held at St-Denis from 11 to 13 August.

On 21 August, Queen Catherine, at the end of the mourning period, performed her last public office for her husband by attending a solemn mass in the chapel of the Palace of St-Germain. Queen Catherine's tears never once stopped flowing and she has taken for her future emblem a broken lance inscribed, 'From this has come my tears and my pain.'

August 1559: Scotland

A conference had been held in July between the Lords of the Congregation and Regent Marie: the former agreed to leave Edinburgh, obey the law, stop molesting the clergy and attacking churches; in return the regent agreed she would not molest their preachers nor allow clergy to do so. Mid-August, 1,000 infantry and cavalry sent by Queen Mary and King Francis landed at Leith with their wives and children, promptly fortifying the town.

The Lords of the Congregation quickly protested that the regent had directly violated the agreement; she denied the charge, claiming there was no such condition within, unaware Knox had secretly published an extra clause that all French were to leave Scotland and no more to be brought in.

The Reformist faction was strengthened by the addition of James Hamilton, Earl of Arran and his father, whom he has convinced to change sides, along with the Earl of Rothes, Lords Patrick Ruthven, James Ogilvy, Patrick Lindsay, John Maxwell, William Kirkcaldy of Grange, Sir John Bellenden, Robert Melville and William Maitland.

10–15 September 1559: State Entry

At Villers-Cotterets, Antoine, King of Navarre had strongly argued for a regency which was resisted as the king is of full age. Told

Francis intended his principal advisers to be his mother and his wife's uncles, Antoine declined to attend any councils. Plagued by a terrible headache, the king delayed his departure and did not reach Reims until 13 September.

Two days later, in tribute to the king taking the sun as his emblem with the mottos Light of the Right and Faith must be Observed, the citizens of Reims had set up a pageant at the gate with a sun enclosing a glowing red heart, which opened to reveal a little girl who gave him the keys and verses of welcome. Riding a white charger and wearing a suit of black velvet, the king rode through the beautifully decorated streets in a great storm of wind and rain which soaked the tapestries and the heralds' plumes. Met by Cardinal de Lorraine in his capacity as Archbishop of Reims, he was accompanied to the west door of the cathedral. There, under a great canopy of crimson velvet, awaited cardinals, bishops and clergy. After the archbishop made his oration, King Francis was conducted to the high altar, where he prayed and offered a gold statue of St Francis and kissed the cross. He was then escorted to apartments prepared in the Palais du Tau. On the morrow, the Duke of Savoy intends to present the king with the Order of the Golden Fleece from King Philip.

Queen Mary made her entry later in the day; her litter got soaked in the rain as the bad weather refused to abate.

18 September 1559: Coronation

Just after midnight, after praying all evening in the cathedral, King Francis entered his oratory, a pavilion made for him of purple damask decorated with gold *fleurs-de-lis*, to make his confession. Less than six hours later, he gave orders for four knights to go to the Abbey of St Remy, taking with them an extra white horse and a white damask canopy for the Grand Prior. The four acted as hostages while the prior conveyed the Holy Ampulla to the cathedral.

An hour later, the ducs de Guise, Aumale, Nevers and Montpensier with King Antoine arrived at the cathedral to assemble with the ecclesiastical peers to form the procession, accompanied by canons and chaplains. With crosses and candles carried before them, they walked to the palace and entered the king's bedchamber, where he lay upon a bed covered in cloth-of-gold damask over crimson silk, his head resting on a crimson velvet pillow. He rose and was dressed in a fine linen shirt and crimson satin camisole, both with slits front and back loosely laced. Over them he wore a long-sleeved cloth-of-silver robe. He was then led in procession to the cathedral's galleried scaffold, called The Heart, erected in front of the high altar. The king knelt in prayer and was then conducted to his gold-covered seat, while those who came with him took their seats in the galleries: ecclesiastics to the right and lay peers to the left, sitting with lords, knights and ambassadors from Spain, Portugal and the Pope. Sat with them were Charles, Prince of La Roche-sur-Yon, his son Henri, Marquis de Beaupreau and Francois, Comte d'Eu, who were to make the offerings of bread, wine and gold.

In the queen's gallery sat the three queens – Mary (shining in silver), Elisabeth and Catherine – plus princesses and ladies of the court with the king's brothers, the Duke of Savoy (whose fever had delayed the coronation by a day), Duc de Lorraine, the Prince of Ferrara and Count d'Egmont.

King Francis, after kissing the Gospels and leaving a hand on them, knelt and made his coronation oath to defend the church, keep the peace, provide justice to his people and hunt down heretics. When he stood the congregation was asked if they accepted him for king. To loud acclamation, the king's silver robe was removed and buskins put on his feet, while the King of Navarre affixed and removed the spurs. The sword Joyeuse in its scabbard was blessed and girded on him, and during the prayers he held the naked blade upright, humbly placing it on the altar, after which the archbishop handed it to Constable Montmorency to carry naked in front of the king until after the royal banquet.

The archbishop, using a golden stylus, took from the Holy Ampulla a tiny quantity of the oil, about the size of a pea, which he placed upon his finger to mix with the chrism. Francis, kneeling before the archbishop, was anointed on the crown of his head, his chest, between his shoulders, on his right and left shoulders and on the bends of both arms. The slits of his chemise and shirt were relaced and he was dressed in an azure blue tunic, dalmatic and mantle (which his father had worn at his own coronation). After his palms were anointed, gloves were placed on his hands and the diamond ring placed on the forefinger of his right hand. In his right hand he held the sceptre; in his left the Hand of Justice. Lastly, the great Crown of Charlemagne, gold and bejewelled with its four large, jewelled *fleurs-de-lis*, was then placed over his head while the peers, summoned at this part of the ceremony, touched it with their right hands. Then the king was lifted up to his throne while the people cheered loudly to the sound of artillery, trumpets, oboes and drums. Mass and offering followed, the king wearing his lighter crown. Afterward, in procession as before, he entered the palace to attend the royal banquet.

Once the festivities are over, the royal family intend to move to Blois for the winter season after visiting Lorraine and Champagne.

Late September 1559: 'Pale as a ghost'

A few days after the coronation, King Francis had an attack of quartan fever. As soon as he felt recovered, 'every day the court saw with astonishment the king, pale as a ghost' go hunting with his dogs, spear or arquebus in hand, leaving before dawn and riding all day, hardly bothering to eat and sometimes taking shelter at nightfall in the first manor house he reached.

October–November 1559: Tyrant

News came from Scotland that Queen Marie, lying sick in Edinburgh Castle, was conveyed by French soldiers to the safety of her house in fortified Leith, when on 18 October the Lords of the Congregation advanced in great strength on the city. Three days later, the Lords demanded by letter that she, being 'deposed' for ruling as a tyrant who had betrayed the country to a foreign enemy, should leave Scotland and take all the French with her. In response she sent Robert Forman, Lyon Herald to tell them she was surprised any person should claim power besides her daughter and son-in-law, from whom her own authority derived: 'As to subduing the kingdom by force, for whom should I conquer it, my daughter being the lawful possessor. As for Leith, how come it is lawful for you to keep an army at Edinburgh and not lawful for me to keep forces at Leith for my own defence?'

They responded by proclaiming with trumpets at the Mercat Cross, in the name of Mary and Francis (with a counterfeit seal that had been procured by the Hamiltons after compelling James Cortry to engrave it), that the regent was no longer to be obeyed. Lyon returned with their message that she and all French soldiers should leave Leith within twenty-four hours or be attacked. She did no such thing, however, and when the Lords marched on Leith the French defeated them. Adding further insult, James Hepburn, the twenty-three-year-old Earl of Bothwell, waylaid John Cockburn of Ormiston and confiscated a large sum of money intended to aid the Lords. Lord James, swearing undying vengeance, pursued him with 2,000 horsemen. Bothwell took refuge in Crichton Castle and escaped with the money before his castle was seized and sacked. The Lords, taunted with jeers and stones, abandoned Edinburgh for Linlithgow on 5 November. The day after, Queen Marie was welcomed back into Edinburgh.

18–25 November 1559: Parting

The royal party left Blois to escort Queen Elisabeth to Chatellerault in Poitou, arriving on 23 November. The king and three queens made solo entrances into the town in the snow. The following days were spent by Queen Catherine and Elisabeth together, mostly in tears, and no less by the heartbroken Queen Mary and King Francis. Even the Spanish ambassador forgot his Castilian stiffness, touched at the sight of the Spanish queen tearing herself from her mother's arms as she entered the litter which will take her, via Poitiers, to Spain.

23 December 1559: Execution

Anne du Bourg was put to death, strangled first and then burned at the Place du Greve.

3 March 1560: Conspiracy

Couriers arrived at Amboise with letters warning King Francis of a conspiracy against him, but unlike the nebulous warnings he has received since January while at Blois, details were specific: a nameless 'great prince' intended to murder him, his wife, his mother and his brothers along with the Duc de Guise and Cardinal de Guise on 6 March.

7 March 1560: Letter

From Amboise, Queen Mary ended a letter to her mother, 'We are seeing things here which we never thought to see, and are no more happy in our traitors and rebels here than you are there. But thank God, they have been discovered.' In the margin she wrote, 'I dare not say more, as I fear my letters are opened and read.'

9–28 March 1560: Tumult of Amboise

Believing the recent threat mere rumour, on 9 March King Francis decided to go hunting. Two days later, small bands of armed men were discovered and arrested in surrounding woods and villages. The chateau went once more into lockdown. To the surprise of many, Louis de Bourbon, Prince of Conde (suspected as being the 'great prince') arrived that same day. He was appointed to guard one of the gates, alongside Mary's uncle Francois, the Grand Prior. A group of soldiers arrested near the Chateau de Noizay complained they only wished to petition the king for their wages. When they came before him, King Francis rebuked them, gave them their wages and commanded them to return home.

Early on 15 March, boatmen on the Loire spotted more than 100 horsemen, wearing white sashes, galloping down the Blois Road towards Amboise and alerted the castle. When the horsemen reached the foot of the castle, mounted defenders awaited them. Would-be attackers not taken prisoner scattered into the woods and were pursued. Two who were taken had been among those pardoned by the king the day before, and he ordered them instantly hanged from the battlements over the castle gate.

One party of horsemen took refuge in a house, wounding many who surrounded it. When the house was set on fire, fifteen men surrendered but one threw himself into the flames and burned himself alive. As defenders returned from all around, they brought in many prisoners. In the evening seven were hanged after questioning. During the day, the king had sent out a summons for men-at-arms, weapons and artillery and issued a general pardon for all who would return to their homes. While they waited, the Duc de Guise continued sending out bands of horsemen to scour the woods. On one such foray, the leader of the enterprise, La Renaudie, was caught and killed when he tried to escape. His papers were gathered for close examination and his corpse was displayed on a gibbet at the court gate for two days.

As interrogations continued, prisoners revealed they had been recruited at Orleans and given arms, provisions and pay of 4 crowns. Told of this, the cardinal dashed his biretta to the ground in a rage and stomped on it several times. The king was indignant and one night at supper he struck the table, saying, 'There are people who court and betray me, I shall make them rue it one day.'

By 20 March, King Francis, tired of being cooped up, decided to visit a heronry a league away, accompanied by his brother-in-law the Duc de Lorraine. Queens Mary and Catherine rode to Chateau de Chenonceau, while Duchesse Claude went by water, not wishing to ride.

Three days later prisoners were tried and many were hanged or beheaded in the courtyard; those quartered had their body parts distributed in the town and surrounding villages.

On 25 March, King Francis gave audience to Catanea, an ambassador from the King of Algiers, who presented him with a gift of six Turkish horses. The ambassador was entertained magnificently in the afternoon by a joust, the highlight being the entry of Jacques, Duc de Nemours dressed like a burgher's wife in a black dress, a bunch of 100 keys chiming like bells hanging from a silver chain on his girdle. His opponent, Grand Prior Francois, came out in Egyptian dress, wearing a velvet gown with puffed silk sleeves and a large round hat, with a monkey dressed in baby clothes on his left arm.

On 28 March, ten men stood on the gallows with ropes around their necks but by mercy of the king were condemned to the galleys for life.

1 April 1560: Proclamation

A proclamation dated 29 March has been received by King Francis from the English queen. She says she is persuaded, thanks to her 'gentle and gracious nature', that the title to the English crown injuriously pretended by his wife proceeds from the ambitious desire of the House of Guise, and that for the security of her realm, and to her great cost, she has assembled sea and land forces provoked by the nearness of French soldiers and threats of their being reinforced. She wants it known she wishes to remain at peace so long as no manifest invasion is made upon her realm or people.

3 April 1560: Protest

After the arrest of his master of horse, Louis, Prince of Conde in council at Chenonceau protested that he heard whispers accusing him of being author of the late conspiracy. He said if any would make such a charge openly, he would absolve himself by sword. Duc Francois spoke in the prince's favour while the Cardinal de Lorraine sat behind the king's chair, keeping his eyes fixed on the floor. The king uttered few words in reply, speaking low as is his wont, so that only the prince could hear him.

24 April 1560: Passing Visit

Riding from Chenonceau, Gomez, Count de Feria and his wife, Jane Dormer, were welcomed on the road by King Francis who invited them to break their journey and dine at his table at Amboise. Queen Mary presented the countess with a jewelled touret and two very handsome gowns, one of cloth-of-gold, the other of crimson satin covered with gold embroidery.

April–May 1560: Scottish News

After Lord Grey of Wilton brought an English army of 8,000 into Scotland in March, Lord Erskine granted asylum to Regent Marie, now so ill she can only walk with a staff. He has refused admittance to Edinburgh Castle to anyone, whether French, Scots or English. To talk to any person, she comes to the parapet in front of the blockhouse while they stand outside the gates. The last few months have seen constant fighting, with the upper hand shifting between the camps. In May the French won a battle, helped by Leith lassies loading French muskets and pouring hot liquid on the heads of those scaling the walls. The queen asked for a parley with Lord Grey, offering to remove from Scotland all the French troops. He conferred with the Earls of Arran and Argyll and returned to tell her there would be no peace until every French soldier, minister and official, along with the queen herself, should depart Scotland, for no longer would they accept any governor except a native Scot. Once alone, Queen Marie was heard sobbing.

28 June 1560: 'Forgive her'

Since Queen Mary had come to realise the danger of her mother's situation, and fearful of losing her kingdom, she had incessantly shed bitter tears and made herself so ill she had taken to her bed, ignoring all comfort given to her by her husband, his mother or her uncles. When news arrived on 18 June of her mother's death seven days before, it was kept from her, courtiers waiting for the Cardinal de Lorraine to break the news. He related to her that her mother on her deathbed had requested the attendance of duke and nobles – friends and foes – and had so generously received them that they were shamed into tears. She had asked them to return to their allegiance, make peace and dismiss both armies. Tiring, she beseeched them tearfully to 'forgive her everything wherein she had displeased them since her arrival in Scotland'. She spoke with Preacher Willock for a while at their request but, losing speech, died around midnight.

July 1560: Treaty of Edinburgh

The Peace Treaty of Edinburgh was signed by the Lords of the Congregation and French deputies led by Henri Cleutin, Seigneur d'Oysel on 6 July. D'Oysel afterwards invited the English commissioners to eat with him. At the banquet neither fish nor meat was served except one dish of horse. Men-of-war are leaving and new fortifications have been demolished.

6 August 1560: Accord

At Fontainebleau the English ambassador, Sir Nicholas Throckmorton, was given audience by Queen Mary. She stayed standing throughout and spoke only in Scots. He affirmed that his mistress had kept her word and proceeded no further for her surety than she had promised. Her forces had left and only an ordinary garrison was at Berwick. Queen Mary replied she was glad of peace and hoped Queen Elizabeth would continue it, as would she.

A touch of pleasure for the queen for from Madrid: the Bishop of Limoges has sent her a book on chess, saying he has heard she enjoys the game. Rumour has it he arrives unexpectedly somewhere, plays and always beats his host; many await his sudden appearance!

12 August 1560: Memorial Service

A memorial service for Queen Mary's mother was held at Paris Notre-Dame on the Feast of St Clare, a nod to the part of Marie's childhood spent in a convent of Poor Clares with her grandmother Philippa of Guelders, Queen of Sicily. Heralds stood at the entrance to the choir while her body was represented by an empty coffin covered in cloth of gold and topped by a white satin cross. The requiem mass was given by Eustache du Bellay, Bishop of Paris and the sermon by Claude d'Espence, who detailed the story of her life and the many good things she had done for Scotland, emphasising that at her deathbed even her enemies wept.

21–23 August 1560: Assembly of Notables

King Francis opened his Assembly of Notables by asking all those present to sincerely advise him on the problems of public debt, unrest in the realm and religion. Many noted the Bourbon brothers, Antoine and Louis, were not in attendance. Cardinal de Lorraine spoke on the first issue, revealing that when Francis acceded to the throne the country was on the verge of bankruptcy, with a deficit of around 40 million livres as a consequence of wars and wedding celebrations, and that royal revenues from taxes raised less than 10,000 livres per annum. Against his inclination he had tried to curb expenditure by freezing pensions and salaries, demobilising soldiers without paying them and leaving merchants and creditors unpaid as there had been no money in the coffers; he admitted this had caused a lot of the present unrest.

Discussion turned to religion. Admiral Coligny presented a petition to the king in which he requested an end to persecutions and for Protestants to be granted freedom to exercise their religion and build their own places of worship. Cardinal de Lorraine suggested that holding their gatherings in private houses should suffice for them. After debate he conceded to the calling of an Estates General to explore ways of reconciliation to calm the realm, agreeing for it to be held at Fontainebleau on 10 December and for it to be followed by a general meeting of the clergy a month later to examine abuses within the French church.

22 August 1560: 'His will is mine'

While waiting to attend Queen Mary, King Francis spent a little time conversing with Sir Nicholas Throckmorton, asking him if Queen Elizabeth enjoyed hunting. Told she did, King Francis approved, calling it his chief exercise and pastime.

Escorted to Queen Mary, the ambassador found her seated under her cloth of estate, attended by her ladies and gentlewomen. She bade him sit on the low stool placed before her. When he mentioned that she had not yet ratified the Treaty of Edinburgh, she answered in Scots that she would conform herself unto her husband, 'for his will is mine'.

He was, she said, to tell his mistress Elizabeth she much esteemed 'her amity' and prayed her to judge Mary by herself, 'for I am sure she could ill bear the usage and disobedience of her subjects which she knows mine have showed unto me. And write unto her from me that as I am her nearest kinswoman, so I will for my part in all my doings make it good, looking for the like at her hands, and that we may strive which of us shall show most kindness to the other.' Furthermore, she had 'forgiven and forgotten the faults of my subjects, but if they forget their duties hereafter, they may be made to learn to know it'. At the end of the interview, she promised to send Queen Elizabeth her picture 'though it not be worth the looking on, because you shall promise me that she shall send me hers'.

September 1560: Conspiracies

All through the summer months a war of pamphlets has been waged, many declaring King Francis 'unfit to rule without a regent', but most are vitriolic against Queen Mary's uncles, concentrating especially on the cardinal, labelled a 'ravening tiger' and 'venomous viper' with woodcuts purporting to show execution scenes from Amboise. Other accusations are that they abuse the 'youth of the king' and usurped a regency which rightfully belongs to Princes of the Blood, calling on all to rescue King Francis from Guise tyranny.

When La Sague, a messenger of the King of Navarre, was arrested, papers were found on him which clearly proved the Bourbons were behind the sedition. The king despatched one of his gentlemen to Nerac to tell Antoine that he was informed from many quarters of a conspiracy against him headed by his brother Louis, Prince of Conde. He summoned both to attend his court with a message: if the prince refused, he was 'very well able to make him understand that we are king'.

Meanwhile, the court ladies have been conducting their own conspiracy, secret whisperings lady to lady asking whether the queen was *enceinte*. On 10 September, the queen showed confirmation by adopting the floating tunic of a pregnant woman, but a few weeks later resumed her ordinary clothes. On 26 September, her uncles consoled the royal couple that they were young and had the future ahead of them.

18 October 1560: 'Delighted the hearts'

At the gate of Orleans on 18 October, King Francis was received with great pomp. Taken to a stage, he reviewed the troops, civic officers, children of the city and archers. Mounting a great horse and guiding it under a gold canopy, he joined the procession through the richly tapestried streets, followed by his brothers and nobles.

Later that same day, Queen Mary made her own state entry riding a white hackney harnessed in gold, wearing a gold dress studded with stars of diamonds and pearls. On her head she wore the royal crown adorned with *fleurs-de-lis* and left her face uncovered. Her grace, beauty and sweetness of expression 'delighted the hearts of the gazers', who cheered her until they were hoarse. She was accompanied by her aunt Anne, Duchesse de Guise.

31 October 1560: Arrest

Today Antoine and Louis de Bourbon finally arrived in Orleans, where they were received by King Francis with extreme coldness. Queen Catherine appeared moved by their reception, having tears sparkling in her eyes. Francis wished to hear from Louis' own lips what defence he could offer for his conduct. The prince began denouncing Mary's uncles and was peremptorily silenced by the king, who ordered him to be removed from his presence. He was taken to a house, already barred, in which he was to have no attendants and be kept in solitary confinement, surrounded by soldiers. He ordered Antoine to go to his apartments where he will also be kept under house arrest.

13 November 1560: Tried

Being a Prince of the Blood, Conde was brought before the grand chamber of the Parlement of Paris and tried by a commission of judges presided over by the First President. Found guilty of high treason, he was sentenced to be executed on 10 December.

17 November–4 December 1560: Collapse

While attending Vespers, King Francis collapsed clutching his head from agonising pains while pus flowed out of his left ear. Then it was remembered he had returned from hunting the day before complaining of sharp pains in his head and a buzzing in his ears. He was carried to his bed where the doctors bled him and applied suction cups. For a few days he improved but he relapsed with fever on 21 November; seven days later the doctors dosed him with rhubarb, which made him sick. Again, he rallied a little but found himself too frail to keep the Feast of the Golden Fleece on 30 November.

On 2 December, though still weak, King Francis was so determined he was recovering that he gave orders for all the tapestries, clothes, furniture and household goods be packed and transported to Chenonceau where he and his wife intended to remove next day. Although during the day he had a 'profuse evacuation' from his nostrils and mouth, he had sat upright and managed to take and keep down a little food.

The following day, still resolved on travelling, King Francis went to the cathedral but the cold caused him such excruciating pain in his ears and head that he collapsed. His servants had obeyed his previous orders so promptly that, when carried back into his apartments, he had to be laid on a mattress until a comfortable bed could be set up. With the king feverish again, through that day and into the next, Queen Catherine refused to let the surgeons carry out a trepanning operation, saying her son was too ill to bear it and too weak having been loose of his body.

On the evening of 4 December, he managed to speak a few words and took a little food before falling asleep.

5 December 1560: Death

An hour before midnight, sixteen-year-old King Francis died in unbearable agony, incoherent and feverish. Queen Mary stayed constantly at his bedside, while Queen Catherine kept vigil in his brother's bedchamber.

6 December 1560: Seals and Jewels

As soon as Queen Catherine rose, she summoned a Privy Council and declared herself regent for her ten-year-old son, now King Charles IX. She had appointed King Antoine, her son's nearest relative, first minister of the council and agreed she would open all state correspondence in their presence so they could advise her. The cardinal broke the seals of the late king in their presence.

The Duc de Guise, who had spent all night in vigil over the deceased king's body, came to Queen Catherine to express his loyalty to her and the new king. The same day Dowager Queen Mary handed to them the crown jewels, including the diamond cross, a large diamond and the Egg of Naples ruby; the forty-two items were valued at 490,914 crowns. She retained a large diamond set in gold with a gold chain and ruby, it being a personal gift from her father-in-law.

23 December 1560: Quiet Funeral

The body of King Francis was carried in the night to the Basilica of St-Denis where he was buried alongside his father. His heart had previously been buried on 8 December in the choir of the Cathedrale St-Croix in Orleans.

15 January 1561: Requiem

The requiem for Francis II at Orleans was attended by Queen-Dowager Mary, cardinals de Lorraine, Tournon, Bourbon and Chatillon, twenty Knights of the Order wearing their collars and a large crowd of courtiers.

February 1561: 'Without counsel'

Audiences were given by Queen Mary at Fontainebleau: first to Henry, Lord Darnley, sent by his mother Margaret, Countess of

Lennox from Temple Newsome to deliver letters of condolence; second to the Earl of Bedford, who came on 16 February to offer Queen Elizabeth's condolences. On 18 and 19 February, the earl with Sir Nicholas pressed her to ratify the Treaty of Edinburgh. On the first day she told them she was 'without counsel', their own queen having advised her to take counsel of the wise men of her realm. Bedford pushed again and she told him, 'The matter is too great for one of our years.' On the following day she replied that 'ere long some of the nobility of Scotland' would be arriving and when she had communed with them, she would send Queen Elizabeth an answer 'she trusts will please her'.

March–May 1561: Proposals

On a visit to Paris, where she arrived on 20 March, Queen Mary oversaw all her robes and jewels before travelling to Reims to spend Easter with her uncles and grandmother. On her way to Nancy to spend time with the Duc and Duchesse de Lorraine, she gave audience at Vitry on 14 April to John Leslie, a canon of Aberdeen Cathedral. He was an envoy from the bishops and Earls of Huntly, Atholl, Crawford, Sutherland and Caithness, to entreat her to land at Aberdeen where they would meet her with an armed force of 20,000 men to escort her to Edinburgh and overturn the reformed church. He advised her to have the leader of the Reformers, her half-brother Lord James, apprehended and detained in France. Mary then met Lord James at St Dizier. She told him bluntly – and publicly – she had no intention of ratifying the treaty with England and found the amity between the realms distasteful.

Duchesse Claude, keen to entertain her 'nursery sister', arranged hunting and hawking parties or shows and plays during the day; the evenings were committed to dances, music and masques. Many rumours drifted abroad that the queen was considering various proposals of marriage. But around 9 May she became so ill she was unable to attend the coronation of Charles IX on 15 May, and her grandmother carried her to Joinville to take care of her.

10–15 June 1561: Farewells

Queen Mary returned to Paris on 10 June, conducted in state from the gate of St-Denis to the Louvre by the Princes of the Blood where Queen Catherine and King Charles awaited to welcome her. River pageants on the Seine and feats of arms at St-Germain were arranged to honour her. The poet Ronsard composed a farewell elegy in her honour, saying the court would miss her as a pasture would miss its flowers, the sky its stars or the sea its waves.

Having been allowed audience on 15 June with Queen Mary, Sir Nicholas Throckmorton once again broached her ratifying the treaty. She advised she would give an answer when she had received the counsel of her Estates and asked for a safe-conduct from his mistress while travelling to Scotland. In conversation she remarked that she hoped Queen Elizabeth would no longer encourage her Scots subjects to continue their disobedience, for subjects should not give a law to their sovereign. Throckmorton replied that Scotland was in no other case than other realms of Christendom and that her mother 'had kept her realm in quietness until she began to constrain men's consciences'.

Mary countered, 'God commanded subjects to be obedient to their Princes.'

'In those things not against his commandments,' he replied.

She replied that she would be plain with him: 'The religion that I profess I take to be most acceptable to God...'

'But,' Sir Nicholas cut in, 'your uncle the cardinal has said great errors and abuses have come into the church', explaining that he sees need for reform.

To end the conversation, she said she 'did not mean to constrain any of our subjects, but trusted that they would have no support at his queen's hands to constrain us'.

20 July 1561: 'Make sacrifice of her'

Allowed a last audience with Queen Mary, Sir Nicholas Throckmorton announced that, because she had violated the condition to ratify the treaty within sixty days, Queen Elizabeth had refused to grant a safe-conduct; that if she ratified it as she was 'in honour bound to do, the Queen would not only give her free passage, but also be most glad to see her pass through her realm'.

Queen Mary sat down and bade Sir Nicholas to sit by her. Signalling her ladies to move away, she pointedly commented that she disliked to have so many witnesses 'of her passions as his mistress had', referring to Queen Elizabeth showing anger when talking with the Scottish envoy. She told him she was aggrieved to so far forget herself in asking for something she did not need, for she could 'pass well enough to her own realm without the Queen's passport or licence' and perceived Queen Elizabeth, though she was her nearest kinswoman, was not minded for amity between them, but seemed to prefer the amity of her disobedient subjects. And though she was young and lacked experience, 'I have age enough and experience to use myself towards my friends and kinsfolk friendly and uprightly'. Ending her harangue, she desired to know what she had done wrong to so offend his mistress. Sir Nicholas offered she had used the style, title and arms of England to which she had no right and had not done in Queen Mary's time. She replied that his mistress should be satisfied she had not done so since her husband died.

When Sir Nicholas returned after taking leave of King Charles, he wished her a good voyage, apologising that he could not wait upon her at her embarkation. Queen Mary told him that had her preparations not been so advanced 'peradventure his mistress's unkindness might stay her voyage; but now she was determined to adventure the matter whatsoever came of it. She trusted that the wind would be so favourable that she need not come on the coast of England; and if she did, then the Queen, his mistress, would have her in her hands to do her will of her: and if she was so hard-hearted as to desire her end, she might then do her pleasure and make sacrifice of her.'

14 August 1561: 'Adieu, France'

Presenting her aunt Anna with a beautiful necklace of rubies, emeralds and diamonds, Queen Mary embraced the Duc de Guise before giving a farewell to all her friends not travelling with her and boarded the galley. She has the comfort that three of her uncles go with her: Claude, Duc d'Aumale, Grand Prior Francois, and Rene, Marquis d'Elboeuf.

They set off around noon but as they sailed outside Calais harbour, a ship coming into port hit the sandbank and sank too quickly so that many drowned. Theirs was a little fleet of two great ships and two galleys. The larger of the two 'was all white, the other coloured red, was well-trimmed and appointed. She bore a white flag with the arms of France, and in her stern another white flag glistening like silver.'

Leaning her arms on the deck rail, Queen Mary murmured, 'Adieu, France, I shall never see you again.' As France receded, tears coursed down her face. At supper she could only manage to eat a little salad. Before retiring she asked to be roused at first light if France remained in sight, but they awoke in a thick fog.

'Will marry where she will'

Scotland, 1561–1568

In accordance with the Treaty of Edinburgh, Parliament convened for 1 August 1560 with full attendance of peers, barons and borough representatives. It lasted nearly the whole month and was considered as valid as if expressly summoned by command of the king and queen. An Act of Oblivion was passed, voiding offences committed since 6 March 1558, and a council of twelve persons, chosen out of twenty-four, was created to govern in the absence of Queen Mary. A petition to reform religion was presented which declared Catholic doctrine contrary to reason, the clergy licentious and exorbitant church revenues ill applied. This resulted in three Acts: the first abolished the jurisdiction of the Pope; the second condemned all Catholic doctrines and practices contrary to Reformist ideals; the third forbade the celebration of mass in Scotland with confiscation for a first offence, exile for a second and death for a third. Meanwhile, the Earls of Morton and Glencairn and William Maitland of Lethington repaired to the English court with a proposal for Queen Elizabeth to marry the Earl of Arran; she graciously declined.

Sir James Sandilands of Calder, Lord of St John was sent to France to gain royal assent to the ratification and the Acts passed. Arriving in early October, he was treated coldly and in November was disdainfully dismissed with a letter from King Francis to the Estates. In this he declared he was displeased at their presumption and intended sending two ambassadors to assemble a legitimate parliament. When, in the month following, they heard of his death, Scottish lords were gleeful, saying he had 'perished of a rotten ear... in that deaf ear that never would hear the Truth of God'.

In March 1561 ministers were dispersed all over Scotland, charged to uphold moral virtues, overseen by superintendents. In May, the Estates received an ambassador from France in Parliament who asked them to renew the Auld Alliance, discontinue the league with England and restore Popish ecclesiastics. In response to his visit, abbeys, cathedrals and churches not previously devastated 'perished in one common ruin'. During that summer there was much debate and sundry public dispute regarding religion but the realm itself was in 'quietness with good justice kept'.

19–22 August 1561: Arrival

When the thick, cold Forth haar lifted, Queen Mary's little fleet signalled her arrival by cannon and sailed safely into the bustling port of Leith on 19 August. She and her ladies were invited to rest for an hour or so in the house of Andrew Lamb until a party of welcome appeared, led by her half-brothers Lords James and Robert and including Duke James and his son James, Earl of Arran. As the ship carrying her horses had gone astray in the fog, hackneys and ponies had to be borrowed – to Mary's private distress, for her arrival in Edinburgh would lack a certain splendour.

At Holyroodhouse, Lord Robert had prepared apartments for her in the ground floor of his house, which was attached to the northern side of the palace. Outside bonfires were lit and she was regaled with violin music and singing. Brantome complained they played the 'vilest fiddles' and sang psalms which were 'out of tune and concord … what a lullaby!' To his disgust, Mary complimented them and asked them to continue, which encouraged even greater efforts. Her reward was three nights of broken sleep before she moved into the royal apartments on the second floor of the north-west tower.

In her presence chamber she hung black velvet which contrasted with the painted armorial shields on the oak ceiling. Her bedchamber had two small rooms leading off it into the turrets: the one in the north-west she decided to use as her private supping chamber and made it cheerful with crimson and green hangings; the other she chose for her dressing room. To the queen's great delight there were two gardens to explore: one on the south side, which was created by her grandfather, has butts for archery and the other, which she can see from her windows, was created by her mother. Nearby there is a tennis court, an orchard, a lion house and, surrounding everything, a deer park.

24 August 1561: Catholic Mass

On Sunday, promised she would be able to hear the Catholic mass in her own chapel, Queen Mary was surprised when Lord James had to bar the door to stop her service being disrupted. Using his own authority, he stopped the zealous Patrick Ruthven, Lord Lindsay, armoured and brandishing his sword, from rushing into the chapel to kill her priest. Her other half-brothers, Lords Robert and John, joined him to prevent her priests being attacked when they returned to their chambers. During the afternoon, crowds gathered around the abbey to shout abuse at hearing mass was being once again performed in Scotland.

25 August 1561: Proclamation

At the Mercat Cross, Queen Mary had it proclaimed she has no intention to interrupt the established form of religion and at a time convenient will take the advice of her Estates, 'desirous for one good order to the honour of God and tranquillity of her realm'. She commanded that no one molest her domestic servants or any French persons within or without the palace.

2 September 1561: State Entry

Leaving Holyrood, Queen Mary rode by way of the Long Gate and North Castle Bank through the triumphal arch and into the courtyard of Edinburgh Castle. After dining in state, at noon a cannon shot gave signal for ordering the procession to leave the castle. The Earl of Huntly bore the sword of state before

Queen Mary, who was met at Castle Hill by twelve townsmen dressed in black velvet. Bidding her welcome, they positioned a gold-fringed purple velvet canopy (lined with red taffeta) over her head. Continuing the ride downhill towards the city, fifty Moors danced around her: black-hatted, black-masked young men with bare arms and legs coloured black. Dressed in yellow taffeta and with gold chains around their necks, legs and arms like slaves, they held jewel-encrusted rings in their mouths. Accompanying them were sixteen prominent citizens wearing velvet gowns and blue bonnets. After them came a cart carrying children with a coffer.

Youthful Moors, respectable citizens and nobility preceded her down to the entrance of West Bow into the High Street. At the 'butter trone', the dairy scales, a circular cloud on a stage parted into four leaves at the queen's command, revealing a little boy dressed like an angel. He descended to give Her Grace the keys to the city, a Bible and psalm book covered in purple velvet. Keeping hold of the keys, she passed the books to Arthur Erskine, her master of horse, while the boy proudly declaimed, 'Welcome our Sovereign, welcome our native queen', the city offering her the volumes 'as gifts most gainful for a godly prince wherein your grace may read and understand the perfect way unto the heavens high and how to rule your subjects and your land...' Ending by saying that all with body and goods were 'ever ready to serve' her, he stepped back into the cloud and was raised up.

On a double stage by the Tolbooth, Fortune sat surrounded by three maids (male actors dressed as fair damsels) on one; a band of musicians played on the other. At the Mercat Cross, the queen was greeted by four fair virgins, dressed in 'heavenly clothing and from the cross the wine ran out at the spouts in great abundance; there was the noises of people casting the glasses with wine'.

At the 'salt trone', after a little speech, three effigies – Korah, Dathan and Abiram, rebels against Moses who had been swallowed up by the earth – were burnt (taking the place of the official pageant, forestalled by the Earl of Huntly, of a wooden priest being burned upon the altar for celebrating mass). Queen Mary quickly departed to the Nether Bow where on another scaffold the Antichrist in the form of a dragon was burnt while a psalm was sung. The queen halted at the entrance to the Abbey of Holyroodhouse to listen to the children in the cart. They made a speech admonishing her to stop hearing mass and sang a psalm. At their departure she made her way to her outer chamber in the palace, where a cupboard of gilt plate was presented to her.

3 September 1561: Luxury

In the evening, Queen Mary gave a grand entertainment. Hangings and arras, brightly lit by silver lamps, made the walls gay with colour. Rushes had been swept from the floors, replaced by Turkey carpets. Scattered around the room and gallery were tables covered with gold-fringed crimson velvet, among them ebony and mother-of-pearl chess boards holding exquisite chess pieces and ornate folding chairs and stools upholstered in red velvet with gold and silver embroidery.

The queen has carpeted her privy cabinet with green cloth, placing within her much-loved harp and lute, two globes (one celestial, the other terrestrial) and shelves containing her books in Latin, French, Italian and Spanish, covering history, chronicles, science and poetry. On the walls are portraits of her mother, father and husband and other ancestors along with geographical charts.

She has set up many beds in the palace, all rich and elegant, including one of frosted cloth-of-gold with red silk, another of crimson velvet decorated with gold phoenixes, a bed half cloth-of-gold and half cloth-of-silver embroidered with violet and grey silk, another decorated with leaves and branches with its canopy and headpiece fringed with gold and violet silk and another of white velvet with gold and violet silk with curtains of white taffeta. In her wardrobe she has sixty gorgeous gowns made of cloth-of-gold or cloth-of-silver, purple or crimson velvet, satin or silk, many adorned with gems or fine embroidery, fourteen cloaks and thirty-three gold and silver spangled masquerade costumes.

4 September 1561: Princes and Subjects

Summoned, John Knox came into Queen Mary's presence. She mildly rebuked him for inciting rebellion against her authority. He responded, 'If, madame, to rebuke idolatry and persuade people to worship God according to His Word is to raise subjects against their princes, I cannot stand excused. But if the true knowledge of God, and right worship, leads good subjects to obey princes from their hearts, who can reprehend me? In religion, subjects were not bound to follow their prince, but the commands of God. If men in the days of the Apostles had been compelled to follow the religion of Roman emperors where would be the Christian faith?'

The queen said, 'But these men did not resist with the sword.'

'Because they had not the power,' he replied.

'What!' exclaimed Mary. 'Do you maintain that subjects, having power, may resist their princes?'

'Most assuredly, if princes exceed their bounds ... it is no disobedience against princes but obedience to the word of God.'

The queen fell silent for a while. 'Well then, I perceive my subjects shall only obey you, and not me ... whilst I must learn to be subject unto them and not they to me.'

Knox replied, 'God Forbid, far be it me to command any from their lawful obedience. My only desire is for both princes and subjects to obey God; that He enjoined kings as foster-fathers and queens nursing-mothers to his church.'

She snapped angrily, 'Yours is not the church that I will nourish. I believe the Church of Rome to be the true Church of God.'

He retorted just as angrily, 'That harlot, the Church of Rome, would never be the immaculate spouse of Christ.' Scornfully he pointed out that her church was full of errors and polluted with vices. She ended his invective when she rose to go to her dinner, bidding him farewell. Taking his leave, he prayed she 'would be blessed within Scotland as ever Deborah was in Israel'.

Thomas Randolph, the English ambassador, noted that Knox had made the queen weep during the interview 'as some of that sex will do for anger as well as grief'. Knox said of the queen, 'If there be not in her a proud mind, a crafty wit and one obdurate heart against God and his truth, my judgement fails me.'

6 September 1561: Council

Crafting her Privy Council, Queen Mary made Lord James her principal minister and retained George Gordon, Earl of Huntly in office as Lord Chancellor. They are joined by James Hamilton, Duke of Chatellerault; Archibald Campbell, Earl of Argyll; James Hepburn, Earl of Bothwell; George Hay, Earl of Errol; William Keith, Earl Marischal; John Stewart, Earl of Atholl; James Douglas, Earl of Morton; William Graham, Earl of Montrose; Alexander Cunningham, Earl of Glencairn; and John, Lord Erskine. Other officers are Master Robert Richardson, Treasurer; Master James MacGill, Clerk of the Register; and Sir John Bellenden, Justice Clerk; John Johnston also took oath as Clerk of Counsel.

Queen Mary has placed a little sandalwood table by her Chair of State to hold her workbasket so she can work on her embroidery while she sits listening to their deliberations.

11–29 September 1561: 'Nearly suffocated'

In autumn's flaming colours, Queen Mary began her progress. In her personal retinue she has fifteen ladies, the Earl of Argyll, Marquis Rene d'Elboeuf and her brothers, Lords John and James. On the evening of 11 September, she arrived at Linlithgow before travelling to Stirling where, on her first night at the castle, she had a lucky escape from being nearly suffocated by smoke when her tester and curtains caught fire from a lit candle. Queen Mary lodged on 15 September at Leslie Castle with Andrew, Earl of Rothes so that on the following day she could make her state entry into Perth, where she was welcomed with a heart full of gold pieces. While riding in procession she suddenly fainted but soon recovered. It is said she often has such attacks, although usually after some unkindness. Next day she rode to Dundee, then crossed the Tay to reach St Andrews where she lodged a few days, before going to stay at Falkland Palace.

5 October 1561: Angered

After hearing Edinburgh Town Council had proclaimed at the Mercat Cross that 'all monks, friars, priests, nuns, adulterers and fornicators and all such filthy persons to remove themselves within twenty-four hours under pain of carting through the town, burning on the cheek, and perpetual exile', Queen Mary angrily ordered better-qualified persons replace Provost Archibald Douglas of Kilspindie and his bailies, or they would answer to her.

26 November 1561: Exiled

Grizzel Sempill, Lady Stonehouse, found adulterer and mistress of John Hamilton, Archbishop of St Andrews (half-brother of the duke), was ordered by Lord Provost Archibald to remove herself out of Edinburgh forthwith.

4–5 December 1561: Dirge

The day before the first anniversary of her husband's death, Queen Mary had a dirge said for him at Holyrood Chapel. The following day she offered a huge wax candle wrapped in black.

7 December 1561: Leith Sands

In a six-to-six running at the ring on Leith Sands to entertain the queen and foreign ambassadors, Lords John and Robert and Marquis Rene took part, their band wearing women's clothes. They defeated the other team who were dressed as exotic strangers.

Lord James said that Queen Mary, with many merry words, wished that either she or the English queen were a man to end all debates. She has ordered William Maitland to correspond with William Cecil, Queen Elizabeth's first minister, to bring about a personal interview between them.

13–15 December 1561: Wedding

Lord Robert married Jean Kennedy, sister of Gilbert, Earl of Cassilis, at the house of one of his bride's friends where Queen Mary had secretly arranged banquets and dances to honour the couple who are very much in love.

15 December 1561: Church Revenues

To maintain the kirk, the General Assembly agreed a third part of church property revenues either seized by nobles or still held by prelates should be given to Queen Mary to administer the monies to be used to maintain preachers, endow schools and provide relief for the poor.

19 December 1561: Feud

In a drunken lark, the Earl of Bothwell with Lord John and Marquis Rene hoped to surprise the puritanical Earl of Arran *in flagrante delicto* with his mistress, Alison Craig. He being absent, they returned the following night to her house and, refused entry, broke down the door but their bird had flown. On 19 December, armed Hamiltons lurked on the causeway intending to slay Bothwell who, being alerted, had raised his own armed force. News of the pending tumult reached Queen Mary's ears and she sent the Earl of Huntly and Lord James to stop the fighting and severely reprimand the miscreants, ordering Bothwell to repair to his castle at Crichton.

New Year 1562: Weddings

There were festivities at Crichton Castle on 3 January for Lord John's marriage to Jean Hepburn, sister to James. The queen attended.

Around the same time, Arthur Erskine, son of Lord John Erskine, married one of the queen's ladies, Magdalen Livingston, sister of Mary. The queen gifted her a skirt of cloth-of-gold with matching sleeves for her wedding attire.

5 January 1562: Refusal

From Seton Palace, Queen Mary wrote to Queen Elizabeth that she had not yet ratified the treaty as it was prejudicial to such title as 'by birth and natural descent may fall to us … we know how near we are descended of the Blood of England' and was 'loath to receive so manifest an injury as utterly to be debarred from the title which in possibility may fall unto us.' She desired rather a new treaty which recognised her interest to the crown of England after Queen Elizabeth and her lawful heirs.

8–11 February 1562: Wedding

Lord James married Agnes Keith, daughter of William, Earl Marischal at Edinburgh's St Giles Church on Sunday in the presence of Queen Mary, the Duke of Chatellerault, the Earls of Arran and Huntly and the English ambassador. At the wedding feast there was served wild venison, poultry and all kinds of 'delicate wild beasts'. In the evening there was a 'great casting of fire-balls, fire spears and running with horses'. To honour her brother, the queen knighted John Ogilvie of Auchindoun, Colin and Matho Campbell, John Wishart of Pitarrow (also to be made comptroller), Alexander Dunbar, William Kirkcaldy of Grange, the captain of her guard John Stewart of Traquair and John Stewart of Minto.

On Tuesday night, Queen Mary drank a toast to Queen Elizabeth and sent Randolph the 18–20 oz gold cup from which she had drunk. The following night she came in state from Holyrood to the late cardinal's house in Blackfriars Wynd to honour the newly wedded pair, the house having been decorated for supper. Afterwards she was escorted back to her palace by young men of the town dressed in 'masking attire'.

March 1562: French News

On Sunday 1 March, the Duc de Guise halted to hear mass at Wassy, a town forming part of Queen Mary's dowry a few leagues from Joinville. Informed that reformers were breaking the law and holding a service in a barn near the church, he decided to remonstrate with them. Some hotheads among his men went ahead and began to forcibly and rudely eject them. Tempers flared on both sides. The duke's men met thrown stones with arquebus shots, killing about twenty men and women and seriously wounding at least sixty more. This event sparked off similar occurrences by Catholics at Sens, Moulins, Angers and other towns. Protestants retaliated by destroying altars, tombs, relics and statues and burning down churches. In Orleans, Joan of Arc's monument was burned along with Queen Mary's husband's heart. At Clery the grave of Louis XI was broken open and his bones burned. At Rouen, Richard the Lionheart's tomb and the sepulchres of William the Conqueror and his wife Matilda at Caen were desecrated. John Knox preached a sermon which moved the queen to angrily send for him. He told her that he considered her uncles 'enemies of God' who 'spared not to spill the blood of many innocents'.

26–30 March 1562: Frenzied

Bothwell and Arran, reconciled by John Knox, dined together at the Duke of Chatellerault's newly constructed house in Kirk o' Field on 26 March and attended church together the day after. Two days later, with Gavin Hamilton, Abbot of Kilwinning, they dined with the duke at his principal palace of Kinneil. During the night the Earl of Arran, using a rope fashioned from his bedsheets, climbed out of his bedroom window. Appearing at Falkland, he demanded to see Queen Mary. When she rose, he said he had come to warn her that his father, Bothwell and the abbot intended to kill her half-brother Lord James and abduct and imprison her at Dumbarton Castle while she was out hunting deer. In the morning, Queen Mary left for St Andrews, taking Arran with her. Lord James has ordered Bothwell and Gavin Hamilton to be arrested and imprisoned at St Andrews.

19 April 1562: Surrender

At the Privy Council meeting Arran spoke wildly and confusedly. His father, with tears trickling down his cheeks, begged the queen to believe his son was demented and all his accusations false. She said he could show his good intent by surrendering the keepership of Dumbarton Castle to her. After the meeting, she invited the duke into her privy garden while she shot at the butts, one of her favourite pastimes.

3–11 May 1562: Lochleven

Recalling the pretty royal lakeside castle of Lochleven from her progress last September, Queen Mary decided to try out its reputation for excellent falconry. On the way from Falkland Palace her horse fell with her so she arrived on 3 May with a sore right arm and bruised face but is still looking forward to her sport. Preceding her she had sent various furnishings: in her presence chamber ten pieces of tapestry showing hunting and hawking have been hung. A gold-embroidered crimson canopy has been set over her throne, its draperies fringed with gold and silver silk. In her bedchamber is set a bed of green velvet, with a green taffeta counterpane, a table covered with green velvet lined with green taffeta, a small ebony sofa and several chairs.

17 May 1562: Marriage

John, Lord Fleming married Elizabeth Ross, one of the queen's ladies-in-waiting. She was married in a gown of silk taffeta trimmed with gold – a gift from the queen, who also arranged triumphs, shows and pageants in Holyrood Park by the side of the loch, the showpiece being the sea battle between galleys and a castle. Queen Mary also invited the Swedish ambassador who had arrived three weeks earlier with a proposal of marriage and a portrait from twenty-nine-year-old King Eric XIV; the ladies agree he is handsome.

23 May 1562: Tears

When Queen Mary talked with Randolph regarding her meeting with Queen Elizabeth being delayed until the following year, he was surprised when 'tears fell from her cheeks' before realising it had made her courtiers think he had brought some heavy news.

14 June 1562: Diamond Heart

At Dunfermline, where Queen Mary has lodged the last few days, Randolph, invited to supper, presented her with a letter from Queen Elizabeth. Reading it after her meal, she placed it in her bosom, next to her skin, saying she had 'a ring with a diamond fashioned like a heart and know nothing better that can show my goodwill to my sister' and would send it with a few verses written in her own hand. Removing the letter and returning it, she said if she could place it nearer her heart she would.

23 July 1562: Outraged

While walking in the garden at Holyrood with Queen Mary, Sir Henry Sidney said Queen Elizabeth was regretful their autumn meeting in York would have to be deferred. To his surprise, she wept copiously, saying that had she not had some inkling of what he had come to say, she would have been driven into a passion and kept to her bed all day. She has suggested a date next year between 20 August and 20 September. While they were in conversation, a Captain Hepburn approached and handed her a document which she gave to Lord James. He opened it to reveal four ribald verses 'and drawn in pen the secret members of men and women'. Queen Mary was outraged and ordered the captain's immediate apprehension for such a lewd gift which impugned her honour.

24 July 1562: Papal Visit

Brought across the fields and along the town walls to Holyrood, Father Nicolas de Gouda was escorted by the royal almoner into the presence of Queen Mary who awaited him in a private room at an hour when all her courtiers were at the kirk for the preaching. The nuncio saluted her in the name of the Pope and delivered His Holiness' letter. Before continuing the interview Queen Mary told him that though she understood Latin she was not well able to reply in that language and agreed to his request to admit Father Edmund Hay, who had accompanied him, to act as interpreter.

She spoke to Father Hay in Scots, excusing herself for it taking a month to receive the nuncio and with so little ceremony, referring to the disturbed state of Scotland. After reading the apostolic brief, she explained that in order to preserve traces of Catholic faith and worship in her realm she had been obliged to do many things she disliked; she could not send Scottish prelates to the Council of Trent, although she herself would forfeit her life for her faith, and she refused to allow letters to be sent to her bishops. Fearful of courtiers returning, she bid the father a farewell with the injunction he should keep to his room and not venture out, impressing upon him that she was prevented from exercising her rights of sovereignty for if she opposed them they frightened her with threats of an English invasion; her confessor and some of her Catholic attendants had already been frightened away, leaving her alone and isolated among heretics, obliging her to receive visitors in secret.

26 August–21 November 1562: '*Wished she could be a man*'

Going north on progress, Queen Mary arrived at Dunnottar Castle on 26 August. There news came to her that the Earl of Bothwell, imprisoned without trial in Edinburgh Castle since 4 May, had during the night prised a bar loose from his cell window, climbed down the castle rock and escaped.

The next day the queen reached Aberdeen. Given audience, Elizabeth, Countess of Huntly begged to be allowed to intercede for her son, Sir John Gordon, who had refused to enter ward at Stirling Castle to await trial after gravely wounding a lord in Edinburgh. Queen Mary refused, telling the countess he had first to surrender and enter ward as ordered, especially as he had impudently harried her retinue while they travelled. The bruit had come to her ears that he believed himself so handsome he could abduct her and win her heart. The heartsore countess invited the queen to visit her and the earl at Strathbogie Castle; this she also declined (she feared they meant to take her captive), but she gave permission for the Earl of Argyll and Mr Randolph to go. The latter thought it the best-furnished house he had ever seen in Scotland. The queen stayed at Balquhain Castle.

Leaving Aberdeen, the party travelled to Darnaway Castle, now held by Lord James after his sister created him Earl of Moray. Holding court and council in the fair and large hall there, the queen sent command to Sir John Gordon to surrender his castles of Findlater and Auchindoun and enter ward.

Reaching Inverness on 11 September, Alexander Gordon, Sir John's brother, refused the queen admittance to her royal castle. On hearing of this, the earl immediately sent word his son must admit the queen. When he opened the gates to her on 13 September, she immediately ordered Alexander executed and his body hung from the battlements. She delighted the citizens of Inverness by adopting Highland dress, having three plaids made from local woollen tartan: one white, one blue and a third black, embroidered in gold and lined with black taffeta. She gave audience to Hugh of Lovat, chief of Clan Fraser. The vain seventeen-year-old, imagining he made a handsome picture, declared he would lead his clan against the Gordons for her, which if she allowed would avenge the deaths of his forebears at the Field of the Shirts eighteen years earlier. She gracefully thanked him, saying she had no wish to cause further quarrels between the clans.

Randolph, having never seen her merrier, was amazed that Queen Mary was unconcerned by the menacing power of the Gordons. As they made their way to Findlater, harried still by Sir John, she said she wished she could be a man 'to know what life it was to lie all night in the fields, or to walk upon the causeway' with a helm, buckler and broadsword. Nearing the River Spey, scouts reported Gordon horsemen were hidden in the woods but no attack came. At the castle, all was silent and calls for it to surrender went unheeded.

Back in Aberdeen, on 22 September, the queen placed the soldiers, cannon and 120 harquebusiers she had sent for under the command of Captain Hay. They were ordered to Strathbogie where George, Earl of Huntly was asked to surrender the formidable cannon that stood in the centre court in front of his castle. He complained he could not understand why he was so badly treated; his son, not he, was the offender. He sent word to Queen Mary that he would send a party of Gordons to pursue and arrest his son. She declined, sending orders instead for the earl to be arrested. Huntly, alerted by the approach of horsemen at midday, abandoned his half-eaten dinner and escaped unseen over a back wall wearing neither boots nor sword. The bearer sent to Queen Mary with the keys to Findlater and Auchindoun was immediately imprisoned. On 16 October, Queen Mary put both Earl Huntly and Sir John to the horn, outlawing them.

The persecuted Huntly mustered an army of around a thousand men. On 28 October, they advanced towards Aberdeen, stopped by 2,000 men led by the Earls of Moray and Errol at Meikle Tap Hill near Corrichie, where Huntly's army was decimated. Sir John and his brother Adam were captured, along with their father who, being put on his horse, toppled off dead before he hit the ground. His body was thrown over fish baskets and carried into Aberdeen while his sons were led like felons through the streets. The Aberdeen surgeon, Robert Henderson, after removing the bowels, embalmed the earl's body with spices, aqua vitae, vinegar and other ingredients making it fit to be transported by sea to Edinburgh so it could stand trial for treason. The many rich furnishings and ornaments of Strathbogie Castle were sent either to Edinburgh or to Darnaway.

On 30 October five of the Gordon clan were executed on Castle Gate. Two days later, Sir John was led out to the same place. To belie the rumours that she had encouraged him by flirting with him, Queen Mary watched his execution. Sir John steadfastly looked at her, saying he suffered for love of her. The executioner was inexperienced and bungled the beheading while the queen wept. She pardoned Adam on account of his youth but, though he had nothing to do with the disturbance, George Gordon, married to Anna Hamilton and living quietly in the duke's house at Kirk o' Field, had the 'doom of forfeiture' placed on him and was ordered to ward himself in Edinburgh Castle.

On 21 November the queen arrived back in Edinburgh and a few days later she had to take to her bed with the new illness of influenza, called by those who suffered from it 'the Newe Acquaintance'.

7 January 1563: Fugitive

News has come that the Earl of Bothwell, though managing to stay in hiding for weeks after being shipwrecked in November and washed up on the Northumbrian coast, has been taken prisoner by the English.

10 January 1563: Wedding

At Castle Campbell, James Stewart, Lord Doune married Margaret, sister of the Earl of Argyll, in the presence of Queen Mary and James, Earl of Moray. After the banquet, there was a masque, with lute players and courtiers all dressed as shepherds in white taffeta with white damask purses.

8 February 1563: Treason Trial

George, Lord Gordon was tried, convicted and declared a traitor. Re-imprisoned in Edinburgh Castle, it is intended he will be sent in a few days in 'free ward' to the Castle of Dunbar. Queen Mary did not attend, being ill at Holyrood.

12–14 February 1563: 'Stab him!'

The French courtier and poet Pierre de Chatelard, while Queen Mary was in a meeting with Moray and Maitland, intruded into her bedchamber at Holyrood. Discovered, the queen's ladies ejected him before she came to bed.

At Rossend Castle in Burntisland where the queen lodged to break her journey to St Andrews, she found Chatelard in her bedchamber. Struggling with him, she shouted for Moray. When he rushed in, she screamed, 'Stab him!' Refusing to draw his dagger, he said killing him outside the law might compromise her and took hold of the poet to remove him.

22 February 1563: 'At last is free'

On the scaffold built for his execution at St Andrews, Chatelard, knowing his words would be reported to her, recited Ronsard's

Ode to Death which begins, 'Means death so much? Is it so great an ill...' and ends, 'And I shall not care. He that escapes desire, at last is free.'

15 March 1563: Assassinated

News arrived that Queen Mary's uncle Duc Francois has been assassinated. Fighting the Huguenots, he had retaken Bourges, Rouen and Dreux and was about to assault Orleans. At dusk on 18 February the duke, going to visit his wife at the Chateau de Vaslins, changed out of his armour into a buff doublet and a hat with a jaunty white plume. As he rode along, a pistol shot came from behind a hedge. The bullet entered below his right shoulder but he made it to the chateau where surgeons removed it. When he failed to recover, they probed his wound again and found an abscess formed around two more bullets linked by iron thread. His fever worsened and he died during the early morning of 24 February, aged forty-four, his wife and eldest son at his bedside.

29 March 1563: Great Sorrow

While on a hunting trip around her brother's house at Petlethie, Queen Mary received a letter and last prayer with a testament from her twenty-eight-year-old uncle Francois, the Grand Prior, who had suddenly fallen ill and had died on 5 March in Provence.

9–15 April 1563: Time Out

Having kept Easter at Falkland Palace, Queen Mary travelled to Lochleven for some 'quiet time'.

19 May 1563: Outrage

In Queen Mary's presence, Archbishop Hamilton and forty-seven Catholic priests were arraigned and sentenced to imprisonment at the queen's will for openly defying the law and holding mass on Easter Sunday, 11 April. Outraged Protestants had initially arrested them. Hearing this, Queen Mary had summoned John Knox to

Lochleven to ask him to persuade the people not to punish any man for worshipping in their own religion. He refused, telling her they had broken the law and she must do justice.

26 May–4 June 1563: First Parliament

At the well-attended state opening of Parliament on 26 May, Queen Mary wore her crown and royal ermine-furred, gold-embroidered purple velvet robes. The Duke of Chatellerault bore the State Crown before her, the Earl of Argyll the Sceptre and the Earl of Moray the Sword of State. Her ladies accompanied her, causing John Knox to fulminate at 'such stinking pride of woman' at Parliament as never before seen in Scotland. The queen made her maiden speech in Scots.

Two days later, during the afternoon session, the chested body of the late Earl of Huntly was brought into the council chamber and stood upright. In the queen's presence he was declared a traitor, his title attainted and his arms torn and struck out of the Heralds' Book. His body was then taken to Blackfriars Priory. Similarly, Gordon, Earl of Sutherland, who had fled into Louvain after being implicated in his cousin's rebellion, was declared attainted and forfeit.

Several Acts were made in the days following: men or women found continuing in adultery to be punished with all rigour, even to death; ditto for any practising witchcraft; no subject, of whatever quality, to raise armed bands, neither horse nor foot; no subject within burghs, without special licence, to wear armour or arms, or 'make sound of trumpet or tabor, use culverins or display banners, ensigns or other bellicose instruments'. Coal exports were banned, hoarding of corn was to cease and no deer, roe deer or other wild animals were to be shot with pistols or culverins as noblemen 'can get no pastime of hawking and hunting as has been had in times past'.

John Knox angered the queen. He gave a sermon on Sunday 30 May, warning the attending lords that if they allowed the queen to marry 'an infidel' (a Catholic), they would 'banish Jesus Christ' from Scotland and bring God's vengeance upon them. When he came into the queen's presence as summoned, she began angrily, 'I have borne with you in all your rigorous manner of speaking against myself and my uncles ... I have given you presence and audience whenever it pleased you to admonish me and yet I cannot be quit of you. I vow to God I shall be once revenged.'

Waiting for her 'to hold her eyes dry ... and the howling besides womanly weeping' which stopped her speaking, he replied, 'True, Madam, I have been at divers controversies but never perceived your Grace to be offended at me, but when God delivers you from the bondage of darkness and error, you will find the liberty of my tongue inoffensive.'

'And what have you to do with my marriage?' she asked coldly.

Knox replied, 'A subject of this realm, Madam, albeit I be neither earl, lord nor baron but yet I am a profitable member of the same.' As he repeated the tenets of his sermon, the queen wept so hard that her page was unable to give her enough handkerchiefs with which to dry her eyes. Knox said he did not rejoice to see her weep nor did she have just occasion to be offended for he was forced to obey God and speak plain. She ordered him out of her sight. He was directed to her outer chamber where her ladies were sat in their colourful dresses. In a merry tone, Knox said to them, 'Fair ladies, how pleasant this life of yours if it should abide and in the end we might pass to heaven in such gay clothing. But that knave Death will come whether we will or not ... foul worms will be busy with the flesh be it ever so fair and tender...' He was summarily ordered to remove himself to his house.

24 June 1563: Portrait

To Queen Mary's joy, Maitland returned from France with a portrait of her mother. He also brought three bodices of red satin with gold thread, three of white satin with silver thread, two coats of green velvet with cloth-of-gold and two of violet velvet with cloth-of silver along with rolls of blue-figured cloth-of-gold, grey satin and colombe taffeta and seventeen silk and gold-embroidered cushions.

November 1563: Death

News has come that Lord John, aged only thirty-one, has died at Inverness. He leaves behind one son, Francis. Grief stricken, the queen said that God takes from her those she loves best.

9–11 December 1563: 'Until death'

Being ill in bed, her attendants said Queen Mary had exhausted herself at the masque 'dancing overlong to celebrate her birthday'; the queen said she had a cold 'caught from being overlong at divine service'. Randolph, after asking for audience, was shown into her bedchamber on 11 December. He presented her with a jewelled ring from Queen Elizabeth which she kissed several times, saying she now possessed two jewels she would always keep nigh to her until death: the one she held and her marriage ring.

23 December 1563: Melancholy

In court, Queen Mary is said to be melancholic. Whispers say it is from the pain she suffers in her side which responds neither to purging nor the medicines she takes; others that it is because no one solicits her hand in marriage; several say it is because her apothecary, having gotten one of her maids pregnant, tried to slay it in the mother's belly, for which both are sentenced to be shortly hanged.

6 January 1564: Two Queens

On Twelfth Day, Queen Mary crowned her 'Flamy' Queen of the Bean and dressed her in a gown of cloth of silver. She then beset Mary Fleming with so many jewels on her head, neck, shoulders and body there was no space left to add the smallest jewel. Randolph said so good accord for one day was never seen 'as to behold two worthy queens possess without envy one kingdom'.

9 February 1564: Request

Queen Elizabeth has been requested by Queen Mary to release the Earl of Bothwell, her 'highly trusted servant', from the Tower and allow him licence to travel to France to take up his appointment in the Scottish Guard. His keepers have only good reports of him: one says 'he has always been courteous and honourable, keeping his promises' and another 'he is very wise, not the man he was reported to be'.

Mid-February 1564: Teases

Invited to court, Randolph complained Mary was contrary. When talk turned to marriage she would sometimes enjoy speculating; other times she preferred a 'widow's life; sometimes she will marry where she will and other times complains no-one seeks her hand'. He asked her to show some compassion for her Four Marys who had vowed 'never to marry if she be not the first'. Idly, she said she would choose an English nobleman; court gossip says she would never debase herself marrying anyone of lesser rank to herself.

Lord James and his sister argued after he defended John Knox. He took leave to spend time with his brother-in-law, the Earl of Argyll. When rumour said he had travelled to England, Randolph was surprised when Mary was over-quick in believing it, 'conceiving evil where none is thought'.

Queen Mary gave a banquet of cheer with such marvellous dishes and entertainments that nothing was 'left undone that might either fill their bellies, feed their eyes or content their minds'. All the ladies, including the queen, dressed in white and black. The Four Marys served Randolph and the queen, who asked him to dine with her, while the chief lords were served by the rest of her ladies. Afterwards, verses were sung in praise of Queen Elizabeth and Queen Mary toasted her. As Randolph gave thanks, the queen handed him a paper with the words of the song.

She intends to leave for Lochleven on 7 March for a few days before travelling to Perth and then will spend Easter at Falkland Palace.

18–30 March 1564: Marriages

While Queen Mary was at Perth, she was pleased to receive Michel de Castelnau, Sieur de la Mauvissiere, who brought with him letters from her friends and family. In conversation with him she revealed she had been asked for her hand in marriage by the Archduke of Austria, the Duke of Ferrara and other princes of Germany and Italy. For herself, she told him she prefers Don Carlos, Prince of Spain, as he is likely to have rule of Flanders, and had secretly reopened negotiations because 'she was born a queen and had been the wife of a king ... and would not marry anyone under the degree of a prince'. Castelnau revealed he had come to offer a proposal of marriage from a French duke. She replied she was honoured and that she 'really loved France, but as she had once the honour of being mistress of it, should not return in a lower station'.

Queen Mary was furious when the news reached her that on 26 March the recently widowed, fifty-four-year-old John Knox had married seventeen-year-old Margaret Stewart, great-niece of the Duke of Chatellerault, without her consent. Margaret will be the stepmother of two young boys, Nathaniel and Eleazar.

And when Randolph had audience with her on 30 March and informed Queen Mary that Queen Elizabeth offered Lord Robert Dudley as suitor, she was shocked into exclaiming that 'your mistress wrote to have special regard to my honour' and so she had 'expected the best in England would be offered to her', assuming Queen Elizabeth would offer Lord Darnley. Randolph, trying to make the best of it, says it meant she was offered the best beloved of his queen and the means by which she might inherit England.

'I look not,' said she, 'for the kingdom, for my sister may marry ... my respect is what may presently be for my commodity and content of friends who I believe would hardly agree that I should debase my state so far.'

May–August 1564: Pastime

Leaving Perth, Queen Mary went to Stirling and Edinburgh and spent time all June at Lochleven. The queen, invited by John Stewart, Earl of Atholl and Elizabeth Gordon his wife, intends to spend much of August hunting in the parklands and highlands of Atholl.

9 October 1564: Proclamation

At noon, it was proclaimed at the Mercat Cross that Mathew, Earl of Lennox, who arrived in Scotland two weeks ago, is restored to his lands, heritage and goods; his doom of forfeiture of 1545 has been annulled, revoked and rescinded.

The earl has given Queen Mary a marvellous jewel, a clock and a dial curiously wrought and set with stones plus a looking glass very richly set with stones. She has given him well-furnished lodgings by the abbey and in his bedchamber set 'a rich and fair bed'.

6 November 1564: Proposal

Queen Mary revealed privately that the Prince of Conde, via her grandmother, had sought her hand in marriage making handsome proposals regarding religion and offering to manage the lords.

25 January 1565: Mischief

Days of great snow and wind have imprisoned the queen in her bedchamber to keep warm and she has sent a letter by bearer to her ambassador in Paris, James Beaton, Archbishop of Glasgow. He is to pretend to be greatly annoyed at the letter being delayed. Then, to make the English ambassador believe she had sent something important, he is to make a big show in soliciting an audience with Queen Catherine.

28 January–3 February 1565: Bourgeois Wife

When Randolph arrived at St Andrews on 28 January, he found Queen Mary and her ladies had taken up lodgings in a merchant's home, dressed in semblance of bourgeois wives. That evening she graciously received the letters from Queen Elizabeth to peruse. When he arrived the next day, it was 'passed wholly in mirth'. Over the next three days, Queen Mary invited him to dine and sup with her at her own table, refusing to attend to any business. When he broached the subject of her reply on 2 February, he was told that if he wanted to interrupt their pastimes with great and grave matters and was weary of the company, he should 'return home to Edinburgh and keep your gravity and great embassade until the queen come thither, for I assure you, you see her not here, nor I know not myself where she is become…'

17 February 1565: First Meeting

While lodging at Wemyss Castle in Fife, Queen Mary was pleased to be reintroduced to Lennox's son, nineteen-year-old Henry Stewart, Lord Darnley and Douglas. The fair-haired teenager she had met in France at the time of her husband's coronation, and later bringing condolences after his death, had become taller than herself. Such a new experience for the queen who said admiringly that he was the 'lustiest and best proportioned long man she had seen'. She was even more delighted that he had a good knowledge of science and excelled in witty conversation. They almost have the same birth date, Mary's being a day later than her cousin, but of course four years apart.

25 February 1565: Dancing

After Lord Darnley accompanied the Earl of Moray to listen to John Knox preach at St Giles, he was invited to dinner, supper and the dancing afterwards; he charmed the queen by dancing a galliard with her.

1 March 1565: Grand Dinner

Although Edinburgh was blanketed by deep snow, Moray invited all the court to a great dinner at his house in Canongate. Queen Mary sent word she wished herself in the company and was sorry she had not been invited. She was merrily told the house was hers and she welcome without being asked. She dined alone but sent word for all to come on Sunday 5 March to be at her banquet at the 'marriage of her Englishman'.

The Lord Moray's house has several splendid apartments and a spacious terraced garden behind it. When the weather is not inclement there is an arbour composed of three or four elm trees with branches grown together, and a fishpond with the statue of a boy fishing.

5 March 1565: Wedding

On Shrovetide's 'Fasterins Eve', Mary Livingston was married at court to John Sempill of Beltrees, (who had been born in England). For wedding gifts, Queen Mary has granted the couple the barony of Auchtermuchty, a bed with silk-fringed embroidered taffeta curtains and a cover of scarlet and black velvet. She gave the bride for her wedding attire a doublet and skirt in cloth-of-silver, with rubies set in gold upon the collar and sleeves. Buchanan composed a masque in their honour and the painter was paid £12 for making props.

Meanwhile, Lord Darnley continues to enchant the queen for he excels in singing and playing the lute and they share a passion for riding, hawking and hunting. He is skilled in swordplay and shooting and enjoys playing tennis and croquet. In the evenings the two enjoy cards, dice and music.

16 March 1565: 'Wept full'

The English ambassador in audience brought a letter from Queen Elizabeth in which she says she will not name any successor to her throne unless she decides not to marry. After Randolph left, Queen Mary 'wept full'.

Circa 19 March 1565: Proposal

In a beautiful Italianate hand, Lord Darnley handed a poem to Mary:

My hope is you for to obtain,
Let not my hope be lost in vain,
Forget not my pains manifold,
Nor my meaning to you untold.
And eke with deeds I did you crave,
With sweet words you for to have.

To my hope and hope condescend,
Let not Cupid in vain his bow to bend,
Nor us two lovers, faithful, true,
Like a bow made of bowing yew,
But now receive by your industry and art,
Your humble servant Harry Stuart.

Offering her a ring, he proposed to her but was refused. Lord Darnley said he would not give up his suit and wrote a lament:

The mourning turtle dove,
Such sorrow may not endure,
As I do for my love, Who has within her care
My heart, which shall be sure
To serve her until death...

He ends,

No pleasure till we meet
Shall make me feel content,
But still my heart lament,
In sorrowful sighing sore,
Till such time she be present.
Farewell, I'll say no more.

April 1565: Rumours

At the beginning of April, a few days after Lord Darnley arrived at Stirling at Queen Mary's invitation, he was 'sweated' after falling sick of a cold, as it was thought, until 'the measles came out on him marvellous thick'. Although served with a mess of meat at his own charge, the queen has sent him dainties from her own table, it being the first Lent she has been known to eat flesh, though she be in good health.

On 7 April Lord Darnley felt recovered enough to compete at billiards, partnering with the queen against Randolph and Mary

Beaton. The latter won and Darnley gave Mistress Beaton a ring and brooch with two agates worth 50 crowns.

During the queen's Easter Mass, the organs were played in her chapel. And on Easter Monday, she and her ladies dressed like bourgeois wives walked 'up and down the town' taking pledge of every man they met for 'a piece of money to the banquet'. Dinner was prepared, 'at which she was herself, to the great wonder and gassing of man, woman and child' and much wondered at of a queen.

As sharp pains in his stomach and head have forced Lord Darnley to repair again to his bed, the queen has delayed her intended journey to Perth. Rumours leak from the palace that 'the greatest and fairest visit his sickbed' and 'her care has been marvellous great and tender over him', and that she has 'such good liking of him' she will be content to forsake all other suitors. Since St George's Day there have been mutterings in the town at her unqueenly behaviour and that she should not think to marry at her own will without advice of her Estates.

2–6 May 1565: Dishonourable

The night before the Earl of Bothwell was to 'to keep his day of law' on 2 May in respect of breaking ward and the so-called conspiracy cited by Arran, the Earls of Moray and Argyll, the latter being the justiciary of the court, entered Edinburgh at the head of 5,000 men. Alexander Hepburn, Laird of Riccarton came to appear on Bothwell's behalf, saying that though innocent he was reluctant to enter the capital before such powerful antagonists. Queen Mary angrily intervened. She told her brother she mislikes his persecution of the earl and forbade the lawcourt to continue. Many sore words were exchanged, ending with her accusation that 'he would set the crown upon his own head'.

On 6 May, Moray was summoned by his sister to Lord Darnley's chamber. Saying he could show himself her most obedient subject, she gave him a document to sign declaring his consent to her marrying Lord Darnley. He told her that to seek his consent in such a way was dishonourable and he was unhappy at her 'hasty doings' in wishing to marry a man who favoured not Christ's true religion. Court rumour says Moray has disliked Darnley ever since he remarked while looking at a map of Scotland that 'the possessions of the Earl of Moray were too great'.

14–16 May 1565: 'Her own choice'

Nobles, summoned to convene at Stirling on 14 May, were asked by Queen Mary to consent to her marriage, which they reluctantly did the following day. In the early afternoon of that day, Lord Darnley rose from his sickbed. Swearing fealty to Queen Mary, he was knighted and created Earl of Ross and Lord Armanoch. After creating fourteen knights for his personal entourage, he returned to his sickroom. Later, when the Justice Clerk was sent by Mary to tell Darnley his dukedom was deferred, he was almost stabbed by the new earl.

To stop any protest by Sir Nicholas Throckmorton from Queen Elizabeth, the gates of Stirling had been 'shut against him'. After the investiture was over, he was granted audience with Queen Mary whereupon, in front of her nobles, he informed her Queen Elizabeth disapproved of her overhasty proceedings and for encouraging Lennox and Darnley – English subjects – to fail in their duty to her. Mary peremptorily told him she marvelled not a little at the queen's misliking, having, as she herself had once suggested, chosen not only an English noble but a kinsman of hers who surely could not be more agreeable to her.

Maitland is in disgrace for intercepting the letter Queen Mary had written to Queen Elizabeth in which she said she had so long been given fair speech and 'in the end beguiled of her expectation' that she was minded to use 'her own choice in marriage ... and be no longer fed with yea and nay'.

25 May 1565: Duke of Albany

The marriage of Henry, Earl of Ross to Queen Mary was proclaimed in the parish kirk of St Giles in Holyrood and Chapel Royal. Between three and four in the afternoon, the earl was created Duke of Albany with great magnificence in the abbey.

1–16 *July 1565: Pastimes*

Having spent most of June in Perth, with a day at Ruthven and another at Dunkeld, Queen Mary and Henry, Duke of Albany were finally leaving the town to attend the christening of Mary's godson. Informed the Earl of Rothes had gathered a band of gentlemen to abduct the duke, the plot was thwarted by the couple leaving on 1 July at five o'clock in the morning, much earlier than any expected. After a hard but exhilarating 30-mile ride, they safely reached Lord Livingston's Callendar House where they attended the Protestant baptism and the three-day celebrations.

They arrived back in Edinburgh on 4 July. A few days later, they rode to Seton to spend a few days enjoying games of golf and pall-mall. Since returning to Edinburgh on 11 July, the queen caused much gossip when strolling dressed in men's clothes around the streets with her betrothed.

28 *July 1565: Proclamation*

At sunset, Mary commanded Lyon King-of-Arms to proclaim at the abbey gates and Mercat Cross that Prince Henry, Duke of Albany was King of Scotland; that after the marriage Scotland would be governed in their joint names. A new coin has been issued: a silver ryal with their profiled heads facing each other with the inscription 'Henry and Mary by the Grace of God King and Queen of Scots'.

29 *July 1565: Royal Marriage*

Between five and six o'clock in the morning, Queen Mary was brought from her chamber in Holyrood to the chapel by the Earls of Lennox and Atholl. She wore her black mourning gown with a wide hood she had worn on the day her husband was buried. She waited in the chapel while the earls left to fetch her bridegroom. Unlike his bride, Henry glittered in an outfit studded with jewels.

Mary and Henry, according to the Catholic rite, were married in front of the nobles, except the Duke of Chatellerault and the Earls of Argyll, Rothes and Moray who had refused to attend. The king placed three rings on Mary's finger: the wedding ring, one for the Trinity and a fine diamond ring as his own token. They knelt together for prayers and benediction, then Henry kissed his bride, leaving her alone to hear mass.

When Mary returned to her chamber, she said she could now 'cast off care' and invited her nobles and husband to remove a pin from her attire. Laying aside her sorrowful garments, her ladies dressed her in colourful wedding finery. To the sound of trumpets, bride and groom passed to the great hall. At the ensuing feast, the queen's sewer, carver and cupbearer were the Earls of Atholl, Morton and Crawford; the king's the Earls of Eglinton, Cassilis and Glencairn. John, Lord Erskine, the son of Mary's guardian, was created Earl of Mar; Lord Fleming was given the office of chamberlain and Lord Robert was knighted.

King Henry threw gold and silver coins around the palace and out of the windows. After supper, before the dancing, a Latin masque was held: Goddess Diana complained to gods and goddesses on Olympus that one of her Marys had been stolen from her by the power of love and marriage.

Other entertainments are to follow, for George Buchanan has devised other masques including an equestrian challenge in which he intends exotically costumed bands of knights to fight either for King Pallas or Cupid.

Though it was her wedding day, Queen Mary promised the kirk's General Assembly they could worship as they pleased but affirmed she would in no way abolish hearing mass at court.

30 July 1565: Repeat Proclamation

At noon, King Henry was again proclaimed King of Scotland in the presence of the Lords but only his father cried, 'God save his grace.' Many think it illegal for the queen to confer the title upon him.

31 July 1565: 'Her whole will'

It is common knowledge King Henry has constantly harangued the queen to receive the crown matrimonial, despite being told by her he must wait until he attains twenty-one years and has the consent of Parliament. Randolph said the queen 'does everything to oblige him' but he will not do a thing to please her and wrote to the Earl of Leicester, 'All honour that may be attributed unto any man by a wife, he has it wholly and fully; all praise that may be spoken of him he lacks not from herself; all dignities that she can endow him with, are already given and granted. No man pleases her that contents not him. And what may I say more, she has given over unto him her whole will, to be ruled and guided as himself best likes. She can as much prevail with him in anything that is against his will, as your Lordship may with me, to persuade that I should hang myself.'

5–6 August 1565: Horning Remitted

On 5 August, George, Lord Gordon's 'horning' was cancelled and he was allowed to go where he pleases. The following day sundry earls, lords, barons, freeholders, gentlemen and men of substance were charged to come with fifteen days' victuals to pass forward with Queen Mary and King Henry to pursue the outlawed Earl of Moray and his adherents. For, though Queen Mary sent a herald-of-arms to them on 1 August, charging them to appear before her and the king within forty-eight hours under pain of being 'put to the horn', no one from Moray's party has appeared.

19 August 1565: Diatribe

Attending St Giles to hear John Knox preach, King Henry suffered a diatribe that God was punishing the people by setting boys and women to rule over them, based on a text from Isiah about Ahab and Jezebel. Furious, the king stormed out to vent his fury in hawking without first dining. The council has ordered the minister to stop preaching for twenty days, his place to be taken by his deputy Mr Craig.

26 August–18 October 1565: 'Nothing done'

With a pistol at her belt and a soldier's helm on her head, Queen Mary, with only one lady attendant, rode out of Edinburgh in pouring rain by the side of her husband, himself wearing a gilt corselet. Taking six pieces of artillery with them, they were bound for Glasgow to confront Moray and his party, now grown to include the Duke of Chatellerault, his son Arran, the Earls of Argyll, Glencairn and Rothes, Lords Boyd and Ochiltree and Sir William Kirkaldy of Grange. They have announced they fear that the queen and king intend to re-establish Catholicism in Scotland, having refused constantly to establish by law 'the true religion'; Mary countered publicly that the rebels want to usurp the crown under colour of religion.

At around five o'clock in the evening on 31 August, the rebel lords with 600 horse rode into Edinburgh. Captain Alexander Erskine sent a messenger to Callendar House where the king and queen – 'well-wet' – were stopped by the flooding. He asked for their instructions, fearing that if he shot the castle cannon he could injure or kill 'a multitude of innocent persons'. That evening he sent a herald to Moray to tell him he was ordered to fire upon them but would give them two hours to depart. His ultimatum ignored, Erskine ordered gunners to shoot three cannons which broke some tenements. The rebel lords left just before midnight.

Next day, Queen Mary travelled through the capital on her way to Stirling Castle. Undaunted by driving torrential rain and terrible floods, she secured the towns of Dundee and Perth before arriving at Glasgow on 10 September. On that day she sent a letter to King Philip of Spain that she was in 'danger of losing her crown ... and all pretensions we may have elsewhere' and asked for his aid and support, it being 'of importance both for the crown and liberty of the church'. She sent out proclamations for men to arm and assemble at Stirling on 30 September. Preparing to ride out on 19 September, her noblemen worried she would fatigue herself by so much riding with the army during inclement weather. They were told, 'We will never cease to continue in such fatigues, until we have led you to London ... and will Elizabeth repent for not recognising us as her heir.'

At Holyrood on the following day, Queen Mary received James, Earl of Bothwell, who had just arrived from France at her command. Restoring him to all his former offices and dignities, she made him Lieutenant of the Borders. Ordering the principal men of Edinburgh to come to her, she made a speech in which she requested a loan of money in order to crush the rebellion. Refused, she ordered six of the richest merchants imprisoned in Moray's lodging. On 6 October, it was agreed to loan the king and queen 10,000 marks while Edinburgh procured certain rights over Leith and for the citizens to remain at home. Two days later, George, Lord Gordon was restored as 5th Earl of Huntly and given possession of all his father's lands and honours. He departed with the king and queen to head for Dumfries, where the rebels were gathered.

They were met on the road on 11 October by Sir John Maxwell, who came as mediator. The queen would only allow him to make his own peace, telling him she was glad to see he repented his cowardly actions. Returning to Dumfries, Sir John told the lords Mary was resolved not to offer them any hope of reconciliation; not even when he had told the royal couple Moray wished to come to an understanding, 'leaving the sword for our last remedy'. Hearing this, the Lords left Dumfries and the following day the royal army disbanded. Queen Mary and King Henry travelled to Lochmaben for a banquet given to them by the Master of Maxwell.

Six days later the king and queen entered Edinburgh from their 'chaseabout raid' in which 'there was nothing done … As for the lords our sovereigns sought, they all fled into England.'

14 November 1565: Clemency

The king and queen, on 7 November, sent Marchmont Herald to Moray's mother, Margaret, Lady of Lochleven. She was to quit the castle with her son William and grandson Robert and their wives, along with their servants and goods, within six hours or be charged with treason. The herald returned to tell them William Douglas was sick to the peril of his life and Christina, Countess of Buchan, Robert's wife, was large with child and they begged humbly for more time to obey the royal command. Pressed by the Earl of Mar, Queen Mary has exercised clemency.

3–17 December 1565: Pregnant

Queen Mary, told by her doctor she is pregnant, has travelled by horse litter to Linlithgow intending to enjoy quiet time and take the air in its gardens, parks and orchards. She has a comfortable bed at Linlithgow in her favourite crimson velvet and damask embroidered with love knots. Her husband also likes the palace for its tennis court and pleasant loch full of fine perch. The queen has given her husband a purple velvet night-coat for a gift.

19 December 1565: Never Forgive

By proclamation at the Mercat Cross, all the rebel earls, lords and knights and others are summoned to appear on 12 March before Parliament to hear the doom of forfeiture laid on them. To the queen's displeasure, both the King of France and Queen Catherine de Medici have added their pleas to those of Queen Elizabeth to pardon Moray and his confederates; the queen remains adamant no one will be forgiven.

24 December 1565: Mass

While Queen Mary played cards until near daybreak, King Henry attended the midnight mass. After Christmas he plans to go hunting in Peebles until mid-January. Being so often away on his hunting trips, an iron stamp has been made with his signature so official documents can be processed without waiting for him to reappear.

3–12 February 1566: Order of the Cockle

At noon on 3 February, Nicolas d'Angennes, Seigneur de Rambouillet, who arrived at Holyrood with a train of thirty-six horse a week ago, invested King Henry in the Order of St Michael by placing round his neck the gold cockleshell chain. The king wore a crimson satin robe edged with black satin and velvet with gold aglets. Afterwards the king and queen, the ambassador and a few lords passed to mass, though the majority of the lords remained away, and then onto a banquet and masque in the old chapel which had been hung with fine tapestry. Six costumes were decorated with gold flames (made out of old cloth-of-gold cushion covers).

At the banquet and masque held the following evening, Queen Mary, her four Marys and other ladies, wearing men's apparel, presented each guest with a whinger which had been artfully made and embroidered with gold.

On the French party's last day, a banquet was held in Edinburgh Castle at noon. When they departed, the artillery was shot in great abundance. Queen Mary has given to the special envoy a silver basin and ewer, two covered cups, a salt, spoon and trencher – all double gilt – and two horses.

13 February 1566: Secrets

In a letter sent to Lord Leicester, Randolph wrote that city gossips said Queen Mary hated her husband and repented her marriage; that the king and his father intended 'to come by the crown against Mary's will' and intended perhaps worse things against her person. It is said that 'with the king's consent, Riccio shall have his throat cut', referring to her close friend and private secretary.

17 February 1566: Accused

When Randolph came to the council expecting to treat upon border matters, he was astonished to find himself accused, and expressly in front of the French ambassador, of giving money to the Scottish rebel lords. His accuser, John Johnston, was brought in. He testified that Randolph had given him three sealed sacks full of money, which he reckoned contained 3,000 crowns, to deliver to Lady Moray at St Andrews. Randolph said he was falsely accused but Queen Mary overrode him, claiming that she was highly offended and that he was unfit to be Queen Elizabeth's ambassador. He replied that he found it strange such a thing was laid to his charge, but she ordered he was to forthwith depart Scotland.

24 February 1566: Marriage

After Queen Mary had obtained a papal dispensation, the couple being related in prohibited degree, the Earl of Huntly's sister Jean Gordon, a close friend of the queen, was married to James, Earl of Bothwell in Holyrood Abbey, an event celebrated with great splendour. The queen gave the bride a wedding dress of cloth-of-silver. The king and queen paid for the banquet for the first day and festivities are set to continue for five days with jousting and tournaments.

2 March 1566: Proclamation

Ministers ordered Edinburgh citizens to publicly fast from eight o'clock on the night of Saturday 2 March until five o'clock the following evening, occupying their time listening to sermons and praying to God that He would mollify and soften the hearts of the king and queen towards the nobles banished in England.

7 March 1566: Opening of Parliament

King Henry refused to accompany Queen Mary to the opening of Parliament. George, Earl of Huntly bore the crown, James, Earl of Bothwell the sceptre and David, Earl of Crawford the sword. The Earls of Huntly and Sutherland were restored to their whole heritage. The Acts of forfeiture to be passed against the lords in exile were drawn up to be pronounced on Tuesday 12 March.

9 March 1566: Murder!

Early Saturday evening at Holyrood, Queen Mary, in the sixth month of her pregnancy, supped quietly in her private supping chamber, an intimate room only 12 feet by 10 feet, with her half-sister Jean, Countess of Argyll, Lord Robert, Sir Arthur Erskine, her steward Robert Beaton and David Riccio, who sat with a cap on his head at the head of the table. Though King Henry had declined to eat with them, around eight o'clock he entered the room from the queen's bedchamber, having used the private connecting staircase from his apartment below. Sitting beside his wife, he placed an arm around her waist. Almost immediately behind him, a pallid Lord Ruthven emerged, whom everyone thought was on his deathbed. The queen demanded to know why he entered and by whose permission.

Ignoring her, he pointed at Riccio and said, 'Let it please your Majesty that David come forth of your privy chamber where he hath been overlong.'

Riccio took refuge in the window recess behind the queen, who had sprung to her feet. 'If Riccio is guilty of any offence,' she declared, 'we will see him punished. And you, Sir, should leave or be deemed a traitor.'

As Lord Robert, Erskine and Beaton moved forward, Ruthven pulled out his dagger. Brandishing it, he exclaimed, 'Lay no hands on me, for I will not be handled.'

As if it was a signal, George Douglas, Andrew Ker of Fawdonside and Patrick Bellenden, with weapons ready, erupted into the room and knocked over the table, sending candles, cups of wine, plates of beef, mutton and pigeon and bowls of fruit flying. Countess Jean managed to catch a candle. In its light and that of the fire gleamed pistols, swords and daggers. Sheathing his dagger, Ruthven pushed the queen into her husband's arms while Patrick Bellenden placed a 'dagge against her belly with cock down' and Andrew Ker threatened to 'fix his poniard' in her left side, though the blade was turned away by Mary's cupbearer, Anthony Standen. Riccio, clutching Mary's skirts in terror, cried, '*Madama, io son morto, giustizia, giustizia.*' The king wrenched at Riccio's fingers, tearing them from her clothes. Struggling and screaming, the secretary was dragged out to her presence chamber. Lord Ruthven followed, bidding them take him down to the king's chamber. As the king continued to restrain her, David's screams died away. Mary, weeping, moaned, 'Ah poor David; God have mercy on your soul.'

Upon returning, Ruthven told the queen he and his accomplices were highly offended that she was heeding advice to restore the old religion and furious at her tyranny for not permitting the exiled lords to return. He said they would be in Edinburgh on the morrow as King Henry had pardoned them in return for the crown matrimonial. As Mary turned to rebuke her husband for his 'foul act', he defended himself: 'You chose me to be your husband, though I be of baser degree, yet I am your head, and ye promised obedience at the day of our marriage and I should be equal with you, and participant in all things.' Instead, 'You have avoided my company for months, and was in company with Riccio more than I.'

She told him it was not 'the woman's part to seek the husband', to which he replied that when he came to her she made herself sick. Ruthven interrupted them to say, 'It is a wife's duty to yield to her husband.'

She retorted, 'Why may not I leave him as well as your wife did her husband?'

He rejoined he and his wife had been 'lawfully divorced and for no such cause as the king now found himself aggrieved; that David was mean and base, enemy to the nobility, and brought shame to her and her country'.

Tearfully she said, 'It shall be dear blood to some of you.' He told her that the more she showed herself offended, 'the world would judge the worse'. Then, asking pardon for feeling feeble, he abruptly sat down and called for a drink. One of the servitors brought him a cup of wine. After he had drunk the queen began to rail, having wept inconsolably the whole time, that if she or her bairn died she should have herself revenged upon him and his posterity, the King of Spain and Emperor being her great friends and 'the King of France my good brother, besides the Pope and many princes in Italy'. Lord Ruthven answered that they were all 'over-great personages to meddle with such a poor man as he'.

Elsewhere in the palace, the Earls of Bothwell, Huntly and Atholl managed to escape out of low windows into the little garden which lodged the lions, and, gathering armed men, endeavoured to reach the queen. They had been driven back by a larger party of better-armed men, led by the Earl of Morton, who had already secured the gates and courtyard. Hearing fighting around the palace, Edinburgh's alarm bells began to ring and a party of thirty-five citizens came, well armed and carrying blazing torches. King Henry went to the window and told them the queen was safe and ordered them to retire. Mary was told plainly by Lord Lindsay that if she spoke otherwise she would be thrown over the wall in pieces.

Once Mary was alone, a maidservant crept in to tell her that Riccio had been stabbed many times just outside her presence chamber. Then his body was thrown out of a window and carried into the porter's lodge, where his clothes were removed and his corpse was buried.

10–21 March 1566: Counterplot

While his father kept watch, King Henry tapped on his wife's door in the early hours urgently asking to see her. Weeping, she refused. He tried again before dawn broke and she let him in. He whispered to her that those he had conspired with were intending to take her to Stirling to be held in perpetual imprisonment; that Lord Lindsay had remarked, 'It would give her plenty of pastime nursing her baby and singing it to sleep … and shooting with her bow in the garden for such things delighted her', keeping her busy while they governed Scotland. When someone wondered about the lords who might oppose them by force, Ruthven had said, 'If they raise any difficulty, we will throw her to them in pieces from the top of the terrace.' Having heard them talk, he told her he was fearful they did not intend to keep their promises to him; that he had been told he must abide by what they said, then removed his attendants and left a guard near his chamber.

Throwing himself on his knees, he implored, 'Ah, my Mary, I am bound to confess, though it is too late, that I have failed in my duty towards you; that the murder of Riccio had never been intended. The only atonement I can make is acknowledge my fault and sue for pardon and plead my youth and great indiscretion to intercede with you for me. … I confess ambition has blinded me and I have been the dupe of wicked traitors and I ask you, my Mary, to have pity on me, on our child, on yourself.' He showed her the bond he had signed agreeing to pardon the lords to gain the crown matrimonial, saying, 'If they knew, I would be a dead man.' Telling him he had done her much wrong and would never 'be able to undo' what he had done, she went on to say that he needed to act with her and for both their own safety they needed to escape, and that first they needed to get the soldiers removed.

He urged her to pretend to be reconciled to the conspirators, perhaps by promising them pardons. Mary refused, saying her conscience would never allow her 'to promise what I do not mean to perform. However, if you think it good, you can promise them whatever you please in my name.' He agreed he would do what he could and left.

During the morning, King Henry issued a proclamation in his sole name ordering all those who had come to vote in the coming session of Parliament to depart the city. Moray, who had arrived the evening before, visited Mary. He told her he had no part in the murder and advised her to admit the lords into her presence. She refused. Left in solitude, no food was brought to her until the afternoon, when it was scrutinised by Lord Lindsay.

On Monday, Moray and the other exiles rode along the High Street to the Tolbooth to protest they had come and had been ready to answer Parliament. Meanwhile, Dowager Countess Huntly was given permission to attend the queen. She had a message from her son: he and Bothwell were raising troops, and if she could manage to descend from a certain window by rope ladder they would get her away. The countess said she could bring it between two dishes as if it was meat. Lord Lindsay, suspecting their low talking, ordered Lady Huntly to leave the room. Although her dress was searched, the letter she carried between her body and chemise was not discovered. In it the queen informed them their plan was impractical as a guard was placed above her chamber opposite the window they had chosen. Instead, she directed them to wait near Seton and she would attempt to escape in the night.

Between four and five in the afternoon, the queen received her brother and the lords in her presence chamber. They knelt before her and sued for pardon, saying they acted not against her but one foreign, mean man of lesser consequence than the lords she intended to ruin. She told them they had offended her in several ways and she could not grant a full pardon so speedily but, as they knew, she was never bloodthirsty nor greedy upon their land and goods. If assured of their good future service, she would endeavour to forget what they had done. Suddenly, as if the child was coming, she ordered the midwife to be summoned and hastily retired to her bedchamber. The king, returning to the lords, gave particulars of the form of pardon which Mary would grant. As they murmured that it gave no guarantee of their safety, the midwife entered to tell them the queen was in some danger of her life. King Henry desired them to propose their own security and he would collect their papers at suppertime, which he did, saying Queen Mary was too ill to read them but he would ensure they were signed and returned to them in the morning. He then suggested the extra guards be removed for he would hold the queen that night in safe custody for 'it would not avail them in law if there were the least appearance of restraint upon her'. They agreed and themselves also left the palace and went to Morton's house for supper.

Around midnight the royal couple crept down the back stairs, through the offices of her butlers and cupbearers and through a door which opened into the burial ground. John, captain of her guard, had horses waiting for her including a tall gelding so she could ride pillion behind Arthur Erskine. Margaret Carwood came to attend upon her and rode pillion behind the captain, and there was a horse for King Henry but not for his father as, when he had asked, his wife had refused saying she had no trust in him and preferred him to stay away from court.

As soon as they were out of earshot of Edinburgh, they set off to cover the 9 miles to Seton at a gallop. As they reached the estate, King Henry took fright at sight of a band of horsemen. He spurred his horse, and tried to make the queen's horse speed up by whipping its hindquarters: 'Come on, come on, by God's Blood they will murder both of us if they catch us.' The queen entreated him to have some regard for her condition. His reply was, 'In God's Name, come on, if the baby dies, we can have more.' She told him to push on and take care of himself. The horsemen, who were in fact awaiting their arrival to be their escort, were astonished when they saw the king speed off by himself.

At Seton, Lord George had new horses waiting and they reached Dunbar Castle safely in company with the Earls of Huntly and Bothwell and Lords Fleming, Seton and Livingstone. They were joined along the road by the Earls of Atholl, Caithness and Marischal and Lords Hume, Yester and Sempill among others. The ride had taken a gruelling five hours and the queen suffered sickness along the way. As soon as she was in the castle, Queen

Mary wrote to Queen Elizabeth that her lords had 'slain our most special servant in our own presence and held our proper person captive treasonably whereby we were constrained to escape about midnight ... to where we are presently, in the greatest fear of our life and ill estate that ever princes on earth stood in...'

Tidings of the escape soon spread and men began flocking to the castle to render their assistance. The Earls of Glencairn, Rothes, Moray and Argyll sued for her pardon and favour and came to her by her permission. The king protested before them all the murder of David was 'sore against his will'. The queen issued proclamation for all persons of an age capable of bearing arms to come to Dunbar within six days and on the night of 18 March reached Haddington Abbey at the head of 4,000 men. Next day the Archbishop of St Andrews met her near Musselburgh. On the following day, accompanied by earls, lords and the archbishop, Queen Mary triumphantly entered Edinburgh and took lodging in the substantial house of Lord Home on High Street near the salt trone.

On 21 March, Queen Mary officially pardoned those involved in the Chaseabout Raid and had proclaimed at the Mercat Cross a declaration of the king's innocence in the murder. She issued a writ summoning Morton, Ker, Ruthven and his son Lindsay, the Douglases – George, Archibald and William – and sixty-three other conspirators to appear Friday next to answer for their crimes on pain of outlawry. Huntley was appointed Lord Chancellor in place of Morton.

28 March 1566: Retaliation

In retaliation for the public proclamation of King Henry's innocence, Morton and Ruthven sent Queen Mary the bond in the king's own handwriting and signed by him which proved he was the chief instigator of Riccio's murder. They revealed they had intended to take Riccio from his own chamber or when he walked through the close but the king 'would have him taken' when he supped at table with the queen, 'that he might be taken in her own presence; because she had not entertained him her husband according to her accustomed manner, nor as she ought of duty'.

2 April 1566: Aspersion

During the day Queen Mary wrote of her recent ordeal to Archbishop Beaton: counselled to sustain 'ourselves with flesh, having passed almost to the end of seven months in our birth', she wrote, her husband 'came to us in our cabinet'. Lord Ruthven entered armed and 'David Riccio took refuge behind our back' while 'Ruthven and his accomplices cast down our table, put violent hands on him, struck him over our shoulder with whinyards', with another 'standing before our face with cocked pistols' and most cruelly took him away.

She is also sending a letter to the Bishop of Dunblane in Rome to ask for papal aid, telling him she was lodged in Edinburgh Castle for her 'greater security', her rebels having fled into England 'bent on negotiating with those of that religion to raise men and money against us'. She expects force to be put upon her to accept their terms or lose her kingdom and life.

11–17 April 1566: Marital Discord

King Henry washed the feet of the poor upon Maundy Thursday and offended many by twice hearing mass openly. He left court on Good Friday; gossip is all of discord between him and the queen. Queen Mary offended many when she had Riccio's body reburied with Catholic rites and placed in 'a fair tomb' in the abbey church.

The king, returning on 17 April, retired to his bedchamber, giving it abroad he is sick. Queen Mary visited him for half an hour in the evening and they have partly reconciled though not so loving as before. Mauvissiere, who arrived on Easter Day, has had audience with the queen but not with the king.

21 April 1566: Laid to Rest

The 4th Earl of Huntly's body, which has lain in Blackfriars unburied since his death in 1562, was conveyed north to be laid in the Gordon family tomb in Elgin Cathedral.

2 May 1566: Freed

The Earl of Arran has been sent to stay at Hamilton under surety of the Earls of Argyll and Moray. Weak and sickly, he has lost his power of speech.

17 May 1566: Grant

After his wife Agnes was granted the barony of Terregles on 8 May, Sir John Maxwell, Warden of the West Marches, became Lord Herries.

May 1566: Secret Plans

Under cover of night, Queen Mary secretly summoned Christopher Rokesby to meet with her in a little closet in the castle to ask him about Queen Elizabeth and Lord Robert. He explained he could tell her little for the last year he had lived quietly in Yorkshire with his wife. Summoning him again the following night, she sat on a little hard coffer while Rokesby knelt beside her. She told him she knew well his brother-in-law, Christopher Lascelles, and that he was obtaining for her a 'true pedigree' of her title to the English crown and discovering her friends in England. She was corresponding with Stanley, Herbert, Darcy and Dacre of the crooked back and meant to win the friendship of the Duke of Norfolk and the Earls of Northumberland, Westmorland, Cumberland and Derby for, she believed, they were of the old religion, which she means to restore and thus win the hearts of the common people. Then, at a meet time, with the help of Spain, France and the Pope, and after stirring war in Ireland to turn away unwanted eyes, she intends to invade England, join with English Catholics and proclaim herself Queen of England.

26 May 1566: Indignant

Not only falsely accused by Queen Mary regarding the affair of the 3,000 crowns, Mr Randolph is most indignant that she now accuses him, on the slenderest information, of writing a book against her.

3 June 1566: Lying-in

Today, Queen Mary entered her lying-in chamber, set up with a royal bed of blue taffeta and velvet, alongside the royal cradle lined with the best Holland cloth and blue plaid canopy. Staying to attend her will be Mary Beaton; her aunt Margaret Beaton, Lady Reres; Margaret Fleming, Countess of Atholl; and midwife Margaret Huston.

After receiving the sacrament as 'one who is in proximate danger of death', the queen made her will: that the infant, if it survives her and lives, will inherit all; otherwise she made some personal bequests. She wishes to add to the Crown Jewels the Great Harry (a diamond cross with chain and necklace, both with rubies and diamonds) and seven large diamonds to ornament future queens of Scotland. She leaves to her husband twenty-six items of jewellery including two gold watches, one with ten diamonds and two rubies, the other with diamonds, rubies, sapphires and pearls; twelve great buttons with roses of diamonds and other buttons set with rubies and sapphires; and, above all, 'a diamond ring enamelled red, with which I was espoused for the king, who gave it to me'. To her most faithful and loyal retainer, James, Earl of Bothwell, she leaves a table diamond and a miniature mermaid figurine set in diamonds holding a diamond mirror and a ruby comb. To the Countess of Mar and her daughter Mary she leaves jewels including a belt of amethysts and pearls, bracelets with diamonds, rubies and pearls, pearl earrings, a zibellino (a sable with a gold head) and a belt carrying a miniature portrait of King Henri II. Smaller bequests include a gold heart with three diamonds, ruby and pearl to her equerry Alexander Erskine and a jewel with sapphire and pearl to his brother Arthur, and various rings for 'well-beloved friends'.

King Henry has been ill for several days and for his ease Queen Mary lovingly had white satin bedjackets made for him.

13 June 1566: Paradise

Patrick, Lord Ruthven died at Newcastle. Some say he was raving like a madman that he could see paradise and a great company of angels coming to take him.

16 June 1566: Gifts

One Harry, the king's man, brought gifts for Queen Mary from Flanders comprising a bearing cloth and banqueting dishes of sugar and quince preserve called marmalade.

19 June 1566: Prince of Scotland Born

Between ten and eleven o'clock in the morning there was a discharge of all the castle's artillery announcing, after a labour of twenty hours, the birth of a prince. To help ease the royal delivery, the relics of St Margaret had been sent for. A puncheon of wine was set up to run at the Mercat Cross. About two in the afternoon, the king came to visit Mary and kiss his son. Earlier in the day he wrote to Mary's uncle proudly announcing the birth, which he said 'will not cause you less joy than ourselves'.

Helena Little has been appointed the prince's wet nurse, assisted by four rockers.

Queen Mary will stay in her apartment for the next month until churched. During her lying-in, King Henry has 'led a disorderly life', associating with dissipated youths and bathing in the sea in remote places. It is assumed he will continue until she is recovered. Given he has 'vagabondised every night', the queen has been forced to order the castle gates to be left open for him. She has ordered the baby's cradle will stay by her bedside at night. In his swaddling clothes the queen has affixed a diamond cross.

24 June 1566: Audience

At three in the afternoon, the special envoy from Queen Elizabeth, Mr Henry Killigrew, was met at the castle by the Earl of Mar who took him to Queen Mary's bedside, though she is not yet entirely recovered. She thanked him in a faint voice with a hollow cough for Queen Elizabeth's letters of congratulations. After, he saw the young prince while he 'sucked of his nurse' and later, when he saw the prince naked, he remarked his hands and feet were well proportioned and he was 'like to prove a goodly prince'.

3 July 1566: Arrest!

After he was seen meeting with Mr Henry Killigrew, Christopher Rokesby was arrested today by Captain Lauder while soldiers searched his chamber and removed all his papers. Accused of being a spy, he was sent under guard to be imprisoned at Spynie Palace, the fortified castle north of Elgin belonging to Bothwell's uncle and where he himself was brought up, with strict instructions for him to be kept in complete isolation.

28–31 July 1566: Invite

John and Annabell, Earl and Countess of Mar, invited Queen Mary and her ladies, with the Earls of Bothwell and Moray, to spend a few days at Alloa Tower where it was remarked the prince is 'one very lusty child'. King Henry made a passing call and the family spent only a few hours together before he returned to Edinburgh. When the king told his wife he bore her brother evil will and wanted to kill him for being overmuch in her company, the queen brought the two of them together in her presence, saying she could not be content they should be 'unfriends'. Gossip says the king even mislikes the ladies Argyll, Moray and Mar keeping much company with his wife.

14–20 August 1566: Hunting

Queen Mary and King Henry were invited for the stag hunting by John, Laird of Traquair. While at supper one evening, Mary whispered in her husband's ear she felt unwell and wondered if she was pregnant and should not participate in the next day's hunt, being unable to gallop her horse. Speaking rudely and loudly to her, he exclaimed, 'Never mind, if we lose this one, we can make another.'

The laird intervened and said he did not speak like a Christian. 'What!' the king said, 'Ought not we to work a mare well when she is with foal?'

22–31 August 1566: Security

Removing Prince James to the greater security of Stirling Castle, Queen Mary raised 500 harquebusiers to escort her and surround the prince's litter. On arrival, she assigned his care to that of the Earl and Countess of Mar. Lady Reres has been appointed the prince's governess and the queen has provided for her a bed with blue woollen curtains, a woollen-filled mattress, feather bolster with one pillow, linen and blankets. Similar was provided for the nurse and rockers plus two coverings of tapestry and sheets for the servants who will lie in the prince's outer chamber.

30 September 1566: Leaving

The royal couple went different ways after they visited their son at Stirling. To her surprise, Queen Mary at Holyrood received a letter from the Earl of Lennox. He wrote that her husband, humiliated at being denied the crown matrimonial, had a ship lying ready to sail to France, intending to use her dowry monies to support himself. Despite all his pleading, his son would not alter his mind.

That evening King Henry appeared at the gates but refused to enter, insisting Moray and Maitland be sent away. Around ten that night the queen went out to him and persuaded him to come to her bedchamber and there they remained together all night. Next morning, she coaxed him to come with her to council, where she informed her ministers of his wish to go overseas and, taking his hand, asked if she had offended him in some way. When he refused to answer, du Croc, the French ambassador, told him bluntly that leaving would dishonour him and his wife. Finally, King Henry said, 'Adieu, Madame, you shall not see my face for a long space.' Before he departed for Glasgow, he left the queen a note that he still intended to leave the country.

7–31 October 1566: Law Days

To conduct the Borders Law-Days, on 7 October Queen Mary with the Earls of Moray, Huntly, Atholl, Caithness and Rothes and Lords Livingston and Seton along with officers and judges left Edinburgh heading for Jedburgh, with an overnight stop at Borthwick Castle.

Two days later the retinue arrived at Jedburgh, where they received news that on 6 October the Earl of Bothwell, who had left earlier with 300 horse to round up border rebels, had been seriously wounded by John Elliott when he resisted arrest. Managing to kill Elliott before the outlaw killed him, the earl was found unconscious by his attendants, who carried him to the Hermitage. Meanwhile those previously arrested and warded had managed to take over the fortress and refused the earl admittance to receive medical help unless they were allowed to go free. After they had gone, the earl, bleeding profusely from wounds in his forehead, thigh and left hand, and thought to be on the verge of death, was admitted.

At Jedburgh, Queen Mary set up court in the Tolbooth enquiring into complaints, giving out fines, imprisoning some; on 12 October she decreed a pint of good ale should cost no more than 5d and 16 oz of fine bread 4d. Free to discuss border affairs, the queen and earls rode to the Hermitage on 16 October. After a conference of two hours, they rode the 25 miles back to Jedburgh.

Next day, Queen Mary complained of her 'old pain' in her side. Taking to her bed, she fell into a fever, vomiting more than sixty times. News arrived that Prince James had been sick but had recovered after vomiting. On the third day of her illness, Queen Mary convulsed and temporarily lost her sight and speech. Two days later, believing she was dying, she asked the Bishop of Ross to hear her confession. Although suffering seriously from his wounds, Bothwell arrived by horse litter. She then summoned all the nobles to her bedside and begged them to love each other, to look after her son and ensure the crown passed to him and not to her husband. She asked Moray to be as tolerant to Catholics as she had been to Protestants; that she died in the Catholic faith and asked pardon of God for her sins.

On 23 October, at ten in the evening, the queen's eyes closed, her mouth clenched shut and her limbs grew stiff and cold. Her servants, believing she was dead, threw open the windows to set her spirit free. But her surgeon, Arnault, finding one arm less stiff, worked frantically to revive her, bandaging her limbs and massaging her for three or four hours, forcing wine down her throat and giving her an enema of wine and herbs. She began to sweat; sight and speech began to return and after vomiting she began to slowly recover. Fruits considered beneficial, such as pomegranates and lemons, were sent for from Edinburgh.

King Henry, who had been hunting in Fife and fishing at Lochleven, arrived on 28 October having only just learned of his wife's illness. Next day he left to ride to Stirling. After a fire broke out and destroyed part of her lodgings two days later, the queen was moved to the four-storey tower owned by the Kers of Ferniehirst. Her misery was made complete when news arrived that her husband had informed the Spanish and French kings she was 'dubious' in her faith, citing it as the reason the Catholic cause in Scotland was disordered. In other letters she was apprised King Philip was intending to make war in Flanders and the Pope would only provide her with support if she executed Moray and other leading Protestants listed by Bishop Mondovi, who had been waiting in Paris since 10 August for her to summon him to Scotland.

15–20 November 1566: 'Wish to be dead'

After holding a week-long justice eyre at Kelso, the queen rode by Berwick on 15 November and was given a salute by English guns. Upon stopping to allow Sir John Foster to cross the border and pay respects to her, his horse reared and bit the queen's horse in the neck and caught her in the thigh with one of its forefeet. Sir John immediately alighted and fell to his knees to crave her pardon. She bade him rise and assured him she was unhurt, though all knew she would be badly bruised for days. By easy stages, they travelled to Eyemouth, Coldingham, Dunbar and Tantallon Castle, lastly arriving at Craigmillar Castle on 20 November, where the queen has taken to her bed, weeps and tells physicians and her ladies she 'could wish to be dead'.

2–7 December 1566: Divorce?

King Henry arrived at Craigmillar on 2 December, stayed one night and then left for Dunbar. Du Croc wrote to Archbishop Beaton that he doubted the two could ever be truly reconciled: the king would not humble himself and she was too aware he plotted against her.

During the ensuing days, Argyll, Huntly, Moray, Bothwell and Maitland met together to discuss ways to ameliorate the queen's distress. Together they approached her to discuss her divorcing the king. She replied she could only consider it if it was lawful and not prejudicial to her son. Earl Bothwell reminded her his parents' marriage had been annulled without prejudice to his own rights. Maitland said they would 'find the means'. She interrupted him, saying she wished nothing done 'by which any spot might be laid upon her honour ... lest you believing that you are doing me a service, may possibly turn to my hurt and displeasure'. To that Maitland replied, 'Madam, let us guide the matter among us, and your Grace shall see nothing but good, and approved by Parliament.'

14–24 December 1566: Christening

Queen Elizabeth's special envoy, the Earl of Bedford, was given audience on Saturday 14 December at Stirling Castle, presenting Queen Mary with a gold font weighing 333 oz (valued at £1,048 13*s*), and smilingly suggested that as the prince had grown too big for it, 'it may be better used for the next child'.

For the christening, the queen has gifted dresses to Mary Beaton and Countess Annabell: the former received a long-sleeved dress of yellow gold satin edged with silver and the countess a dress of crimson velvet decorated with silver passementerie. For the earls, Moray was gifted a suit of green, Argyll red and Bothwell blue. King Henry was gifted cloth-of-gold with a frieze of silver for a horse caparison.

At five o'clock on Tuesday evening, Scottish barons holding waxen tapers drew up in double columns between the palace and chapel royal. To the sound of clarions, a body of handsome youths holding torches passed between them, preceding the Countess of Argyll, bearing the royal infant wrapped in silver damask in her arms. She wore a gown of gold-embroidered crimson-violet damask with bands of gold. On her right was Jean, Comte de Brienne, deputising for the French king (who had brought the queen a gift of a pearl and ruby necklace and earrings), and on her left du Croc, deputising for Moretta, the Duke of Savoy's ambassador who had been delayed. After them the Earl of Atholl bore a large wax candle, the Earl of Eglinton 'the salt fat', Lord Sempill the cross and Lord Ross a basin and ewer. The Earls of Bedford, Moray, Bothwell and Huntly stayed outside the chapel.

Queen Mary was already inside the chapel with John Hamilton, Archbishop of St Andrew (strictly instructed not to spit in the baby's mouth), along with the Bishops of Dunkeld, Dunblane and Ross, and the Prior of Whithorn with several deans and archdeacons. Countess Jean presented the baby at the altar. Mass over, heralds to the sound of trumpets thrice proclaimed the prince 'Charles James, James Charles, Prince and Steward of Scotland, Duke of Rothesay, Earl of Carrick, Lord of the Isles and Baron of Renfrew'. The choristers then sang, accompanied by the organs.

At the torchlit banquet, Queen Mary invited the deputies to sit at her table, de Brienne to her right, Bedford to her left and du Croc at board end. Queen Mary was served by the Earls of Huntly, Moray and Bothwell (carver, cupbearer and server respectively); the Comte de Brienne by the Earls of Mar, Cassilis and Atholl; the Earl of Bedford by the Earls of Rothes, Eglinton and Crawford; and du Croc by Lords Maxwell, Boyd and Livingston. Trumpets and musicians led in the meat and dancing took place for the rest of the evening.

Next evening there was a musical fete and on Thursday, at supper, musician Bastian Pagez had dressed twelve men as satyrs with long tails and whips to run in before the meat, which was bought in on a stage moving as if by magic, with musicians clothed like maidens singing and playing alongside, and servers dressed as nymphs on the table to pass dishes to the satyrs to serve. As the satyrs wagged their tails, every Englishman turned his back to their table, offended as for years Scotsmen had contemptuously called Englishmen longtails. So indignant was Christopher Hatton he later told Sir James Melville that he would have killed Bastian on the spot if Queen Mary had not been present. The queen and Bedford, becoming aware of the uproar, immediately restored harmony. After the four courses were served, all went to view the pageant beside the kirkyard in which wild men dressed in goatskins fought with Moors armed with cannon. Once the fort was aflame, there was a display of fireballs and fire spears.

Christmas Eve saw a parting of the ways: King Henry, who had stayed the whole time in his rooms, left for Glasgow to spend Yule with his father; the Earl of Bedford to spend the season with Moray; Queen Mary to spend Christmas at Lord Drummond's castle and New Year with Countess Annabell's father, Sir William Murray, at Tullibardine. She intends to be at Stirling on 2 January. Her last act was to grant pardon to the Earl of Morton and seventy-six other exiles, on condition they do not come within 7 miles of court for two years. Only two were excluded: George Douglas and Andrew Ker. She also restored Archbishop Hamilton, being primate and legate of Scotland, to all his consistorial jurisdictions.

25 December 1566: Public Repentance

By the General Assembly, the Countess of Argyll was ordered to make public repentance in Stirling's chapel royal one Sunday in time of preaching 'for assisting at the prince's baptism', it being performed in 'papist manner'.

3 January 1567: Succession

In reply to Queen Elizabeth's letter, delivered by the Earl of Bedford, Queen Mary thanked her for consenting to look into the matter of the succession and to examine the will 'supposed made by the king your father' which is said to bar her.

6 January 1567: Marriage

At Stirling Castle, Mary Fleming married William Maitland of Lethington as his third wife. He is eighteen years older than her but has romantically and faithfully pursued her for nigh-on three years and won her love.

8 January 1567: 'Great pox'

Queen Mary sent her physician to Glasgow after being informed King Henry had fallen ill barely a mile from Stirling on the day he left and that he arrived at Glasgow in great pain. 'Livid pustules' had broken out all over his body, his hair was falling out, and he had covered the blisters on his face with a white taffeta mask. At first all thought the king had caught smallpox but the queen's physician has diagnosed he has the 'great pox'.

20 January 1567: Glasgow Bound

Queen Mary left Edinburgh to go to Glasgow to see her husband. Before leaving, she wrote a letter to Archbishop Beaton to advise him she had attempted to get to the bottom of rumours that her husband was planning to seize the prince and govern in his name, or that her nobility planned to imprison the king. The only thing she said she could be sure of was that her husband's father and his supporters bear ill will towards her but their power was not equivalent to their minds and God takes 'the mean of execution of their pretensions from them'.

1 February 1567: Royal Arrival

Having taken the trip in easy stages, resting for a few days at Linlithgow, Queen Mary and King Henry arrived in Edinburgh. The king, deciding against lodging at Craigmillar Castle and unable to lodge at the Hamilton mansion at Kirk o' Field with the archbishop living there, was taken to the Provost's House. It is a two-storey structure, with six or seven large chambers, kitchen and cellar, set within a well-enclosed area and secure, having only three doors: one into the ground floor from the quadrangle with a turret stair connecting it to the second floor; on the city wall a door which bolts on the inside and gives access into the cellar and vault; and a third door on the east side, opening into pleasant gardens with a postern gate leading into a walled garden and an orchard bounded by a hedge with the vista of open fields beyond.

For his comfort, turkey carpets have been laid and tapestries hung in the rooms he will use for his bedchamber, presence chamber and wardrobe. In his bedchamber, a black velvet bed was removed, replaced by his own royal purple velvet bed, with roof and headpiece and curtains of purple damask, the whole covered in gold and silver embroidery and gold silk flowers, which was the queen's gift to him last August. It also has bolster and pillows of violet velvet and a blue taffeta quilt. For his further ease, he has a chair covered in purple velvet with velvet cushions, a little table covered in green velvet, a small Turkey carpet and a chamber pot for night-time. A bath was placed in the room for the king's treatment, a door covering it when not in use. The room also has a timber gallery and window overlooking Flodden Wall. In his presence chamber has been set a chair of estate on a dais of black velvet beneath a cloth of estate fringed with silk.

The queen also decided to furnish a bedchamber for herself, taking the room directly below the king's, bringing over from Holyrood a bed of yellow and green damask with its coverlet of green taffeta, so she can sleep there if she desires.

9 February 1567: Festivities

As Moray was on his way to St Giles for the preaching, he was intercepted and informed his wife had miscarried and lay dangerously ill. Ordering a horse to be saddled, he went to Queen Mary to ask her leave, refusing her request to defer his journey until the morrow.

At noon, the queen attended the wedding breakfast of her musician Bastian Pagez and his betrothed, Christily. The bride wore a gown of black satin, gifted by the queen who, having to leave for Moretta's farewell banquet in Canongate, promised to attend the evening masque the bridegroom had devised to celebrate his marriage. She attended the meal, accompanied by the Earls of Bothwell, Argyll and Huntly. The Earl of Bothwell looked particularly fine in black satin fringed with silver.

Early evening, about seven o'clock, the queen and her lords rode to Kirk o' Field to spend the evening with the king. While Mary and Henry chatted, earls Bothwell, Argyll, Huntly and Cassilis played at dice. Between eleven and midnight, the queen told the king she had to leave to keep her promise to Bastian and would sleep that night at Holyrood. When he demurred with a grimace, she said as he was having his final treatment bath, they would be together next day and as a token of her pledge gave him a ring. Mounting her horse in the quadrangle, the night being very dark, the queen's procession made the torchlit three-quarter-mile ride to Holyrood. It was very cold and the frosty roads – Cowgate, Blackfriars Wynd and Canongate – were covered with a light sprinkling of snow.

10 February 1567: Regicide!

Two hours after midnight, all Edinburgh was woken by a massive explosion, like a volley of thirty cannon, which shook houses. People came running out into the streets. Finding the Provost's House had been entirely destroyed, people rushed to the scene of devastation, some in their nightclothes, some carrying lanterns. Swaying on top of Flodden Wall, the blackened, shocked figure of Thomas Nelson stood crying for help. Rescuers helped him down and gave him clothes to cover himself. He, along with Symons and Taylor's boy had all had a miraculous escape. People began digging in the rubble looking for survivors, or bodies, but especially for the king. In the debris, two mutilated bodies were pulled out which proved to be those of two servants, Andrew McCaig and Glen, who had slept downstairs. Feverishly, rescuers searched for the king. Three hours later his body was found where none had thought to look: under a pear tree in the orchard in the south garden, sixty to eighty steps away from the house. A yard or two away was the body of Taylor, his faithful attendant who had served him since the king was a boy. Both were nearly naked, clad only in short nightshirts. The king lay on his back cupping his genitals with one hand; Taylor had on one slipper and a night-bonnet, his nightshirt rucked up around his waist, his head resting on his crossed arms. To huge astonishment, no one could see a mark on either of them: no burns, marks of strangulation, violence, fracture, wound nor bruise. Strewn around them were a velvet mule, a purple velvet chair, rope, a dagger and the king's furred purple velvet nightgown.

10 February 1567: Investigation

The Earl of Bothwell, as Sheriff of Edinburgh, was roused from his bed and told the king's house had been blown up. Having lodgings on the outer part of Holyrood, he quickly dressed and gathered a band of guard to go and investigate. Finding a barrel which had stored powder, he impounded it for the markings to be examined later. When the king's body was found, it was carried into a house and kept under guard. Certain people were apprehended and kept in custody so they could give their statements.

Between nine and ten o'clock, French Paris went to attend upon Queen Mary and found her bedchamber already hung with fine black cloth and lit only by candle and fire. Bothwell arrived and conferred with Mary and she ordered a post-mortem examination. This took place in the presence of her Privy Council. The doctors discovered that 'one rib in the king's body was found broken by the distance of the jump of the fall' and that he also had grave internal injuries. They concluded he had been blown into the garden by the explosion. When they were finished, the king's body was carried to Holyrood for embalming, completed by the queen's apothecary, Martin Picavet, who sent a bill to the treasurer for £40 for drugs, spices and necessaries for opening and perfuming the body and £46 for 'coals, tubs and barrels used in the bowelling'. The king was then laid out in state in the chapel. The queen ordered her mourning: black Florence serge and black plaid for a gown and cloak, silk chamlet lined with taffeta for her skirt and sleeves, plus cambric for her headdress.

During the afternoon, Thomas Nelson was called by the council. Questioned, he replied to his understanding: at first the king was to lie at Craigmillar, then the duke's house, but he was conveyed to the Provost's House. The keys were in the doors and the rest delivered by Robert Balfour, the owner. The queen slept there on Wednesday and Friday nights. The key to her bedchamber was given to her usher, Archibald Beaton, and he and Paris both had keys to the garden door for the queen 'used with Lady Reres to go into the garden to sing'. The queen had a door taken down to cover the bath and she had a new black bed removed to set up an old purple bed. From the first time she stayed, the king's servants never had the key to her bedchamber again. After the queen left the king had stayed up another hour before retiring, William Taylor staying in his room. He, with Edward Symons and Taylor's boy, lay in the little gallery outside the king's bedchamber; this had a window overlooking Flodden Wall and they never 'knew of anything until the house wherein they lay was fallen about them'.

11 February 1567: Wedding

The favourite maid of the queen, Margaret Carwood, keeper of the royal pantry, married John Stewart in the chapel royal on this Shrove Tuesday morning. Queen Mary attended the wedding but not the banquet and gifted her 'pantrice' black satin and velvet for her wedding gown.

Later in the day, the queen sent letters to her father-in-law and Archbishop Beaton. To the latter she wrote that the murderers had not been completely successful for she believed the murder 'was designed for us as for the king, for we lay most part of all last week in that same lodging ... and of very chance tarried not all night by reason of some masque in the abbey, but we believe it was not chance, but God that put it in our head'.

The Privy Council met and took depositions from some townsfolk who had heard men running but little else. A proclamation was issued offering to the 'first revealer' of the crime, 'although he be one culpable and participant of the said crime', a reward of £2,000 and an annuity.

15 February 1567: Funeral

King Henry was buried alongside the queen's father in the royal vault at Holyrood today according to Catholic rites.

16–19 February 1567: Seton

For her health, Queen Mary travelled to Seton with an entourage of 100 persons including Maitland, Archbishop Hamilton and Lord Livingston. She left her son in Edinburgh Castle in the care of the Earls of Bothwell and Huntly.

Above left: Henry II. (Courtesy of the Rijksmuseum)

Above right: Queen Caterina de'Medici. (From *Vita di Caterina de'Medici* by Eugenio Alberi, 1838)

Fontainebleau. (Courtesy of Aurele Martens from Pixabay)

Above left: Francis II. (From *Royal House of Tudor*, 1866)

Above right: Mary Stuart as Dauphine. (Courtesy of the Metropolitan Museum of Art)

Amboise. (Courtesy of Laure Gregoire from Pixabay)

Above: The Tumult of Amboise, 1560. (Courtesy of the Rijksmuseum)

Below: Edinburgh Castle. (Courtesy of kolibri5 from Pixabay)

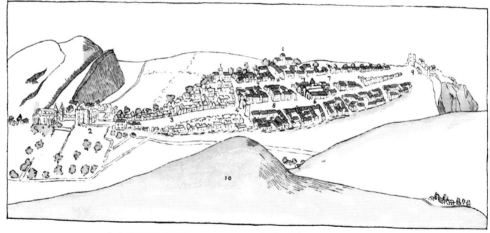

1. Kirk o'Field Church	6. St. Giles's Church
2. Holyrood	7. Cowgate
3. Canongate	8. Wynd leading to Kirk o'Field
4. Netherbow Port	9. Castle
5. Netherbow	10. Calton Hill

Above: Sketch map of Edinburgh. (From *The Mystery of Mary Stuart*, 1902)

Left: Lord Darnley with his brother Charles. (From *James I and VI*, 1904)

Stirling Castle. (Courtesy of Shelley Murray from Pixabay)

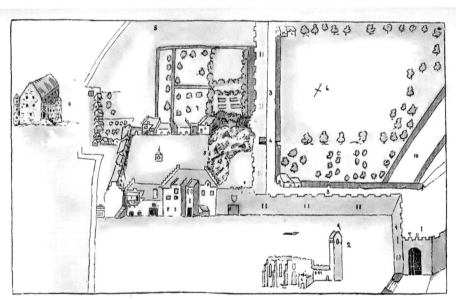

1. Kirk o'Field Port
2. Church of St. Mary-in-the-Fields
3. Thieves' Row
4. Door from Darnley's House into
   Thieves' Row

5. Ruins of Darnley's House
6. Darnley's Body
7. Darnley's Garden

8. Grounds of the Black Friars
9. Hamilton House
10. Potter Row
11. Town Wall

Sketch map of Kirk o' Field including the aftermath of the explosion. (From *The Mystery of Mary Stuart*, 1902)

Surrender at Carberry. (From *A History of the Family of Seton*, 1896)

Lochleven Castle. (Courtesy of Anita from Pixabay)

Queen
Elizabeth I.
(Courtesy of the
Rijksmuseum)

Thomas Howard,
Duke of Norfolk.
(Courtesy of the
Rijksmuseum)

Chatsworth of Queen Mary's time. (From *The Stately Homes of England*, 1891)

Above left: Mary in later life. (Courtesy of the Rijksmuseum)

Above right: Execution of Mary, Queen of Scots as drawn by Robert Beale. (From *Tragedy of Fotheringhay*, 1895)

28 February 1567: Placards

Two placards mysteriously appeared on the Tolbooth door during the night: one with the queen's initials and a hand holding a sword, the other with a mallet painted above Bothwell's initials.

8 March 1567: Audience

The queen consented to see Henry Killigrew, who found her in a dark chamber and was unable to see her face but noticed she was very doleful in her speech.

Meanwhile, placards proliferate in the town, bearing several names as the alleged murderers of King Henry.

23 March 1567: Requiem

By command of Queen Mary, a solemn requiem was sung for King Henry in Holyrood Chapel.

28 March 1567: Prayer

It being Good Friday, Queen Mary, with two of her ladies, attended Holyrood Chapel and remained in prayer from eleven at night until three the next morning.

During the previous weeks, letters between the Earl of Lennox and Mary have flown. To his first letter, in which he asserted that Mary should have the murderers of his son tried in Parliament, she replied on 21 February that Parliament was summoned to meet on 14 April; by return he requested an earlier trial, asking that she arrest and imprison every man accused on the placards. In return she asked who he would accuse given so many had been named (including her own servants and officials)? He then predictably offered a list of eight names with that of his enemy, the Earl of Bothwell, prominent.

In the Privy Council today, a defiant Bothwell stated that, being innocent, he is ready to stand trial. The law demanding fifteen days betwixt summoning and trial, the court of assize was appointed for 12 April and, as accuser, the Earl of Lennox was publicly summoned to appear, proclaimed at the Mercat Crosses of Edinburgh, Glasgow, Dumbarton and other places.

29 March 1567: New Guardian

To the initial discontent of Edinburgh citizens, Queen Mary transferred the captainship of the castle from the Earl of Mar to James Cockburn, her comptroller. The earl was being honoured having been appointed governor of Prince James and keeper of Stirling Castle. His orders are to prevent anyone from entering the castle with more than two or three attendants.

A letter has arrived from Queen Elizabeth, dated 24 February, in which she says, 'My ears have been so astounded and my heart so frightened to hear of the murder of your husband ... I urge you to preserve your honour rather than look through your fingers at revenge on those who have done you "*tel plaisir*" as most people say. I counsel you to take this matter to heart to show the world what a noble princess and loyal woman you are...'

7 April 1567: Licence

Queen Mary has given Moray licence to go to France, Flanders or other parts beyond sea for five years. He has made a will giving the guardianship of his only child and daughter, two-year-old Elizabeth, to Queen Mary should he die while abroad.

12 April 1567: The Trial

Queen Mary, waving from a window with Lady Lethington by her side, watched the Earl of Bothwell ride out of Edinburgh Castle on a magnificent courser (rumoured as the king's), flanked by Morton and Lethington. They, and fifty of Bothwell's followers, rode through densely packed streets to the Tolbooth. The trial began at noon before Justice-General Archibald, Earl of Argyll. Bothwell's procurators, chosen by him in court, were David Borthwick and Edmond Hay. The Earl of Lennox was summoned but did not appear. His advocate, Robert Cunningham, stood and protested the time of trial was too short and his client was absent because he was in fear of his life. He produced copies of his client's letters to Queen Mary dated 26 February and 17 March in which the earl accused Bothwell, James and Gilbert Balfour, David Chalmers, Francis Bastian, John de Bordeaux, Joseph Riccio and 'blak' Mr John Spens, one of the queen's advocates – who was attending on her behalf in court with her other advocate, Robert Crichton – of being the murderers of his son. The queen's advocates produced her replies to Lennox. The judges, headed by George, Earl of Caithness, were the Earls of Rothes and Cassilis and Lords John Hamilton (son of the duke), Boyd, Sempill, Herries, Ross, Oliphant, plus lairds and others to the number of fifteen. After long reasoning they took a vote. At seven in the evening, James, Earl of Bothwell was unanimously found innocent of 'art and part of the slaughter of the king', no evidence having been brought by his accuser.

13 April 1567: Accusations

Earl Bothwell set up a signed writing on the Tolbooth door announcing his innocence in the king's murder: if any say other, he gives him the 'lie in his throat' and will fight him according to the law of arms. Someone set up a placard alongside, the writer offering to prove by the same law 'that Bothwell was the author of that foul and horrible murder … and the king's murderer now occupies his place'.

On the market cross, another placard declared the devisers of the murder as James, Gilbert and Henry Balfour, 'black' Mr John Spens, Archibald Barton, James Borthwick and young Sandy Durham and 'their hands' the black Laird of Ormiston, the Laird of Branston, John Hepburn, young Laird of Tully, William and Edmund Blacater, Hames and William Edmonston, Herre Lauder, James Cullen, Patrick Wilson, 'wanton' Sym Armstrong and several others.

14–19 April 1567: Fitting Husband

At the opening of Parliament, Queen Mary with her nobility passed to the Tolbooth, the crown borne before her by Argyll, the sceptre by Bothwell and the sword of honour by David, Earl of Crawford. Forfeiture laid upon the Earls of Huntly and Sutherland was revoked. The acquittal of Bothwell by the Court of Assize was ratified. Lastly an Act was issued that those devising and setting up placards defaming any person of the king's murder without proof would be, if discovered, punished. At close of the Parliament on 19 April, the queen returned to Holyrood; now the Earl of Huntly bore the crown, Argyll the sceptre and Bothwell the sword.

In the evening, Bothwell invited the earls and lords to supper. Many of them signed a bond agreeing they would defend him against defamers and recommend him as a fitting husband for the queen. The Laird of Grange revealed he had heard the queen say she would not care if she lost 'France, England, and her own country for him' and would go to the 'world's end in a white petticoat' before she leaves him.

Queen Mary intends to spend a day or two at Seton and then go to Stirling to visit her son.

24 April 1567: Abducted?

Having broken her journey from Stirling at a private home the previous night, her small escort of thirty, which included Huntly, Lethington and James Melville, had just reached the two bridges over the Almond and Gogar Burn when the Earl of Bothwell with hundreds of spearmen stopped them. Taking hold of her bridle, he told her there was danger for her in Edinburgh and for their safety would escort them to the safety of Dunbar Castle. Captain Blackater, who took hold of James Melville's rein, told him to have no worry, for all was done with the queen's own consent.

Disturbed at events, Simon Preston, Provost of Edinburgh had the common bell rang. Men ran to armour and weapons, the port was shut and artillery of the castle shot, but common bruit is the abduction was already known; many suspect a ruse devised by the queen to staunch the mouths of people who allege the earl was more familiar with her grace long before.

3 May 1567: Divorce Petition

Countess Bothwell, who petitioned Edinburgh's commissary court on 26 April for a divorce on the grounds her husband had committed adultery at Haddington with her sewing maid, Bessie Crawford, was today granted her suit.

6 May 1567: Entry into Edinburgh

Dismounting from his horse, the Earl of Bothwell took the queen's steed by the bridle and respectfully led her into Edinburgh via West Port, along Grassmarket and into the castle. She had been twelve days at Dunbar. That they were to marry was already known by the people.

7 May 1567: Annulment and Banns

By virtue of his authority as papal *legate a latere*, Archbishop Hamilton, asked by Queen Mary on 27 April to investigate the validity of the marriage between James Hepburn and Jean Gordon, nullified it on the grounds they were related in the fourth degree of consanguinity.

Thomas Hepburn, in the queen's name, immediately instructed John Craig to publish the banns for Earl Bothwell's marriage to Queen Mary. Craig refused, saying he saw not her handwriting. The Justice Clerk brought her signed order but still he refused. He talked with the couple, who said they would proceed whether the kirk would have it or not and so he proclaimed their marriage.

12 May 1567: Dukedom

Queen Mary, on her way to Holyrood, stopped off at the Tolbooth to declare to the assembled magistrates and nobility that she had pardoned and forgiven the Earl of Bothwell and intended to promote him to higher honour. That evening, between seven and eight, the earl, already hereditary Great Admiral of Scotland, was made Duke of Orkney and Shetland and Marquis of Fife with great magnificence. She placed the coronet on his head with her own hands. He made four knights: James Cockburn of Langton, Patrick Whitelaw, James Ormiston and Alexander Hepburn.

14 May 1567: Marriage Contract

The queen and the new Duke of Orkney signed their marriage contract, witnessed by Archbishop Hamilton and others. She also signed a short declaration saying she was not offended by her nobles signing the bond of 19 April nor deemed them unfaithful subjects.

15 May 1567: Wedding

In the great hall at Holyrood, Queen Mary was married to the Duke of Orkney in a Protestant service witnessed by the Earls of Crawford, Huntly and Sutherland and Lords Arbroath, Oliphant, Fleming, Livingston, Glamis and Boyd and Archbishop Hamilton and Bishops of Dunblane, Ross and Orkney with other gentlemen.

The queen wore a black velvet gown edged with gold. Afterwards, she changed into a yellow silk gown decorated with gold embroidery. The queen has gifted her new husband a night-coat adorned with genet fur.

Dissenters against the marriage placed a placard on the palace gates with the words *Mense malas maio nubere vulgus ait* (Wantons marry in the month of May). Later that day, Mary told du Croc, who had refused to attend the ceremony, she could not rejoice and wished she was dead.

17 May 1567: 'Stab or drown herself'

Everyone in earshot was astonished to hear Queen Mary, closeted with her husband, scream for a knife so she could stab herself, or else she would drown herself. Since her marriage she has shed endless tears.

23 May 1567: Council Meeting

By the advice of her 'dearest husband' and her Privy Lords, Queen Mary has thought it expedient to declare her mind regarding the first Religious Act, ordinance and proclamation made when Her Highness first arrived in the realm to have full strength, force and effect and that Her Majesty did not mean to violate, prejudice or derogate such Act. London merchants were also granted ground at Newhaven for the making of salt.

27 May 1567: Greetings

The queen's husband wrote a respectful greeting to King Charles IX of France, whose Scottish Guard he had formerly commanded. His letter to Queen Elizabeth was bolder, saying he was aware she disliked him but was resolved to maintain friendship between the two kingdoms and none was more willing than he to show her every attention.

It is noted that the duke uses great reverence to the queen, staying bareheaded, but sometimes she will take his cap and place it on his head.

10–14 June 1567: Subterfuge

Three days after Queen Mary and her husband departed Edinburgh for Borthwick, as they were sitting at table, they were surprised to be informed that James, Earl of Morton and Alexander, Lord Home with 1,200 men were galloping to the castle. As the first troop arrived, they called out they were fugitives. Rightly suspicious, the couple refused them admittance. During the night the duke departed quietly and rode to Dunbar Castle. Seeing he had gone, those surrounding the castle departed for Edinburgh, to show they did not act against the queen. Along the way, they were joined by the Earl of Mar, Lord Lindsay and the lairds of Tullibardine, Lochleven and Grange. The Earl of Mar had the gates of Edinburgh broken open and marched in, forcing the queen's adherents to retreat into the castle.

After the queen sent out a proclamation charging persons between sixteen and sixty to come to her and her husband's assistance, on the night of 11 June she slipped from Dunbar around ten o'clock disguised in men's clothing and rode to join her husband who awaited her half a league from Borthwick. The next day, the rebel lords proclaimed that James, Earl Bothwell on 24 April put violent hands on the queen, detained her against her will, pressed her to an 'unhonest' marriage and intends to have the prince in his keeping. They therefore adjudge him the principal deviser of the late king's murder and demand all lieges, on three hours warning, to pass with them to deliver the queen from her captivity, revenge King Henry and preserve Prince James.

Two days later there was alarm just before midnight in Edinburgh when word came that Queen Mary and her spouse were on their way with their army, meaning to cause the rebels to flee or fight. They convened their supporters with great diligence and 'left to meet her either to revenge her dead husband or die'.

15–17 June 1567: Carberry to Lochleven

Having spent the night at Seton, the royal army, informed their opponents had gathered around 4,000 good, well-drilled soldiers, marched before sunrise in order of battle to Carberry Hill, setting up the royal standard prominently on the eminence. Queen Mary, wearing a black hat and black velvet jacket over a red and yellow skirt, made a short speech saying hers was the better right to avenge the king; that her husband had been found innocent when tried and though the rebels talked of defending the young prince it was they who held him. Dismounting from her grey charger, she went to sit on a stone, Mary Seton sitting with her.

Fearing Mary arriving at Edinburgh Castle, the rebel lords and their force left at two in the morning, but upon reaching Musselburgh at daybreak they were surprised to see Carberry Hill already occupied. They drew their men into two divisions: the first under the command of Morton and Hume; the second under Mar, Glencairn and Atholl. Their standard was a 'green tree with broken branch, the king's corpse lying beneath', the little prince holding a sign: 'Judge and avenge my cause, o Lord.'

Du Croc, arriving later, found the armies separated by a running brook with a mere half-league between them, but no engagement had yet occurred. He reminded the rebels they were acting against their sovereign; they replied that bloodshed would be prevented if the queen was out of her husband's power. Knowing the queen's goodness, he asked to be allowed to mediate, to which they assented, allowing him to ride over to the queen's army, where Captain Cladre with thirty horse met him. Taken to the queen, he kissed her hand and asked if the two sides could at all be reconciled. The queen said the lords showed themselves 'very evilly disposed to her', having persuaded her to marry him whom 'they had vindicated of the deed of which they now accused him'. Nevertheless, she said, if they acknowledged their fault and asked her pardon, she 'was ready to open her arms and embrace them'.

Having been busy ordering the army, Orkney came to them and in a loud voice asked if he was the one they wanted. Du Croc, equally loudly, told him that 'the other party had assured him they were the queen's humble subjects and servants' and *sotto voce* that they were his mortal enemies. He countered that they were simply envious for not 'one among them that would not like to be in my place'. Wanting to avoid bloodshed, he said he was ready, notwithstanding his royal marriage, to engage in single combat with any who would meet him. The queen refused to hear this action, saying none would be his equal in rank. Du Croc noted the duke's skill in marshalling his army, and recalled the earl was known to have many books on mathematics, geometry and military matters. As he left to return to the other camp, the duke advised him like the unsuccessful peacemaker 'between the armies of Scipio and Hannibal' to take up a position to watch 'the greatest pastime'. The ambassador replied he 'should never see anything which would distress' him more.

From morning until evening, messengers shuttled back and forth between the two camps. Morton's palace of Dalkeith being nearby, refreshments were brought to his troops while the queen's soldiers, becoming fatigued by the great heat of the day, dispersed into villages for refreshment. As the day grew late the queen complained she still had no idea whether her lords were her subjects or enemies meaning to deprive her of her crown. After further consultation, she agreed she owed a duty to severely punish the murderers of the late king, pointing out it included certain persons of the lords' party.

About eight that evening, rebel horsemen began moving to cut them off from Dunbar and others behind a hill out of sight, presumably to attack. The queen requested she might speak again to Kirkcaldy of Grange, deeming him an honourable man. She told him if he gave his word the lords would receive her as their mistress, and not seek to do injury to her men, she would go with them to Edinburgh. While Kirkcaldy rode back with her latest message, her husband pleaded with her to ride to Dunbar with him and await her supporters or let him fight; that their fair words only concealed treachery. She refused to listen, begging him to go to Dunbar without her. For her security he gave her the signed bond which named those who were guilty of conspiring the death of the late king and told her to keep it secret and safe, and again begged her not to 'perish through her own kindness'. She told him to await her at Dunbar for either she would shortly come to him or send him news. He, with visible emotion, mounted his horse as she requested, and galloped away with a small company.

The Laird of Grange returned. Assured by his words, she said loudly, 'Laird of Grange, I render myself unto you, upon the conditions given.' She gave him her hand which he kissed and he then took her horse by the bridle. Reaching the first rank of the army, she was received with respect. But as they came to the second division she was stunned when she was met with cries of 'Murderess', 'Drown her!' and 'Burn her!'

They arrived in Edinburgh late that night, and as she rode by the common people cried out against her, standing at windows and stairs. She wept and cried out to all the gentlemen and others on the causeway that she was their native princess and they should not suffer her 'to be so mishandled'. She was lodged in Sir Simon Preston's house. The best chamber looked over the High Street opposite the Cross. Banners and ensigns were set up, some showing the king lying dead under the tree; one painted placard pictured Queen Mary as a crowned mermaid and below, within a circle surrounded by seventeen swords or daggers, a hare to signify James Hepburn. Before Atholl and Morton left her presence, she raged in bitter terms she would have 'them hanged and crucified'. Though supper was brought to her, she refused to eat.

An hour past midnight the dishevelled queen, jacket torn and hair hanging about her ears, appeared at the window, raging and weeping, calling for rescue. During the night, she wrote a letter to

Bothwell, addressing him as 'dear heart', whom she should never forget nor abandon for absence, that she sent him away 'only for his safety, willing him to be comforted and be upon his guard'. She promised a reward to one of her keepers if he saw it safely conveyed to Dunbar but he delivered it instead to the lords.

All next day Queen Mary stayed in one room strictly guarded. Around nine that night, surrounded by guards, the banner of the dead king carried before her, she walked to Holyrood between Morton and Atholl. Her ladies, Mistresses Sempill and Seton, pressed as close to her as they could, while women sitting on house forestairs reviled her as she passed. Allowed to rest, the queen was roused at midnight. In the morning, she was welcomed to the island and castle of Lochleven by Sir William Douglas, with his brothers, Robert and George (only two years younger than the queen). She was conducted to ground-floor rooms, simply furnished with the laird's own furniture. Only two ladies had been allowed her, Jane Kennedy and Marie Courcelles, along with her cook, Estienne Hauet, and her private surgeon.

24 June 1567: Hanging

Captain William Blackater was tried for murdering the king and condemned as a traitor on 24 June. His arms and legs were broken and he was hanged and quartered. On the scaffold he swore his only crime was drinking with a friend and coming outside at the sound of the explosion. The assize was made up mainly of vassals and servants of the Earl of Lennox, who vows retribution on any servant, friend or relative of Bothwell. The Duke of Orkney has gone to see Huntly and Argyll to attempt to raise support for his wife.

2 July 1567: 'All is lost'

The French ambassador, du Croc, left Edinburgh on 2 July for France, going by way of England, leaving because 'all is lost'; he said the queen's adversaries 'assert positively' she was complicit in her husband's murder, 'proved by letters under her own hand', copies of which they had given him.

9–29 July 1567: 'Will live and die with him'

Sir Robert Melville managed to gain audience with Mary alone on 9 July. Lord Ruthven had been sent away for being charmed by her into giving her intelligence and favour. Since 1 July, she had been allowed more ladies and two chamberers. Speaking alone with him, she told Melville she refuses to abandon Bothwell, and avows she 'will live and die with him' and if she had to make a choice between him or her crown, she would choose 'to live as a simple damsel with him'.

Melville visited her again on 16 July. She asked him if he would take a letter from her to send to her husband. When he refused to accept it, she threw it onto the fire. When he urged her to divorce Bothwell – a sentiment echoed by the letter from Sir Nicholas Throckmorton smuggled in Melville's sword scabbard – she sent word to Sir Nicholas that she took 'herself to be seven weeks gone with child'. Melville also smuggled in a turquoise token from the Earl of Atholl and from her Flamy, Lady Lethington, a small gold ring with Italian writing referring to Aesop's fable of the mouse and the lion.

In the English ambassador's letter, he told her Queen Elizabeth was perplexed at how she could marry a man charged with murdering her husband and who had a lawful wife alive which would make any children illegitimate; that she was earnestly bent to punish the murderer no matter how dear she held him but would do 'all in her power for her honour and safety'. Melville returned with requests from Mary to be moved to Stirling to be with her son; if they refused to move her then she desired them to send her apothecary, her embroiderer and a valet.

During the month the queen received from her chambers at Edinburgh a silver basin, soap, a silver cockerel and a small lockable cabinet along with various clothes and sleeves, 5,000 pins, stockings, shoes, furred boots, a case of confits, six skeins of Spanish silk and eighteen small flowers painted on canvas traced in black silk.

On 24 July, Lord Lindsay and two notaries visited her. When they left, they took with them her signed abdication and letters of regency. She said out aloud her signature did not signify consent and she would repudiate them the instant she was free. Lord Lindsay said especial care would have to be taken that she never had the opportunity. On the same day, the Countess of Moray left Lochleven to go to St Andrews; there was great sorrow between her and Mary at meeting – and at their parting. The queen has taken to her bed and has since had 'two fits of ague' and miscarried twins.

When Sir William ordered bonfires to be lit and the ordnance to be shot from the castle walls, Mary learned her son was being crowned.

29 July 1567: Coronation

At Stirling, John Knox gave a sermon, then the queen's abdication and her authority for Moray to be regent during her son's minority were read out aloud. The Countess of Mar brought the baby prince, wearing royal robes, into the chapel. The Earl of Morton and Lord Hume took the coronation oath on his behalf. He was then anointed, the crown placed carefully over his head, the sword laid by his side and the sceptre gently placed into his palm. The ceremony finished with prayers in the Scottish tongue. The new king was returned to the castle in the arms of the Earl of Mar, while Atholl bore the crown, Morton the sceptre and Glencairn the sword of honour.

The inhabitants of Stirling with men of war stood upon the castle guarding it all afternoon. In Edinburgh they made 'near a thousand bonfires', the castle's cannon being shot while the people danced and cheered.

30 July 1567: Fines

By order of Edinburgh Town Council those inhabitants who did not set out fires for the coronation are to be fined £10 40s, the proceeds going towards common works of the town.

6 August 1567–2 May 1568: Escape Plans

Fearing an escape attempt, Queen Mary, still refusing to relinquish Bothwell, was moved for safer keeping to rooms on the third floor of the square tower of the keep; the second floor houses the castle's principal dining hall and rooms. She has a sitting room on the east side with sleeping apartments on the other. Sir William's daughter and niece, both about fourteen, sleep in her bedchamber. Above her rooms, the fourth floor is divided into sleeping apartments for her servants.

There is only one doorway from the courtyard and a partition separates the hall from the entrance which creates a long corridor leading to the spiral staircase linking the floors.

Having arrived from France only a few days before, on 15 August her half-brother Moray visited. She was about to eat supper and he refused to join her. When he did not pass her napkin to her, she commented he had not found it beneath him before to do so. After she had eaten, they walked in the garden, he principally talking of her marriage and suspected complicity in King Henry's murder. She told him she was 'innocent in all that could be laid to her charge' and any man who usurped her position whatever his motive would lose her favour. She reminded him that, being a bastard by birth and origin, what had been done to her could just as easily be done to him with less scruple. He told her he had accepted the regency and would do what kindness he could for her. That visit 'cut the thread of love and credit between the queen and him forever'.

George Douglas, charmed by the captive, soon began smuggling out letters in which Mary implored aid from friends and kin, home and overseas, from 'her prison in the Tower of Lochleven'. On 4 September, she wrote to Robert Melville to obtain silk materials and thread, including sewing gold and silver, also shoes, her white and black satin doublets and skirts, a red doublet, a loose taffeta gown with other clothes, along with her maidens' clothes for 'they are naked' and to send some silver. She also requested he ask Servais, her wardrobe officer, to send pairs of sheets along with black sewing silk, feathers, pearls, a dozen needles and any other bed coverings.

Sir William did his best to cheer his captive. When the weather allowed, he took her boating on the lake. George suggested she ask to be allowed to hawk on St Serf Island where he could hide men in the monastery ruins to overpower her guards and spirit her away.

Returning to the castle on one boating trip, the servants in fun were making a mock assault on the castle from a boat; defenders and attackers pelting each other with clods of turf.

Moray visited Mary again on 23 October and found her working embroidery on a folding screen. He was told she often worked patiently at her needlework and received regular deliveries of silk and cloth. In November she received her clock with a morning alarm. Meanwhile, plotting continued and letters were smuggled in and out. One scheme was to assault the castle, the queen being able to reveal to Lord Seton and John Beaton that the coal and heavy goods vessel could carry eighty armed men, the garrison comprising only fifteen or sixteen soldiers, but the plan was scuppered for one of her servants was overheard enquiring how many men the boat could carry; thereafter it was secured by chain and a smaller boat used, large enough only for seven people. George mused on whether she could be carried out in a chest of papers.

That George Douglas was in a 'fantasy of love' with Mary came to the attention of Moray in December, when he gave orders Douglas should leave Lochleven and stay away on pain of death. Riding along the far shore, George would wave to the queen while she walked in the garden. Once he rode his horse into the loch as far as he dared; Sir William ordered the cannon fired upon him.

During February, Queen Mary was too ill for plotting. Willie Douglas, a sixteen-year-old orphaned relative who had also succumbed to the queen's charms, devised disguising Mary as the laundress due to visit on 25 March; this failed when the boatman became suspicious of his passenger's beautiful hands and she was returned to the island. When Willie was caught giving her some letters, Sir William angrily expelled him from Lochleven for a month. Lady Douglas asked the queen to stop her plots, for she was sure Moray and she would reconcile. Mary told her while she was kept at Lochleven against her will she 'would do her best by any means to escape'. In April, in addition to her usual prayers, when she was walking in the garden the queen would suddenly kneel, raise her eyes and hands to God, always looking much happier when she rose.

On 30 April, Lady Margaret travelled to Kinross to say goodbye to George, who intimated he was leaving for France. On her return she sent a maid to deliver a pearl pear-drop to Mary, saying George said a boatman had found it and he, recognising it, wanted to restore it to her. It was the signal for another escape attempt.

The optimal time to escape was when the garrison took their supper for then the courtyard was deserted and the gates locked, which during the day stood open but guarded. The key was then placed on the table where Sir William sat and it remained with him until morning. On 2 May, Sir William waited upon the queen while she supped as usual. Afterwards, he went to sup with his wife and the household in the dining hall below. Saying she was going to pray as she usually did after eating, she and Jane Kennedy disguised themselves as countrywomen. As Willie served Sir William with wine, he managed to steal the gate key by dropping a napkin over it. Mary Seton, dressed in her mistress' robe, stood at a window while Mary and Jane silently descended the spiral stair and glided swiftly along the corridor to the tower entrance, into the courtyard and out through the gate. Locking the gate behind them, Willie threw the key into the mouth of a cannon, having already nobbled all the boats except the one they were using. She and Jane laid down in the bottom. All anyone would see if they looked out of a window was a single boy rowing. Once out of range of being seen or shot at, she rose and gaily waved aloft her white veil to alert those waiting for her. Rising from the damp ground where he had been lying flat, the lovelorn George Douglas waded out to meet her. He and Sir Alexander Hepburn, Laird of Riccarton had horses waiting to escort her to where Lord George Seton and his men awaited her. At the gallop, the party reached Lord Seton's castle of Niddry about midnight, having been met at the ferry by Lord Claud Hamilton, youngest son of the duke. There she was feasted and provided with dresses and necessaries befitting her estate. The following day she revoked her abdication, claiming it had been extorted from her under threat of death, and proclaimed Moray a traitor. She entrusted Riccarton to attempt to take possession of Dunbar in her name; afterwards to travel to Denmark to convey a message to her husband. Taking a few days to rest, everyone moved to Hamilton, which the queen intended using as her base.

13 May 1568: Forty-five Minutes

Several earls and lords flocked to Mary's cause at Hamilton, and a council of war was held the day before they set off. Queen Mary elucidated she wished not to 'seek nor hazard battle but to pass to the Castle of Dumbarton' in the keepership of Lord Fleming and wait for her subjects to draw into obedience. The idea was sound: Dumbarton, on the north side of the Clyde, was considered impregnable and convenient for awaiting reinforcements from the north parts. By making a wide circuit around Glasgow they could bypass Moray who had been holding Law Days there, march towards Rutherglen via Langside, Crookston and Paisley and reach Dumbarton. She appointed Argyll lieutenant of her army, which now numbered around 6,000 men. Riding with her were the Earls of Cassilis, Eglinton and Rothes and Lords Seton, Livingston, Borthwick, Maxwell and Herries among many others.

During the same time, Moray had assembled 'the king's army', led by himself and the Earl of Morton. With them were the Earls of Glencairn, Mar and Menteith, Lords Home, Lindsay, Ochiltree and Ruthven and Secretary Lethington, with many other lairds and royal officers; this force numbered nearly 4,000 men. Cannon had been brought from Stirling by Mar and from Edinburgh came hackbutters and royal archers. Spies had told him of Mary's plan, and in the early morning of 13 May, Moray drew up his troops outside Gallowgate Port and waited with his men in full array on the Moor of Glasgow for hours while Kirkcaldy viewed the ground between the Clyde and Langside, waiting to see which way Mary's larger forces intended to travel.

Meanwhile, as the queen's army marched and nothing of moment happened, they became convinced their larger numbers had won the day. As soon as they moved through Rutherglen, Moray's plan became clear: he sought to seize Langside Hill, where the high ground commanded the road between Hamilton and Dumbarton, and force a confrontation.

Dividing into two wings – the left commanded by Moray with the Earls of Mar and Glencairn, Lord Cathcart, barons and Glaswegians, and the right wing by the Earl of Morton and

Lords Hume, Lindsay and Sempill – they marched on and across the bridge and awaited the approach of the queen's vanguard, commanded by Lord Hamilton. Mounting hackbutters behind 200 horsemen, Kirkcaldy forded the Clyde by the ford on the east side of the bridge and rode with all speed to the village of Langside to hide marksmen among the village gardens and thorny hedges of the narrow lane through which Mary's army needed to travel, and placed his cavalry in a position which meant he could support either wing at need and 'encourage and make help where greatest need was'.

Seeing their way blocked, the queen's army occupied Clincart Hill. She rode to high ground about half a mile off, a bog between her and Moray's troops. The two forces engaged. Hamilton attempted to force a passage through but met the close fire of the hackbutters, which cut down many almost instantly, throwing survivors back into those following. When Hamilton managed to gain the top of the hill it was to find the main enemy drawn up in front of him in good order. Fighting moved to the village, both sides sending pikemen forward to become crossed and interlaced owing to the narrowness of the lane. Moray's wing began to waver but reinforcements arrived, striking 'flanks and faces', and pressed so hard that Mary's army began to break ranks. Those retreating broke into the main body, forcing the whole army to crumble. Those fleeing were pursued by Highlanders but Moray cried 'Save, not slay' in hopes of reducing the bloodshed.

The battle had lasted forty-five minutes. Four of Moray's men were killed, Lord Hume was wounded in the face and leg, Lord Ogilvy in his neck by Lord Herries, and Andrew Ker of Fawdonside was severely wounded. On Mary's side, all her cannon were captured, fourteen men surnamed Hamilton were killed and 300 taken prisoner including Lords Seton and Ross and Sir James and Gavin Hamilton, the Masters of Cassilis and Eglinton and many lairds and gentlemen. Lord Herries brought news of the defeat to the queen; with a small escort of horsemen, she made her escape.

16 May 1568: Adamant

By roundabout ways, Lord Herries brought Queen Mary to his castle of Terreagles in the borders. He advised her to stay in Scotland while they raised a new force. Giving no reason, she told him she intended to go to England. He reasoned she would be better advised to sail for France, where she had revenues, estates and access to French support. Ignoring all persuasions, she adamantly insisted she intended to go to England. She did not head straight for Carlisle, near to the border, but on the morning of Sunday 16 May, at a small creek by Dundrennan Abbey, Queen Mary, with twenty attendants, embarked in a fishing boat to sail across the Solway Firth to England.

'Practise with her friends for the crown'

England, 1568–1587

On Mary's arrival in England, William Cecil, Queen Elizabeth's chief minister, wrote a memorial outlining his concerns. Foremost was that Queen Mary had openly challenged the crown of England 'not as a second person after the queen but afore her'; were she allowed to go into France, he believed she would try to 'revive her title as she believes'. If she brought an army with her, it had to be noted that England no longer commanded the 'narrow seas with the loss of Calais' and France was superior in size, soldiers and artillery. If she remained in England, meanwhile, she believes she has 'a great party' to support her and would 'practise with her friends for the crown'.

This was before considering the question of her culpability in her husband's murder. If innocent, could she be restored where she might not have long continuance? If guilty, how 'to cover the dishonour of the crime'? Mary must have been equally aware of the political ramifications of her decision to enter England. It had been perfectly plain since 1558 she believed herself the rightful Queen of England, plotting to bring the dream about, setting the stage to blame Queen Elizabeth for all her ills. She may have anticipated, as Cecil suspected she did (and the writings of Claude Nau, her secretary, seems to suggest), that once in England Catholics would flock to her and she would march in triumph on London.

Mary's machinations at home and abroad were well known to Cecil and, by extension, Queen Elizabeth. However, unlike her ministers, who were concerned only with protecting England and their queen, Queen Elizabeth faced a different quandary: how to protect Mary and the rights of queenship. Her own inclination was to find a way for Mary to be safely returned to Scotland, for as she had written to Throckmorton when Mary was in Lochleven, 'we find her removal either here or to France not without great discommodities to us'.

One thing Mary would not have known was that the papal nuncio, the Bishop of Mondovi, had in December 1566 sent Father Edmund Hay, a kinsman of Huntly and a native Scot, into Scotland to find out what was really happening. In June, Father Hay wrote to the bishop, 'The queen is no longer able to keep from showing the excessive affection which she bears the Earl of Bothwell. In view of this last offence against God's honour and her own, there is no more occasion to send anyone to her, unless inspired by God to amend her ways.' This the bishop sent to the Pope before leaving Paris.

Mary's secretary, Nau, ended his unfinished memorial with some aide-memoires as to events after Langside: 'The road which the queen took after the loss of this battle to reach England; how she drank some sour milk in the house of a poor man; how she borrowed some linen; how she caused her head to be shaved; how she was twenty-four hours without eating or drinking; how John Gordon, Laird of Lochinvar gave her some clothes and a hood.'

16–18 May 1568: Arrival

About seven o'clock in the evening on 16 May, Queen Mary sailed into Workington. Her small retinue included Lords Claud Hamilton, Fleming, Livingston and Herries, plus George Douglas and one waiting woman. When she disembarked she fell over; someone joked she had 'taken possession' of England. Lord Herries sent a messenger to his friend Henry Curwen of Curwen Hall, whose manor, held of the Earl of Northumberland, was near the sea: he had arrived in England 'bringing with him a young heiress for Curwen's son'. The messenger returned to say Henry and his wife were away 'at the Bath' but they were welcome to lodge at the house. As soon as Mary crossed the threshold, she was recognised by a Frenchman who remarked to

Lord Fleming he had seen the queen in better plight. News soon went abroad that Queen Mary was in England. 'Seeing that she was discovered Her Majesty thought it prudent to let it be known she had come in reliance upon the promise of the Queen of England.'

Later that evening, Queen Mary wrote to Queen Elizabeth complaining that, as she well knew, her subjects who had attempted to seize her and King Henry, 'from which God protected us', who had been expelled by her from Scotland but been allowed to return at Elizabeth's request, had then 'held her prisoner and killed a servant in her presence while she was pregnant'. Next, they 'devised, favoured, subscribed to and aided in a crime for the purpose of charging it falsely upon us'. Placing herself in their hands to avoid bloodshed, she had been seized and imprisoned and kept 'without servants except two women, a cook and a surgeon' and threatened with death if she did not sign an abdication of her crown. And though they proceeded against her in Parliament, it had pleased God to deliver her when they thought of putting her to death; and at Langside God had preserved her; escaping to Lord Herries, she had come to England trusting her 'for the safety of our life' and to aid and assist 'us in our just quarrel'. She asked her 'dear sister' to send for her as soon as she could, being 'in a pitiable condition, not only for a Queen but for a gentlewoman', having nothing but the clothes on her person when she made her 'escape, travelling sixty miles across country the first day' and afterwards only at night, signing herself 'your most faithful and affectionate good sister and cousin, and escaped prisoner'.

Riding into Cockermouth in the morning, Queen Mary found the townsfolk turned out in their best attire to see her. When 400 horsemen arrived, it heralded not the arrival of the Earl of Northumberland (then absent from his castle) but that of Sir Henry Lowther, deputy warden and sheriff. Immediately, he ordered her charges to be defrayed and a black dress to be made for her, and arranged credit for other matters. For her night's lodging she was entertained by Merchant Fletcher at his large house in the Market Place. Before leaving for Carlisle the next morning, Queen Mary held court for the ladies. For a parting gift, Henry Fletcher gave her rich crimson velvet for a dress.

At suppertime, the French ambassador arrived at Carlisle Castle, bringing tidings that some of her 'true subjects' were facing execution. She wept all evening.

21 May 1568: Not His Seignory

Thomas Percy, Earl of Northumberland, having ridden from his house at Topcliffe near Thirsk, arrived at Carlisle and insisted on a private audience with Queen Mary. Leaving her chamber, he demanded Sir Richard give up the queen into his care. Sir Richard refused, saying he was charged with her safety. The earl became abusive, calling him a 'varlet' and 'too mean a man to have such a charge'. Highly offended, Sir Richard firmly told him Carlisle was not in his 'seignory' and Queen Mary would stay in Carlisle until he received instructions otherwise from Queen Elizabeth. Meanwhile, Queen Mary sent a letter to the Earl of Cassilis telling him she hoped with God's help 'to return about 15 August with good company'.

28–30 May 1568: Innocence

Lord Henry Scrope and Sir Francis Knollys, having travelled from London, arrived around six o'clock in the evening on 28 May. With them was Lord Herries, who had ridden from Carlisle to meet them and regaled them with the cruelties experienced by Mary, her innocence in her husband's murder and her earnest wish to see Queen Elizabeth for aid to chasten her subjects or gain relief from France. To his surprise, they told him Queen Elizabeth would look with disfavour at French soldiers in Scotland; nor would she receive Queen Mary at court unless she was proved innocent of Lord Darnley's murder. They were welcomed by Lord Scrope's wife, Margaret Howard, having herself arrived from Bolton Castle to attend on the queen; she had come with instructions for Northumberland to depart.

Later that evening, the queen received them in her presence chamber. Reading Queen Elizabeth's letter, she fell into a 'weeping passion'. Leading them into her bedchamber, she declaimed she was innocent and Queen Elizabeth should either subdue her enemies or allow her passage to France for she had 'come of good will and not of necessity' for most of her subjects remained loyal to her; nor did she doubt the kings of France and Spain would help her. After they left, she wrote passionately to Queen Elizabeth entreating to be allowed to 'discharge ourself of the calumnies they dare to prefer against our honour', complaining that it had only been at her request she forgave her ungrateful subjects to her 'detriment and ruin'. She would tell her the truth 'in contradiction to all their lies'; and if not so allowed, after she had 'freely thrown herself, as her best friend, into her arms', she asked permission to request assistance from her allies.

Two days later, complaining still to Lord Scrope and Sir Francis, Queen Mary was surprised when the latter asked her, 'If a prince should fall into madness, might not his subjects lawfully depose him and restrain him?' At her silence, he asked, 'What difference is there between lunacy and cruel murder?' That one derived from melancholy and the other from choler, he continued, and if she was 'guilty of murdering her husband, how should they be blamed that have deposed you?' Tears falling, she began to clear herself in her accustomed manner before departing to her bedchamber.

12–15 June 1568: 'Bloody appetite'

A letter from Queen Elizabeth arrived at nine on the morning of 12 June to inform Queen Mary she intended sending a diplomat to her, and to Moray, to stay hostilities. Queen Mary said rather than submit to Moray in any way she would rather all her party were hanged and she 'would go into Turkey rather than have peace or agreement with him'. And further, Queen Elizabeth should be disabused she had entered England to save her own life; it was to recover her honour and receive aid to 'chastise our false accusers not to answer them as their equal'.

The next morning, Henry Middlemore was presented to Queen Mary, who told him she was unhappy at any cessation of hostilities. Sir Francis said it was clear she would be happy 'to satisfy her bloody appetite to shed the blood' of her enemies. Weeping, she complained she was evilly used. When Middlemore counselled patience until her innocence was proved, she stopped him angrily, saying she 'had no other judge but God'. She immediately wrote to Queen Elizabeth that she 'regretted' coming into England and wanted leave to seek aid from other princes.

Two days after the angry scenes, Sir Francis and Queen Mary walked on the green when twenty of her gentlemen entertained them with a game of football – two hours in nimble and skilful footwork and no foul play. He prevented Queen Mary from hare hunting; she had twice impishly galloped off, outpacing her escort.

Queen Mary has taken note that five watches are kept and said the bars on her bedchamber window, which looks out towards Scotland, might easily be filed and with a knotted cloth she would be able to climb down easily to the ground; other windows are less useful, looking into an orchard within the town wall.

21 June 1568: 'Much ado'

After composing a letter for all Christian princes requesting 'assistance in this her very grievous affliction; finding herself oppressed so cruelly by the disloyalty and treasons of such wicked and unjust subjects', Queen Mary wrote to her uncle the cardinal that, though in England, she might as well still be in Lochleven despite most of her nobility being on her side. She asked him to hasten French support, for her rebels 'openly invent falsehoods against me', and to have compassion for his poor niece and 'send money for I have not wherewith to purchase bread, linen nor clothes'.

She assured him that, though God tried her severely, she would die a Catholic; that she had 'endured injuries, calumnies, imprisonment, famine, cold, heat, flight, not knowing whither, ninety-two miles across the country without stopping or alighting, and then I have had to sleep upon the ground, and drink sour milk, and eat oatmeal without bread, and have been three nights like the owls, without a female in this country, where, to crown all, I am little else than a prisoner'.

Later that day, Sir Francis brought into her presence Jacques Bochetel, the French ambassador in England. Bidding Sir Francis to stay, she instructed Bochetel to request Queen Elizabeth to release her and let her go to France or Dumbarton unless she intends to hold her 'prisoner or put her into Lord Moray's hands'; otherwise, she would seek aid from France and Spain, ending, 'We have made great wars in Scotland and we pray God we make no troubles in other realms.'

Sir Francis replied he prayed that God of his mercy would defend England and his queen from such troubles as 'through our own tenderness, by her attempts might arise'. She replied if she was detained a prisoner, 'they should have much ado' with her.

28 June 1568: Compliments

To the queen's delight, her favourite lady, Mary Seton, arrived yesterday bringing with her coifs, various coloured silk hair ribbons, wigs and hairpieces including 'four Italian-wrought hair in different colours and styles', coifs, pearl headdresses, a black velvet cap, pearl earrings, a box with eighteen veils, sleeves, collars, ruff, garters and hose in various colours (also including measuring sleeves, collar and cap), crepe cloth and silk cloth, perfumed and plain gloves, eighty pearl buttons along with seven pairs of Holland sheets. Ellen Bog, the cook's wife, came with her and brought a chest containing some of her gowns from Lochleven: two velvet, four silk and one camlet.

When Sir Francis complimented Queen Mary today on how pretty she was looking, she told him that Mary was the finest dresser of hair and that the wig she was wearing had been curled by her.

Christopher Lascelles attempted to see Queen Mary but was turned away at the gates.

Lord Fleming having been denied a passport, the queen is sending George Douglas to France to request her brother-in-law take him into service; in reality he is taking all her letters, including her request to the king 'to lend her two thousand infantry and money to maintain 500 light horsemen' with artillery and munitions to recover her strongholds; such 'forces will unite nearly all the nobility', she says, requesting victuals and ammunition be sent to Dumbarton Castle.

5 July 1568: 'No enchanter'

Asked whether she would remove to Bolton Castle, 'a sweet, pleasant and commodious place', Queen Mary said she would not remove 'one whit' further into the realm unless compelled. Angrily, tears running unchecked, she said she 'would seek and get aid' from other princes; that she came freely, is a queen 'subject to none, and would not be made equal to traitors'. She accused Queen Elizabeth and English noblemen of purchasing jewels belonging to her, revealing Bochetel had told her Queen Elizabeth had bought six cords with twenty-five pearls, some as large as nutmegs, from her collection in May. Abruptly, she departed into her bedchamber.

Later she complained in a letter to Queen Elizabeth of Scottish commissioners being 'sent to be heard against me, as if I were the meanest subject'. Allowed audience, she would 'declare to you our innocence and ... thought to satisfy you wholly if we might have seen you'. She ended that she was no enchanter, nor of the 'nature of the basilisk, and less of the chameleon' to turn her to her likeness, nor 'so dangerous and cursed as men say: you are sufficiently armed with constancy and justice'.

15 July 1568: Bolton Castle

When 'stout threats, lamentations [and] anger' were ignored regarding the remove to Bolton, Queen Mary changed tack, becoming pleasant and tractable. The party arrived at Bolton Castle in the Yorkshire Dales an hour after sunset. Although isolated amongst hills, the building lies on a gentle slope covered in wildflowers. It appears very strong, having only one entrance, a great archway, around which no one had assembled to see her arrive. At five storeys high, it must be the tallest house ever to be seen. The queen was escorted to Lord and Lady Scrope's own apartments in the south-west tower. To move all her belongings took four carriages and twenty packhorses.

20 July 1568: Apparel

Today, Sir Alexander Hepburn arrived, along with Borthwick, to attend upon the queen. In the evening five cart loads and four packhorses arrived bringing all the rest of the queen's apparel from Lochleven.

28 July–5 August 1568: 'Goodly gelding'

Trusting that Queen Elizabeth's commissioners will be 'persons of distinction', Queen Mary agreed for her cause to be heard and for Moray and Morton, her adversaries, to be summoned to defend the accusations they bring against her.

A message arrived secretly from the Earl of Northumberland that he has a 'goodly gelding' for the queen. Out hunting in the park, she instructed the messenger, one of her guards, to thank the earl but tell him she lacked no horse, sending him a diamond ring and gold rosary beads for his wife. In return the earl sent her a gold ring with a little table diamond, which the queen commented would never fit any of her fingers. She sent John Livingston's wife with some fine lawn ostensibly to thank the countess for the gold jewel but in reality to give notice how many horsemen it would take to carry her away.

8 August 1568: 'Free princess'

Queen Mary burst into a great tearful passion, wishing she 'had broken one of her arms' before coming into England; Queen Elizabeth had written in reply to one of her letters she 'might freely return home into her country like a free princess'. Tears dried up instantly with news Agnes Fleming, Lady Livingston will be arriving on 18 August to attend upon her. She was discommoded by a letter from Moray, who after an assassination attempt upon him wrote that had he been as willing to shorten her days, he had possessed greater means to do so than 'ever will had entered his heart'.

22 August 1568: French Soldiers

Calling God to witness, Queen Mary wrote to Queen Elizabeth she had not sent for French soldiers to arrive in Scotland and prayed to speak personally to her for 'all our actions are distorted and falsely reported' and asked her to send for her, promising she would not leave Bolton but 'with your good grace, whatever liars may say to the contrary'.

1 September 1568: 'Safe harbour'

In about her twentieth letter to Queen Elizabeth detailing the usual litany, Queen Mary begged her not to listen to false reports, nor let her be 'lost for want of a safe port; for like a vessel driven by all the winds, so are we, not knowing where to find a haven', unless she would consider her long voyage and bring her into 'a safe harbour'.

George Douglas sent word he has arranged for 1,000 French and munitions to go to Scotland with the Duke of Chatellerault, who had received her 12 July 'power, might and authority to govern, command, act and rule'.

To deflect Sir Francis' suspicions of the goldsmith after he was asked for a print of his seal, Queen Mary gave him a pretty chain of gold pomander beads finely laced with gold wire as a gift for his wife, Catherine Carey, together with her first attempt at a letter in English for her 'schoolmaster' as she has affectionately termed him.

The last six carts from Scotland brought more chests of clothing and, to the queen's joy, her small chiming clock inside a grey and silver purse, a gold oval pendant with a small white and black ring within it, a small case of crimson satin and silver housing a plain gold crown and her gold-embroidered satin cloth of estate which she immediately set up in the great chamber.

George Carey, second cousin to Queen Elizabeth, upon calling into Bolton was received courteously by Mary, who recalled they had met before at her son's christening. She told him she thought his father, Lord Hunsdon, had been discourteous for passing so near without visiting 'a poor stranger' and prayed they would not believe what they heard until they knew the truth. He told her great spoils had been done on the borders by her followers; she said if Lord Hunsdon sent their names to her, she would cause them to be punished.

18 September 1568: Conference

John Leslie, Bishop of Ross arrived out of Scotland to attend his mistress. Informing him of the proposed conference at York at which her disobedient subjects are to answer before English commissioners for their unnatural and unjust proceedings against her, the bishop was concerned. He told her they might utter all they could for their defence and it would have been better to negotiate an agreement. She told him he had no need to worry: the principal commissioner, Thomas Howard, Duke of Norfolk, bore her good will; his sister, Lady Scrope, had assured her he would persuade all the commissioners in her favour.

24 September 1568: 'Hazard all'

Glad at receiving her childhood friend Ysabel's letter, Queen Mary wrote apologising she had been unable to write, having been for 'eleven months imprisoned … ten days in Scotland in a castle only five miles distant from my enemies … lost the battle and obliged to take refuge' in England. She asked for her friend to get King Philip to send an ambassador to Queen Elizabeth to tell her she is under their protection and should be restored to Scotland and punish her rebels. She knows she would not dare refuse them, not being 'greatly beloved' while she, herself, had 'gained the hearts of a great many good people of this country … so that they are ready to hazard all they possess for us'. She asked Ysabel to keep it secret, in case it cost her life, but she hoped to send her son to Spain to marry one of the Infantas.

29–30 September 1568: Commission

Robert Melville came to Bolton and presented Queen Mary with copies of the letters Moray intended to produce against her; Lethington had procured them for his wife to copy. Meanwhile, she chose her commissioners – Bishop of Ross, Lords Livingston, Boyd and Herries, Gavin Hamilton, Sir John Gordon of Lochinvar and Sir James Cockburn of Skirling – to attend York on 4 October. She instructed them 'they came in her name' to state her grievances against her rebels and are to firmly protest that although she is 'content for the causes to be considered … she is not subject to any judge, being a free princess'. They are to list her subjects' 'unreasonable and undutiful proceedings' and insist their complaints against her are to be given in writing in order for her to read them and fully advise as to her answer.

If they allege 'they have writings of mine … you shall desire the originals to be produced … and affirm in my name … such writings are false, feigned, forged and invented by them … there being men and women who can counterfeit our handwriting. And if they allege we demitted our crown … tell them, we being in prison, the law is of none avail.'

16 October 1568: Secret Conference

The Bishop of Ross arrived at Bolton from York, ostensibly to obtain Queen Mary's response to Moray's complaint against her of 8 October and to discuss the answers made in reply to her complaint of him. He brought advice from Norfolk: Queen Elizabeth believed Mary to be her enemy and he advised she should write to the queen she would use her counsel in all her affairs and offer to stay in England to her content. Thus, Moray would be stopped uttering his worst and within six months she could be restored with honour intact, quit of 'present infamy and slander', while time worked the rest.

3 November 1568: Casket Letters

Queen Mary received news that on 28 October English commissioners had been shown the silver casket with its letters, poems and various documents reputedly illustrating her love for Bothwell and hatred for her husband. Queen Elizabeth adjourned the York Conference to Westminster.

10 November 1568: Argument

There was a huge argument between Sir Francis and Queen Mary, who accused him of telling the Privy Council she had instructed the Abbot of Arbroath to levy men for an escape. He said he merely warned of the possibility of an escape attempt, seeing whenever it is 'dry overhead' she rides out hunting the hare and often continues hunting after sunset, or 'to take air, the wind never so boisterous'. Life is less frenetic on the coldest days for Queen Mary sits by the window or by the fireside playing her lute or sewing and talking with Lady Scrope while her husband and Sir Francis play chess.

25–26 November 1568: Westminster

In the Star Chamber on 25 November, the Bishop of Ross reiterated the protestation made at York and then he and the other commissioners withdrew on the grounds Moray had been permitted a private audience with Queen Elizabeth while Queen Mary was not allowed 'place to answer for ourselves as justice requires'.

The following day Moray announced his 'chiefest grounds' had been kept back. He accused James, Earl of Bothwell of being the main executor of King Henry's murder and asserted that that Queen Mary was the 'persuader and commander of the murder', who maintained and fortified the murderer before marrying him, and that this was why the Estates had deemed her unworthy to reign and crowned her son.

30 November 1568: Sorrow

News arrived today that Queen Ysabel died after giving birth to a premature daughter. After her ladies laid flowers on her coffin, she was buried on 18 October. Queen Mary immediately wrote to King Philip: 'I cannot speak to you as yet about this loss or even think of it without my heart melting in tears and sighs, while the love I bore to her comes up continually before my memory.' As to him being told she is inconstant in religion, it is a 'calumny invented by my enemies so as to lose your support'. She told Pope Pius V the same day that 'her enemies contrived to introduce an English minister who recited prayers in the vulgar tongue and, being deprived of her religion, she did not refuse to hear'; she asks for forgiveness and absolution if she sinned.

1–17 December 1568: Withdrew

At Westminster on 1 December Queen Mary's commissioners accused Moray of hiding his own treason and usurpation by slandering his queen, and asked that she be allowed to appear in person before the queen, her whole nobility and all foreign ambassadors to declare her innocence. Two days later, at Hampton Court, the Bishop of Ross informed the Earl of Leicester and Sir William Cecil that although the Earl of Moray had made a grievous accusation against Queen Mary, she had prohibited them from making further answer. Next day they were told Queen Elizabeth had sharply rebuked the Earl of Moray and his company for their disloyal accusations against their queen. On 5 December Mary's commissioners asked for her to be allowed audience or they would withdraw.

Moray produced the originals of the 'casket letters', plus depositions and other documents, for perusal by the commissioners on 7 December, leaving them to be examined and compared against other letters from Queen Mary held in the archives. On 9 December Mary's commissioners withdrew.

A day later, and on ensuing days, Queen Mary sent letters to Scotland declaring Queen Elizabeth had made league with her rebels to have her son brought to England, the castles of Edinburgh, Stirling and Dumbarton put into English keeping and Moray to be legitimised to rule Scotland. She further alleged that Moray had leagued with the Earl of Hertford, one for the Scottish crown and the other the English crown, so both would seek her son's death. She prayed all her subjects assemble and do 'all the hindrance and evil that ye may to the said rebels, and stop their returning home'. In like manner she apprised the Earl of Mar on 17 December to take 'care my son is not stolen from you' for it is 'certain and true' they intend to remove him.

26 December 1568: 'Great grief'

In her letter of 21 December to Queen Mary, Queen Elizabeth wrote she had long been sorry 'for your mishaps and great troubles, so find we our sorrows doubled in beholding such things as are produced to prove yourself the cause of all the same and our great grief increased … to have seen or heard such matters of so great appearance and moment to charge and condemn you … in friendship, nature and justice, we are moved to cover these matters and stay our judgement'. She also hoped her commissioners, though they had broken the conference at her command, would advise her to agree, for her honour, to make answer.

Queen Mary told Sir Francis that if Queen Elizabeth had reconciled her and those of her subjects agreeable to her honour she would have been content, but she never meant to answer as her rebels were not her equal, and she would never submit herself to be 'weighed in equal balance'. Sir Francis countered she would be better to answer 'the odious accusations' rather than condemn herself. She said she had reserved her 'freedom of a princess and safeguard of her honour'. He said he perceived that she wished Queen Elizabeth to end the cause to her honour by saying her adversaries' accusations are false because, on the word of a princess, she says they are.

27 January–5 February 1569: Charge

Indignant at being, as she said, moved by force to a new abode without reason, while her entourage travelled between Ripon and Wetherby Queen Mary contrived to send a messenger with a gold enamelled ring for the Earl of Northumberland, requiring him to remember his promise. At Ripon, Sir Robert Melville had arrived to ask if she consented, as the bruit was, to marrying the English Duke of Norfolk. She told him she had received word that Norfolk had found Moray content for them to marry and had asked her to stay her assassination attempt on him, which was supposed to have taken place when he passed by Northallerton.

The English queen has had proclaimed on the borders that neither King James is to be delivered into her hands nor Moray be declared legitimate to succeed to the Scottish throne and any league between the Earls of Moray and Hertford a 'malicious invention'. Sir Francis tasked Queen Mary with writing letters with such 'manifest untruths' to stir her people; she utterly denied writing them.

The weather being continuously grey and cold, Queen Mary became more unwell with a pain in her side. They had lodged at Pontefract and then at Rotherham, where Lady Livingston fell ill. On 1 February, the party stopped at the house of Mr Geoffrey Foljambe at Chesterfield, which the queen said was the fittest place she had seen so far, although she was fretting at having to leave behind Lady Livingston.

In the afternoon of 5 February, the party finally arrived at Tutbury Castle, where she was placed under the charge of George Talbot, Earl of Shrewsbury. In his forties, he has seven mansions in vast estates; his wife, Elizabeth, has two mansions in her own right. Tutbury, rightfully said to be beautiful and good for hunting, stands on an eminence over a river valley and is surrounded by a high wall with a single gateway.

The earl was heard to say that the queen seems quiet, modest and affable. Sir Francis, having been the recipient of her bitter sarcasm and strong invective, told him he was 'amazed to see her sharp tongue so bridled', even more so when the earl reduced her household. She was allowed to retain her masters of household and horse, carver, server, apothecary, physician, surgeon, secretaries, ushers and valets, tailor, master cook and assistants, pastry cooks and baker, wine steward, wardrobe officers, upholsterer, embroiderer, horse keepers and pages; with her nine ladies-in-waiting and their maids, the household still comprises fifty members. The earl and countess have ensured her food – sixteen courses at each meal, served buffet style four times a day – will be delicately served on silver plate. Her rooms are hung with tapestries, and on the floors Turkey carpets have been laid. Chairs and footstools are covered with cloth-of-gold on crimson satin and her maids have embroidered stools. Privately, the queen complained Tutbury is not habitable and despite its hangings and carpets is cold, afflicting her with rheumatism and headaches.

26 February 1569: Visitor

Hearing a visitor, a Mr White, had come to see Lord Shrewsbury, Queen Mary came out with an English Book of Psalms in her hand, having been listening to the service. Trying out the newly acquired English she has been taught by Sir Francis, she enquired after Queen Elizabeth. He told her the queen did very well, though mourning the death of her kinswoman Lady Knollys. He asked how she liked Tutbury, to which she replied that she preferred Bolton but that Tutbury was nearer her dear sister, whom she so desired to see. He asked how she passed the time given the atrocious weather hampered outdoor pursuits. She replied that she plied her needle all day, devising works while sitting with her ladies and the countess until pain made her stop, laying her hand upon her left side. She began a 'pretty dispute' with him as to which of carving, painting or needlework was superior; in her opinion, painting was best.

Conversing later with Sir Francis, Mr White said the Scottish queen has an alluring grace, pretty speech and a searching wit, although he did not understand the riddle she had embroidered on her cloth of estate, *En ma fin est mon commencement*. Sir Francis said the queen believes she has been brought to Tutbury so he can do away with her, being near to the Earl of Huntingdon who she says pretends to the English crown. Mr White noted the care Shrewsbury has of his charge, who overwatches them all for she never goes to bed before one o'clock in the morning; she is watched in turn, and two guardsmen search below her bedchamber window every morning.

10 March 1569: Pills

With Queen Mary complaining of pain for the last fortnight, the earl sent Leveret, his own physician, to examine her. He diagnosed *obstructio splenis cum flatu hypondriaco* and said her great pain comes from windy matter ascending to her head, which makes her swoon. Her physician gave her some pills which made her sick, and afterwards she felt better.

20 April 1569: Wingfield

On moving to Wingfield Manor in Derbyshire, Queen Mary's spirits lifted for it stands high on a wooded knoll with countryside views. The outer court, to the east, is large with outbuildings, lodgings and stables enough to house her four horses. The inner court, entered by a gateway with a porter's lodge, has the chief rooms set around it. Stairs from the porched entrance lead into a great hall with a richly decorated bay window and five great windows framing country views. The queen and her servitors have all the west-side apartments running from the tower.

26–30 April 1569: Warning

Disbelieving the English queen's information that Chatellerault and the regent had come to terms, Mary sent Alexander (Sandy) Bog to Scotland. At his return on 26 April, she wept at the news he brought and took to her bed. At suppertime, her lips and whole face were greatly swelled and she refused to eat, just sat weeping, notwithstanding the earl and his wife trying to comfort her. Adding to the two letters already sent to Queen Elizabeth, she wrote again on 28 April, saying the Duke of Chatellerault and others were imprisoned in Edinburgh Castle and she was giving full warning she was to either 'return us directly into our own country or altogether refuse us', and that any other reply or delay she would regard as a direct refusal that will force her 'to embrace any other aid'.

The letter she had begun writing on 18 April to Bertrand de Salignac de la Mothe-Fenelon, the new French ambassador, informing him her supporters were destitute of all succour while her rebels received English money, horse and foot, she finished on 30 April with a request for the King of France to send munitions, large artillery and victuals to Dumbarton Castle, it making an excellent base for French troops and a safe place for her should she manage to escape.

2 May 1569: League

In a letter from the Bishop of Ross, the queen was informed he had talked with Queen Elizabeth in the gardens of Westminster where she had told him she had no liking for Mary going to France. She believed the cardinal would encourage her to 'claim her crown'. At his proposal on how a reconciliation and a league between the countries could be forged, the English queen had said she thought it reasonable and will write to Moray to gain his agreement.

10–11 May 1569: Illness

After Queen Mary took her pills on the morning of Tuesday 10 May, she suddenly began trembling and vomiting and had several convulsions, recalling her illness at Jedburgh. Around noon, she abruptly said she felt quite restored and immediately wrote to both bishop and ambassador that she had been ill but was recovered.

While abed next day, Queen Mary wrote personally to Norfolk about her ciphers, reassuring him her 'keys are not in that peril you took them in' as only she and those she trusts oversees them; she has no 'matters in head than them you have in hand' for she has had little ease last night for pain and fever and 'pray you not to leave your care of me...I send the Bishop of Ross with letters from Scotland; do you in them as you think best' and she will do her best to recover but her 'trembling hand here will write no more'.

At eleven o'clock that night Queen Mary went to the Earl of Shrewsbury's bedchamber, weeping and complaining with much passion at the stoppage of her servants, having just been informed that George, Laird of Gartley was stopped at Carlisle on his way from Scotland.

22–25 May 1569: Unwell

Informed by Ross of Mary's illness, Queen Elizabeth sent two physicians – Cawdwell and Francis – to attend her. When they arrived, Queen Mary said tearfully to the earl if only her true heart were known to the queen, then she might see her.

Since their coming 'a very unpleasant and fulsome savour, hurtful to her health by continual pestering and uncleanly order of her own folks' and the physicians have advised the earl to move her in a litter in a few days to Chatsworth for five or six days until her apartments 'be made sweet'.

4 June 1569: 'Never reconcile'

The Bishop of Ross has informed Queen Mary that Moray has written to Queen Elizabeth saying it was his belief Queen Mary would never reconcile with him. In response Queen Mary is sending Lord Boyd to rebel lords to assure them that if she is restored she will freely remit all offences. Having procured from Malmo the Duke of Orkney's assent to their marriage being annulled, Lord Boyd is also to action a divorce.

24 June 1569: Remitted All Her Causes

Late this evening, Queen Mary replied to the Duke of Norfolk's two letters to tell him personally she was glad her goodwill is agreeable to him, though 'unworthy of being so well liked of one of such wisdom' and would esteem and respect him so long as she lived, thanking him for his care of her: 'I have remitted all my causes to you ... I write to the Bishop of Ross what I hear from the Duke of Alva; let me know what I should answer.' As for the death of his ward, 'I wish you had another in his room to make you merry.' She said he had forbidden her to write but it was no pain when her health permitted, it being such pleasure to receive his letters, and sent by the messenger a cushion made and embroidered by her own hands. On it were her own arms with a picture of a hand with a pruning knife cutting down green vines with the motto *Virescit Vulnere Virtus* (virtue thrives by wounding).

3 July 1569: Arthritis

On 3 July, aware he had frightened his household, the Earl of Shrewsbury declared he would soon be perfectly recovered. In June when he had ridden the eight miles to Chatsworth he had 'felt a great pain in his back and legs' but felt better after taking a bath. On 13 June he had insisted on being carried in an open litter so he could return to Wingfield. Six days later, he worried his wife by completely collapsing, wishing 'rather to die than live' because of the pain. The countess sent for Dr Francis, who arrived on 27 June. He diagnosed *ex arthritide*. Though recovering, the earl is intermittently feverish with pain in his arms and hands, which are swollen, though his legs begin to mend.

On the same day Dr Francis also attended Queen Mary who complained of 'the old grief of her side'.

August 1569: Denied

At the beginning of August, a letter from Lord Boyd arrived informing Queen Mary that the Great Assembly held at Perth on 25 July had unanimously voted against her restoration and denied her divorce application.

The queen wrote to Norfolk for his advice after Leonard Dacre managed to secretly meet with her on the roof-leads with a plan to liberate her and, dependent upon events, to either set her up in England or take her to Scotland.

20–29 September 1569: Removal

When the Earl of Huntingdon and Viscount Hereford were seen to arrive on the previous day, Queen Mary sent a bearer to Mothe-Fenelon with a letter saying she is being put in the hands of her 'two greatest enemies' and is 'alarmed for her life', enclosing a ring for Norfolk. After evening prayers, when the two newcomers were granted audience, she immediately began lamenting the unkind dealings of their queen, from whom she had expected aid. They told her they were come to oversee her removal to Tutbury Castle, to which she said this was to her utter despair, being 'fromward her home'. She insisted she would send a messenger with letters. They refused, saying they would take them for her. She declined.

As soon as she was in her bedchamber Queen Mary burnt many documents, including ten to twelve letters from Norfolk, angrily saying, 'He had not helped us when he could, nor suffered us to depart with them who would have fetched us away.'

On 22 September, when Queen Mary loudly complained at being removed, she was told she herself had caused it; that Queen Elizabeth had laboured for her reconciliation while she had laboured otherwise. Three days later she wrote again to Mothe-Fenelon that he could judge what safety she was in being in the hands of Huntingdon, who pretends a right to the English succession, and begged him firstly to have 'compassion on a poor prisoner in danger of her life without having offended' and asking him to warn Norfolk to take care; he is threatened with the Tower. She also sent four of her own servants to warn him.

Tutbury was reached on 29 September. The reduction of her attendants down to forty-two persons left the queen fuming that she could not manage with so few, outraged at being used 'not as a prince but a common person'. During the evening her coffers were searched; one or two of the men entered her chamber with pistols and the earls, seeing them, stopped them and commanded them to lay aside their weapons so as not to frighten the women.

1 October 1569: Bodily Fear

Writing 'from her prison at Tutbury', Queen Mary complained to Queen Elizabeth she has 'evil reward' for her long forbearance, with her good sister taking suspicion of her, removing her to Tutbury and changing her keepers. Moreover, her poor dismissed servants were left without means or to be hanged if they return to Scotland, and she was 'left with only 20 men unless she dismisses her women … by which number it is impossible for me to be served', forbidden to go out, her trunks rifled, men 'entering my chamber with pistols and arms, not without putting me in bodily fear'. Being a prisoner, she entreats for a ransom be put upon her and not leave her 'to waste away in tears and complaints'.

10 October 1569: Prisoner

News has come that the Duke of Norfolk was sent to the Tower two days ago.

5–25 November 1569: Rising

On the evening of Sunday 5 November, Queen Mary began complaining to the earl of terrible pains in her side, heart and head. She then suffered a fit, followed by another the next night, after which she told everyone she was dying. That night, she wrote letters 'without light' to Mothe-Fenelon complaining of being ill treated. Taking her physician's usual medicine, the queen took to her bed complaining she was very ill. But this was a ruse, allowing her to remain unseen while she awaits the arrival of Anne, Countess of Northumberland, who intends to enter the house disguised as the midwife of Christily, wife of Bastian Pagez. She and Mary will exchange clothes and she depart without being missed. She wrote to Norfolk saying that 'by way of friendship she had the means to escape', but the countess never arrived.

On Friday 10 November Queen Mary dictated a letter to Queen Elizabeth importuning her to 'perceive the malice of my enemies who strive to trample me to the earth', asking her to pity 'one of your own blood – your equal', having placed herself freely 'into her hands and power ... and at least do not permit my life to be endangered without having deserved it', having heard the Abbot of Dunfermline has come to request her to be handed to Moray.

A message smuggled in from Norfolk caused the queen to send a letter on 14 November to the Earl of Northumberland 'to stay for a time from rising but keep themselves strong'. When Shrewsbury on 16 November received news which caused him to increase his armed retinue by another 100 men and order mounted scouts to patrol every night, she knew her warning had not arrived in time. On 19 November she heard the Earls of Northumberland and Westmorland had reached Tadcaster, 9 or 10 miles south of York.

25 November 1569: Coventry

Late at night, surrounded by 400 soldiers, Queen Mary was escorted into Coventry and lodged in the Bull's Inn in Smithford Street. She was allowed thirty-one persons to attend her including Bruce and Courcelles (who lie in her chamber), Lord and Lady Livingston with their servants, her physician, her tailor, her valets Bastian and Balthasar, her secretary Gilbert Curle, Archibald Beaton, Willie Douglas, two of her pantry officers and two cooks for the kitchen, a launderer and a horse keeper. The Earl of Huntingdon is most discontent, grumbling that 'there is nothing written which is not told her', although he cannot discover the method nor the culprit.

2 December 1569: Lodging

In the evening, Queen Mary was taken to lodge in the meetest house in the city, a mansion within the gateway opposite the church. Coventry citizens keep watch day and night at every gate and no one passes without examination.

29 December 1569: Diamond

A letter from the Duke of Norfolk was smuggled to Mary by Lord Boyd. Huntingdon had told the queen he would never be released from the Tower unless he refused her. She replied that the duke would not be worth a wart if he did. The diamond Norfolk sent her she wears unseen around her neck; she has sent a letter to tell him she would love him 'faithfully till death'.

2 January 1570: Early Start

Though the queen's servants attempted to delay an early-morning start from Coventry, the earl managed the removal to Tutbury Castle so promptly that hardly anyone saw her leave. The queen managed some pleasant conversation, with one of the guards talking of her spaniel, the inclement weather, the redness of her hand and her innocence.

15 January 1570: Letters

The queen spent all day dictating several letters. The one to Mothe-Fenelon was to instruct him not to allow her to be given over to her rebels and to say she was glad to hear the French king prospered; to the Bishop of Ross she wrote that she was sorry to hear of his imprisonment and needed to know what help she could expect from Flanders, saying Queen Elizabeth intends to take her son by force so she can be disposed of; and she asked Norfolk to write of his health for she will be ill at ease till she hears he is mended, ending, 'I pray you, my good lord, trust none that shall say that I ever mind to leave you, nor do anything that may displease you ... I remain yours till death ... your own D.'

22 January 1570: Gifts

On 29 December Queen Elizabeth granted passports for James Lawder and Sandy Bog to pass into Scotland by way of Berwick with two ambling horses, a learning aid and apparel made by Queen Mary as gifts for her son. In her letter to her boy, she asked how he was doing, saying he has a loving mother who wishes him to 'love, know and fear God'. Writing to Countess Annabell she said she was sending her son 'his first doublet and longhose', plus a little hackney with saddle and harness, the other being sent by the Earl of Shrewsbury. James is to be told he has a mother to whom 'he owes obedience and love, to whom he is commanded by God to obey'.

The earl is sending his servant Henry Downes with them as Queen Mary has sent for hawks for him.

29 January 1570: 'The gude regent'

News arrived Moray was assassinated at Linlithgow six days ago, sending all Edinburgh mourning the 'cruel murder of the gude regent' on Linlithgow High Street. He was shot through the belly beneath the navel by James Hamilton of Bothwellhaugh, who was standing in a window of the house his uncle Archbishop Hamilton had acquired years before. Moray died of his wound ten hours later.

31 January 1570: 'Care not for danger'

In a daring letter to Norfolk, Queen Mary said she 'wrote before to know your pleasure whether I should try to make an enterprise; I care not for danger and wish you to seek to do the like for if both of us could escape we should find friends enough ... Our fault were not shameful, you have promised to be mine and I yours ... if you think the danger great, let me know what you please that I do, for I will ever be for your sake a perpetual prisoner or put my life in peril ... let me know your mind and let me know you are not offended at me, for I fear you are seeing I hear no news from you... your own faithful to death, Queen of Scots, my Norfolk.'

13 February 1570: Plain Speech

This Monday the earl removed the lock from Queen Mary's outer chamber door so her servants could be viewed any hour of the night and she herself looked unto if any alarm ensued; he had been given warning her servants had devised a way for Queen Mary to escape out of a window. The earl has increased watchers and warders and used 'very plain speech' to her about her practices at which she was much offended.

11 March 1570: Bitter

Finding her servants with the clothing and horses for her son were stopped, Queen Mary wrote to the Countess of Mar accusing her of denying obedience to her and stating that she and her husband show themselves ungrateful.

19 March 1570: 'Faithful to death'

In a letter for Norfolk, still in the Tower, Queen Mary acknowledged his fear of the consequences of writing her but wanted to remind him, 'I will die and live with you, your fortune shall be mine.' Ross advises her to make certain offers to Queen Elizabeth 'but would enter nothing until I know your pleasure', it being a hard matter to yield her son and strongholds in pledge. Hearing his friend Pembroke had died at Hampton Court on 16 March, she was 'heartily sorry … with heartfelt recommendations to you of your own faithful to death'.

30 March 1570: 'Never offended'

In a flurry of letters to Mothe-Fenelon, the French royal family, her uncle and the Archbishop of Glasgow, Queen Mary spread word that Queen Elizabeth is sending an army to the Scottish borders under 'colour to pursue and seek her fugitive rebels in my country' and she is 'much grieved that this queen, to whom I am so nearly related and whom I have never offended', pays so little regard to her prayers. She asked her uncle to hasten his efforts to help or she will lose her kingdom and her son.

8 May 1570: Disquieted

Disquieting news has much grieved the queen who hears that some Scottish castles and places have surrendered. To ease her troubled mind, she began 'to exercise her longbow' and mutters she hopes other princes will have care for her and her country.

24 May 1570: Chatsworth

Preparations complete, both households removed to Chatsworth, a pleasant place surrounded by moorland and woods, with lovely walks around the house. One of the countess's servants said she keeps a small portrait of Queen Jane in her bedchamber, on a little table by her bed.

14 June 1570: Treaty

After Queen Mary read the submission that Norfolk intends to make to Queen Elizabeth, renouncing thoughts of marrying her, she said she greatly misliked it, even though he does it of necessity and promises he is still honour bound to her. She said Ross is hopeful of working toward a league between herself and Queen Elizabeth for her restoration and has replied to the duke that she will be advised by him 'to accept or refuse whatsoever conditions you think for both our weal, for without yours, I will not have any' and that 'she remitted all to him', signing herself 'your own, faithful to death'.

Afterwards she wrote to Queen Elizabeth asking for a secret interview, assuring her she would make no attempt to assert her rights to the English crown against her or her heirs and would maintain any of the conditions of the treaty to be made between them as she has instructed the bishop. To the bishop she has sent a gift for the queen made by her own hands.

In a letter to the Countess of Mar she reminded her that by entrusting her son to her she had shown much love; nor would she dwell on her offences, leaving her a way to recover her favour, especially as Queen Elizabeth is 'pleased to enter into a treaty with her' and she will shortly be in Scotland with her son brought to England: 'Remember that I am queen, ... my goodwill will profit you... my godmother, remember our old friendship and show me the fruits of it. The day will come when I may have your son in my hands, as you have mine.'

For days Queen Mary has sent letter after letter into Scotland advertising she will shortly be restored. To her 'true subjects' writes that after her delivery, she will have 10,000 English and themselves at her devotion; and if force does not favour her, she will sail to France and cause France to war on England.

10 July 1570: Danger

Using her son coming to England as an opening, Queen Mary has written to the Countess of Lennox despite her 'words and deeds' testifying 'manifest misliking' of her, asking to receive her advice, ending that 'despite your unkindness, will love you as my aunt and respect you as my mother-in-law'.

The same day she wrote to Queen Elizabeth to say she was gratified the small works made by her hands had been liked by the English queen with a request the treaty be concluded without delay; that if Elizabeth would only admit her to her presence she would save her from imminent danger but dared not use pen nor messenger to impart it.

28 July 1570: New Regent

News arrived that the Earl of Lennox was elected and took his oath as regent during the minority of his grandson King James on 17 July.

1–24 October 1570: Articles

Sir William Cecil and Sir Walter Mildmay arrived at Chatsworth with Ross on 1 October. They, with Queen Mary, over the next few days scrutinised the articles of the proposed treaty item by item, the queen objecting to some and suggesting alterations. On 11 October the bishop wrote to Norfolk, now under house arrest in his London home, that Cecil found the queen clement and gentle-natured, disposed to be 'governed by counsel of them in whom she reposed her trust' and enclosed a letter for him asking his advice on the conditions. Norfolk replied she should in no way consent for delivery of her son nor her castles: the first might lead to her overthrow, the second the destruction of her friends.

On 16 October Queen Elizabeth returned her own comments on the articles, with some mistrust of some of the alterations. Instantly Queen Mary sent reply that she was sorry to see her 'mistrust of my sincere intentions' when she gave proof of them by pledging her 'most valued jewel', her son, and wishes to 'cast anchor and terminate my weary voyaging in the haven of your natural goodwill towards me'. On 24 October the English commissioners returned to Windsor to await the king's commissioners from Scotland and she to send her own.

31 October 1570: Catholic League

Though having a problem with her eye, Queen Mary has written to the archbishop of her 'deep sorrow' at the death of his thirty-two-year-old brother, John Beaton, who recently died of dysentery and is to be buried in Edensor church. She has asked the archbishop to send his brother Andrew to her, to be her new comptroller.

Replying to the Pope, she mused what advantage might be derived from a close league of Catholic princes uniting their efforts against the common enemy who could be overthrown once and for all and 'if her determination was matched, all would soon be over'.

21–27 November 1570: 'Evil words'

Furious that Randolph has sent to Burghley a gold jewel made for her by the Countess of Atholl, Queen Mary has written to the bishop to get him recalled from Scotland, having 'evil will' towards her, and has a copy of his letter in which he wrote that 'the lion of Scotland looks to be lord of all' – a reference to the motto under a picture of Mary enthroned in royal robes with a lion worrying a leopard, around them a motif of roses and thistles entwined – and that 'maybe they have overlong nourished so cruel a beast that will devour the whole estate'.

In other letters, she informed the bishop she had caused her rebels' ships to be arrested in France and complained that the usurper Lennox pretends under colour of law to pursue her subjects, is spoiling her of her jewels and caused her son to say evil words of her. This last news she says has left her lying sick, almost to death; that the pain in her side and rheum in her head takes away all appetite, but since she had been outside on horseback she felt better, and the earl hopes the change of air when they move to Sheffield Castle on the morrow will do her good.

28 November 1570: Sheffield Castle

The ride from Chatsworth took nearly four hours. The terrain turned less wild the nearer the party came to Sheffield, moorland becoming woods and fields. The castle could be seen on a gentle hill from miles away. Nearer, it could be seen that it stood between two rivers. A spacious building with two enormous courtyards, it is said to cover more than 4 acres. The outer court houses an armoury, barns, stables and lodgings entered on the south side over a drawbridge. Around the castle across the water lie gardens and orchards, and huge oak trees rise beyond in a great deer park, said to be 8 miles around.

8–11 December 1570: Hysteria

The bishop arrived on 8 December with two doctors. Queen Mary told them she could not eat and had not slept though she had been in bed for the past fortnight; that she has been vomiting a great quantity of slimy phlegm and has the old pain in her left side. The following day after another 'vehement fit of hysteria' the physicians gave her a gentle potion to cleanse her stomach, which she vomited; they tried again the day after but again she could not keep it down and they decided to leave 'nature and youth to work'.

On 10 December the queen felt well enough to send word to Lethington and Kirkcaldy of Grange to remain constant, 'that friends beyond sea hold good, awaiting convenient time to put to their hand', and the Duke of Alva has granted 10,000 crowns to Lord Seton.

The following day the bishop advised Cecil and Queen Elizabeth that his mistress is ill for want of exercise, 'which if not procured will lead to her death'.

24 January 1571: Request

Because the bearer was going to court, the earl allowed Queen Mary to write to the bishop requesting the wine the perfumer left with him, along with cinnamon water and any other medicine he thinks to send with the virginals.

20–27 March 1571: Instructions

Jointly, Queen Mary and Norfolk prepared instructions and their ciphered credentials for the Florentine nobleman Roberto Ridolfi to go first to the Duke of Alva, then the Pope and lastly to King Philip. Queen Mary has instructed Ridolfi to declare to them the cruelty and tyranny inflicted on Catholics and the indignities and cruelties to which she is personally subjected, and the 'dangers to which her life is daily exposed with menaces of poison and other violent deaths' and how she has been mocked by Queen Elizabeth, who pretends a treaty to set her at liberty while using 'every means in her power to injure and hurt my faithful subjects'. He is to expressly declare Queen Elizabeth had 'often been on the point of putting me to death and even gave this charge to one of her pensioners'. The Duke of Norfolk has fully embraced her cause; he and her Catholic supporters are resolved 'to take up arms in my favour against those whom in their conscience, and as bastards, they consider unworthy to reign'. Lastly, she testifies to His Holiness and King Philip that Norfolk will do 'all I, and they, shall order'. She wishes to entrust her son to King Philip but they must be careful not to let her French relations know. The required assistance she leaves for the duke to advise. To the Pope alone Ridolfi is to declare her great grief at being imprisoned by the Earl of Bothwell and being compelled to marry him against her will; she asks to be freed.

The Duke of Norfolk iterated Mary's instructions regarding the cruel persecution waged on her and her supporters and his desire to bring England back to the Catholic fold, being the most numerous and influential in the kingdom, who will take up arms under his guidance. The assistance required, to be undertaken before summer passes, is for 'an experienced general bringing 6,000 arquebusiers, 4,000 muskets for arming our men in like manner, ammunition, money and 25 pieces of field artillery'. With the aid of God, he writes, they would be successful. Suitable landing places in his view are Harwich – within his own liberty – or Portsmouth, and he thinks greater security would ensue if 2,000 men were sent into Ireland and 2,000 men into Scotland, forcing Queen Elizabeth to divide her troops; otherwise, he will 'try the chance of one battle to extricate Mary by force' and seize the Queen of England. Ridolfi left on 24 March, first stop Brussels, taking with him a list of names of favourers of the enterprise.

30 March 1571: Suspended

Shrewsbury says that Queen Elizabeth, despite earnestly travailing on Queen Mary's behalf for the treaty, was told by Morton on 23 March that he had neither commission nor authority to treat upon a matter which required the assent of the Estates. Immediately, Queen Mary wrote to Morton that, as the English queen was minded to restore her to her crown, she could find it in her heart 'to set aside all the evils, griefs, unnatural extortions and displeasure committed against us and remit the same to anyone who first acknowledge their faults and crave our pardon and continue in their "bound" duty as loving subjects'.

18 April 1571: Plots

Shrewsbury has been warned there may be plots in hand and he should look out for the queen feigning sickness for a few days and changing apparel with a gentlewoman who would take her place in bed. Other methods, he is told, might see her dressing in men's apparel and getting to horse; cutting her hair, blotting her face and body with filth and walking out of the gate; or, when out hunting, changing into a page's dress to be commanded by her double to go on an errand.

20 April 1571: Poison Her

Word has come that Lennox took Dumbarton Castle and immediately hanged Archbishop Hamilton, and that Lord Fleming managed to escape but his wife was captured. The queen pretended the news meant nothing to her, but she has been sick and is eating very little. She told Shrewsbury to look to his officers, for she has been warned that she could be poisoned.

Now the French envoy, M. Verac, is removed out of Dumbarton, the queen has written for him to send her a letter of testimony confirming that he heard the Earl of Lennox propose to poison her.

3–4 May 1571: Vexed

After the earl attempted to reduce Mary's attendants to thirty, the queen wrote to Ross that some 'sinister information has been made by her enemies' and now her attendants are ordered to remain in their lodgings between nine at night and six in the morning. Among other restrictions, only Beaton is allowed a sword; no one may enter or leave the house or town without licence; if she wishes to walk abroad she must give an hour's notice; and if any alarm is given, night or day, her people should stay in their chamber or be at peril of death. Now she is 'vexed by sickness, great vomiting of blood, then congealed blood, phlegm and with pain from my side, proceeding from daily displeasures heaped upon me that may be my death'. She has instructed Ross to seek permission for her to visit Buxton Well, for French physicians who understand her sickness, and to be allowed to hawk and hunt. If she dies, he is to remind the queen, it would be upon her head.

18 May 1571: Questions

Letters have arrived from the English queen and from Cecil, Lord Burghley since February, for the earl to relay to Queen Mary that the Bishop of Ross has 'of late attempted sundry practices ... to move new troubles' in England and is now imprisoned. Weeping, she said she had long waited for some quarrel to be had against him for her sake. At Burghley's request, the earl has written out certain questions to ask her. She made reply she had never written nor received any open or ciphered letter to anyone called Ridolfi; the bishop has no cipher wherein she is codenamed '30' or '40' and if any such were, she would not disclose it; and since England would give her no aid, she was forced to write to all her friends for aid against her rebels but refused to name any, saying the earl had no authority to question her.

20 June 1571: Bothwell

Queen Mary often writes letters of comfort to Bothwell and sent instruction to Mothe-Fenelon to stop the efforts of Scotland and England to extradite him from the protection of the King of Denmark for it would destabilise her affairs. She has received rings from King Philip, who has liberated Scotsmen imprisoned in Spain at her plea, and the Duke of Feria, the latter with the motto *Enjoy the present and hope for better things*. By return, she sent King Philip a book covered in gold.

14 July 1571: Scotland

A reply came from M. Verac assuring Queen Mary that Lennox had never spoken 'any proposal that might threaten your life, be it by poison or otherwise'.

8–9 September 1571: The Storm Breaks

Urgent letters came for the earl in which he was ordered to despatch Queen Mary's attendants and reduce her household to ten persons. Consent was given to allow Lady Livingston, who has lain sick for eight weeks, and her husband to depart at their own time.

Shrewsbury came to the queen to inform her that Lennox was assassinated on 4 September, his dying words expressing concern for the safety of his grandson and love for his sweet Meg; the Earl of Mar has been elected regent in his place. The Duke of Norfolk has been committed to the Tower and all her ciphered letters and discourses to him are discovered.

She haughtily told the earl she had placed herself in his queen's hands of her own free will, relied upon her promises, and had been forcibly detained. If the English queen suspects she 'desire to escape', she is 'a free princess' and as such implored aid from France and others; 'it is false and malicious to assert it was to excite rebellion here'. She immediately dictated a letter to Queen Elizabeth complaining that 'if the treatment that I now have is continued, my strength will not suffice me to bear it ... and I will declare to you, and to all the world I have given you no occasion to treat me thus'.

November–December 1571: Complaints

By command of Queen Elizabeth, at the beginning of November the earl told Queen Mary she was to be allowed only as many women as were needful for her person, and can retain her master of the household, physician, apothecary, cooks and grooms of her chamber but the rest are to be sent away either to Scotland or France. When the queen began complaining, she was told that 'her intentions and practises against' Queen Elizabeth and her realm with Norfolk 'deserve a more straiter dealing than this is'.

She responded, 'We have not dealt with the duke since the time of his restraint, nor gone about to stir up a rebellion, nor intended harm to the queen or her subjects.' This unlike Queen Elizabeth, who had maintained rebels against her to the taking of her crown.

Weeping, she continued, she 'looked shortly that her life should end, for thus doth the queen use me', and asked for a priest to be with her at her death to witness that she died a true princess in the Catholic faith.

Exasperated, the earl told her she had no cause to use such words or think evil of his queen. Asked to choose whom she wished to attend upon her, she told him she would name none. Going into her chamber, she immediately wrote to Queen Elizabeth that she sees not only is she in disfavour but, what is worse, she is esteemed by Queen Elizabeth 'as an enemy instead of a friend, a stranger instead of a relative ... you put the worst construction upon all my actions, influenced by the opinion of others'. She prayed to be allowed a Catholic priest and to write to her son, who had been torn from her arms; granted these, she would prepare herself to receive life or death.

Writing to Mothe-Fenelon, she complained her people are not permitted beyond the castle gates and all the earl's servants are forbidden to speak to hers: 'I am confined to my chamber where they wish to again to wall up the windows and make a false door by which they can enter when I am asleep ... this cruelty will only terminate with my life.' While walking on roof-leads with the earl, she had informed him how she had asked Queen Elizabeth for someone to come from France about her affairs before she died, along with a Catholic priest and word from her child.

Asking the ambassador not to forget to send the riband and cinnamon water, she also requested that her soiled linen, and that of her women's, be not inspected by male officers before going to the wash. On 18 November she complained to him the ointment she used to rub on her side and stomach is used up and begged him to send some cinnamon water and nutmeg confits, as air and exercise are denied her and thus her health declines. She also sent one of her blanks with the new bearer to test if he was a safe messenger.

On 19 November the earl delivered a letter from Ross. She told him after reading it that 'it was Esau's hand but Jacob's voice'; that the bishop may have 'used his hand, but some other guided the pen. The bishop did as they would have him do ... they shall find us to be a Queen and have the heart of a queen.' As though, said the earl later, the 'evils discovered were nothing of hers'. She wrote back to the bishop she has been strictly restrained these 'ten weeks within the bounds of our chamber, and considering our disease dangerous to our life', even though the earl, at her continually complaining of being unwell, allows her to walk on the leads and around the courtyard or his large dining chamber. When she complained at not being allowed more, the earl told her plainly and roundly she was the cause thereof herself by her unlawful practices against his queen and that the world judges her to be the only cause of 'the destruction of the Duke of Norfolk'. Her disinterested gaze told him she was unmoved.

3–10 January 1572: Arguments

Sir Ralph Sadler, in audience with Queen Mary, said he was come to Sheffield to supply the absence of the Earl of Shrewsbury on his queen's affairs. When she complained she felt herself 'somewhat hardly dealt with without her desert', he said he thought 'her own conscience' could inform her better.

Six days later the queen and Sir Ralph clashed again when she began to complain of Queen Elizabeth's strict dealing. He told her, 'Perceiving her practises, no prince would use her so graciously nor so courteously', for all she pretends innocence.

She argued, 'What the Duke of Norfolk and others have done, she cannot tell; let them answer for themselves and she will answer for herself that she has done nothing but what she might do for her own help.' She warned her sister she would seek other friends and that Ross was 'a flayed priest who will say whatsoever you will him to say … and if he was free would unsay all'. As for Ridolfi, she neither knew him nor had anything to do with him.

Cuthbert, the bishop's servant, has brought her two little stone boxes full of salves and ointments, a tin bottle of cinnamon water and some lemons and oranges. Hearing he had brought a letter from Mothe-Fenelon, she went to Sir Ralph at ten o'clock at night to insist on receiving it. He told her she could wait until the morning.

The next day, the weather being fair, Queen Mary walked in the courtyard to take the air with the Countess of Shrewsbury. Seeing Sir Ralph crossing the yard, she called to him for the letter he had not yet delivered. He said he had no commission regarding letters, seeing what practices had been wrought by them. She rejoined that for her own part she was sure she had done nothing. She sent her secretary to speak to Cuthbert to ask the ambassador to make means to gain licence from Queen Elizabeth that she might write to France for money, having none at all, neither to buy her clothes or other necessaries, nor to pay her servants' wages.

20 January 1572: Condemned

The Countess of Shrewsbury came into the queen's chamber to inform her that on 16 January the Duke of Norfolk was arraigned and condemned to death, but her servants had already given her the news. The countess found her weeping very bitterly. Asking what ailed her, the queen replied she was sure she knew and that the duke was 'unjustly condemned and had been a true man to her sister'. The countess replied that 'if his offences and treason had not been great and plainly proved against him', those noblemen at his trial 'would not, for all the good on earth, have condemned him', at which rebuke the queen fell silent. She has told her attendants she intends for the next fortnight to stay in her chamber fasting and praying.

She also wrote a memo for her French tailor to make her robes and mantles, two in Florence serge double trimmed with black satin, black taffeta and buttons; a robe and doublet in tawny satin and a doublet of black satin; a furred mantle of tawny damask; a tawny satin skirt, body and sleeves; six pairs of stockings; sixteen pairs of shoes; three pairs of velvet slippers; a velvet hat and one of taffeta; twelve nightshirts and twelve day-shirts and others; and two dozen white handkerchiefs, half embroidered in coloured silk, the other half in white, to be sent to her via the French ambassador when they arrive.

5 February 1572: Rebuked

The earl informed Queen Mary his queen had not answered her several letters because she had seen nothing requiring an answer. However, her last letter with its 'many uncomely, passionate, and vindictive speeches' had decided her to, rather than writing a long letter with 'sharp and injurious words', instruct the earl to read aloud a memorial to her:

First, Mary had done wrong by taking title to the English crown, which Queen Elizabeth had not reciprocated when her subjects had willingly offered her the Scottish crown. For more than twelve years the treaty she promised to sign remained unsigned. She had been charged with murdering her husband, adulterously marrying the murderer and maintaining him in open tyranny, yet who had managed that her life should be saved? Yet she utters injurious words because she is disallowed her full liberty to undertake her evil intentions or take revenge on those in Scotland who would not suffer Bothwell to reign tyrannously over them. Furthermore, many marvel that she says she is in a prison when she is in a nobleman's house, served like a queen, and asking to be freed and restored to her crown, which can only be done by force against her own son, who was invested and crowned. Queen Elizabeth had earnestly solicited the Estates of Scotland for her restoration, and when they refused she pressed them to consider how it could be brought about, to which they had finally assented; yet at that time, as the dates of her letters testify, she sent Ridolfi overseas to procure the aid of strangers to invade England. In conclusion: 'And now she thinks it sufficient to write that, because the queen's majesty refused her, she sought for foreign aid' and makes 'a new offer and reasonable words, promising forthwith to forget all former injuries, and to do all that she can to honour and please her... none can think it unreasonable but that her majesty should clearly see and try what shall be the assurances hereof before she accepts them'.

18 February 1572: Snow

The queen, having spent all the last days in high indignation writing a lengthy refutation to Queen Elizabeth, was so eager to walk abroad she walked in the courtyard in the snow.

March 1572: Letters

The Earl of Shrewsbury has found many ciphered letters hidden under a stone which he has sent to Lord Burghley. Queen Mary is dejected that the earl has also discovered that Thomas Morgan, one of his own servants, has carried secret letters for her and discharged him. Thomas has acted as her secretary and go-between for the last four years. The earl is determined to uncover all her passages after Lord Burghley notified him to look out for a Scots boy who has letters sewn in the buttons and seams of his black frieze coat. So far, he has not discovered letters brought cunningly hidden in a leather bag with a double bottom.

10 June 1572: Duke Executed

Though his execution was stayed twice, the Earl of Shrewsbury came to tell Queen Mary that the Duke of Norfolk was executed at eight o'clock on the morning of 2 June. Queen Mary had a passion of weeping and sickness, declaring her deadly hatred of Queen Elizabeth, and took to her bed. She immediately wrote to Mothe-Fenelon that, despite bathing and medicines, the pain in her side is worse than ever; that the 'Duke of Norfolk had sealed with his blood the testimony of her innocence ... But the pain which I bear from his death so touches my heart, that it surmounts every other apprehension.'

DOLCE VITA

The whole of Europe – and Mary herself – must have waited for the axe to fall upon her neck. Parliament petitioned for her to be executed. Even King Philip thought Queen Elizabeth had been given ample cause. Commissioners arrived at Sheffield on 16 June with a long list of charges. She made a haughty protestation she was 'Queen of Scotland, a free and sovereign princess, nearest blood relation and next of kin to their queen and in right of succession after her to the English crown' and denied all knowledge of any plot, claiming she was merely asking to obtain money from the Pope. In July, it became clear Queen Elizabeth was not going to proceed against her.

With the castle being sweetened during the summer weeks, the households removed to Sheffield Manor, situated within the park about 2 miles from the castle. It had two courts, two gardens and three yards. A flight of steps led into the great hall and to a long gallery.

Then shocking news arrived from France: on St Bartholomew's Day, 24 August, thousands of Protestants had been massacred by Catholics in Paris, sparking off massacres in towns throughout France. In an outcry, there were calls for Queen Mary to be put to death. When the news reached the earl, he increased the number of his soldiers and told Queen Mary she could not walk outside the castle gates.

In December the Earl of Mar suddenly died at Stirling Castle and Morton became regent, at which news Queen Mary wrote to the archbishop that Morton would, to her peril, deliver her son to Queen Elizabeth. In May 1573, Kirkcaldy and Lethington were forced to surrender Edinburgh Castle ending the civil war in Scotland. Her French treasurer, M. de Vergier, was allowed to visit her in July; he was to ask her if she would prefer in future to defray her own charges using her dowry monies. Immediately, she viewed it as a way of increasing her already extensive communications network and agreed. After he left, she was taken to Chatsworth, and thence to Buxton where the earl had finished building a handsome four-storey mansion, situated between the river and the principal bath. It had a great hall, goodly lodgings and gardens. Around the baths were seats interspersed with chimneys for fires to air garments. The poor were allowed to visit so long as no great personages were visiting. On her first visit, his men had overlooked one 'poor cripple' who begged for a smock and had one passed to her through a hole in the wall. Back at Chatsworth at the end of September, Queen Mary was quick to complain to Mothe-Fenelon that she had been entirely deprived of servants and liberty, neither allowed 'to go on foot and horseback'.

In the spring of 1574, a new secret communications method was worked out and a spate of letters arrived and were answered. The earl, often taken by surprise at Queen Mary's knowledge of current events, asked her how she learnt her news. She told him to 'stop plaguing innocence'. During April, the queen turned businesswoman, poring over her lawsuits, wages, accounts and leases, commenting that some of the contracts were 'a mere farce', some forged and fictitious items caused a difference in her receipts of 10,000 francs. She compiled strict instructions regarding her finances. The archbishop was rebuked for questioning her 'harsh instructions' and explained that though she dictated her letters, none were ever signed nor sent without her scrutiny. She asked him to send some genuine '*terra sigillata*' or a bit of 'fine unicorn's horn' because she was fearful of being poisoned.

Several requests were sent to Mothe-Fenelon for white silk, silver thread and crimson satin, saying her only exercise was reading and working, the product of which was presented to Queen Elizabeth via the French ambassador in the summer: a red satin skirt finely worked with silver made by her own hands. He wrote that Queen Elizabeth had prized it very much. There was another visit to Buxton. Outwardly, Mary might seem to have entered into a certain quietness, indulging in favourite pursuits such as raising little birds in cages. She asked the archbishop to procure her turtledoves, red partridges and Barbary fowls and took great pleasure in her dogs, making them blue velvet collars. Mid-July, George Robinson smuggled in letters hidden between the double soles of his shoes. Finding that her brother-in-law, twenty-three-year-old King Charles IX, had died at Vincennes of tuberculosis on 30 May and his brother declared Henri III, she busied herself writing condolence letters, all to be sent on via the archbishop, who was also asked to send Jean de Compiegne with 'patterns of dresses, and of cloth of gold and silver, and of silks, the handsomest and the rarest that are worn at court' and from Poissy 'a couple of head-dresses, with a crown of gold and silver' such as she had worn before and to remind Bretan to send from Italy 'some new fashions of head-dresses, veils, and ribbons with gold and silver'. Intending to create a headdress for Queen Elizabeth, she also asked for gold lace with silver spangles.

And letters continued to flow: she instructed Sir Francis Englefield to reserve any 'final resolution' until there was a safe plan for her liberation, and told the archbishop that Leicester was considering marrying her and that the more 'her friends' were persecuted the more she found herself loved and esteemed by them. She requested he acquire a watch with separate alarm as a gift for Mary Seton. His brother Andrew asked him to send the silk hanging he had ordered for Mistress Seton and declared how proud he was of drawing designs for the queen's needlework. She wrote to her uncle the cardinal, asking him to write to Leicester thanking him for the courtesy he had shown her and to send him 'a handsome present which would do her some good', perhaps a crystal cup or some fine Turkey carpet which 'will perhaps save me this winter' and make him 'ashamed, or suspected by his mistress'.

In October a storm fell on the earl's household. His stepdaughter Elizabeth Cavendish had fallen in love with seventeen-year-old Charles Stewart, Earl of Lennox while they walked together around Rufford Abbey while his mother recovered from an illness she contracted during their visit with the Countess of Shrewsbury. Lady Lennox told Leicester that when she left her bedroom, she found 'the mischief done' and her son had so 'entangled himself' the pair had to marry. Queen Mary commented that Queen Elizabeth would be most displeased as it made Elizabeth Cavendish Mary's sister-in-law and aunt to her son.

On 8 November, Mary was delighted at receiving a letter from the cardinal, commenting he had not forgotten her. She immediately wrote to inform him of her daily 'afflictions, alarms and fears', and that her death was sought for no good reason; she requested money to have the means of assisting herself, along with requests for a gold mirror she could hang by a chain from her belt, with ciphers of herself and Queen Elizabeth with an appropriate motto and four portraits of herself set in gold.

She wrote to the Spanish ambassador saying she accepted the marriage proposition of Don John of Austria, the half-brother of King Philip, sure that the victor of Lepanto would undertake the 'English enterprise' and marry her to have 'the crown of England alight on his head'. A couple of days later, to show her devotion and affection to the English queen, she sent to her half of the sweetmeats she had received from France. The French ambassador sent her half a pound of mithridate, cinnamon water, oil of nutmeg and unguents for stomach and spleen which arrived on Christmas Eve. The day after Christmas she ordered the archbishop to notify King Henri she had no intention of her seven-year-old son being given the title of king; especially as James had shown himself completely attached to her, having written to say he will always follow her orders. She was proud of his excellent French and hears he speaks Latin well, 'is pretty in speech and dances well'.

On 28 December news came that Queen Elizabeth was so angry at the Lennox–Cavendish marriage that Lady Lennox had been sent to the Tower and the young couple put under house arrest at her property in Hackney, while Lady Shrewsbury was ordered to court.

The New Year opened with death and life: her uncle the Cardinal de Lorraine died at Avignon on 26 December, a few weeks short of his fiftieth birthday. She later wrote to the archbishop that she was unable to 'command her feelings or prevent her tears flowing ... God has bereft me of one of those persons whom I most loved ... bereft me at one blow of my father and uncle.' It was followed by news that the fifty-five-year-old Duke of Chatellerault had died at Hamilton. Meanwhile, Mary Cavendish, married to the earl's son Gilbert, gave birth to a little boy at Sheffield who was christened George.

26 February 1575: Earthquake

There was such an earthquake this Saturday evening that neither the queen nor her ladies could sit steady on their stools and chairs while they sat working around her.

11 March 1575: Hesitated

Mothe-Fenelon has written that when he gave the queen's gift of three nightdresses to Queen Elizabeth, she hesitated before accepting, praying him to remind 'her good cousin of the difference in their years, and to say that those who are advanced in life willingly take with two hands, and only give with one finger'.

31 March 1575: New Arrival

Queen Mary welcomed her new secretary, a Frenchman called Claude Nau, recommended to her by King Henri. He replaces Pierre Raulet who died last August after a long illness.

18 May 1575: Warning

The French ambassador has warned Queen Mary that three of the earl's servants are being interrogated in the Tower regarding how and by whom packets of letters and ciphers are conveyed to her and what negotiations are taking place between her and Guaras, the Spanish ambassador.

September 1575: Adieu

Mothe-Fenelon, returning to France because of ill health and unable to say goodbye personally, sent his two nephews to visit the queen. He is being replaced by Michel de Castelnau de Mauvissiere.

November 1575: Birth

A baby girl was born to Elizabeth, Countess of Lennox at Chatsworth who was christened Arbella. Queen Mary sent a token and letter to the Dowager Countess of Lennox. Her mother-in-law replied to thank her and say that, like herself, she had been careful of their Scottish 'jewel'.

January 1576: Curious Watch

Four boxes of apparel made in France by the queen's tailor arrived, along with hoods and linen, two boxes of preserves, bonbons and fifty to sixty letters and cards from relations, friends, servants and others. There was also a curious watch which greatly pleased Queen Mary, having 'pretty devices'. The cover is decorated with two ovals: in one a skull with crossbones at the foot of a tree; in the other moon, sun and stars with the motto *Her virtue attracts me*. On the dial a moon and stars surround a tower with the motto *When they fall they rise*. Around the outside are the arms of France and Scotland and between them pictures and mottos: a tree on a mount with a cityscape and hills behind (*Grows through bonds*); a castle and hill with a shrub (*As seen above*), two castles with a flowering shrub between (*Even when trampled gives ample fruits)* and a palm tree (*Inner virtue withstands burdens*). At the bottom was an eclipse of the moon with the motto *She thus takes away the light she envies*.

12 March 1576: Unwell

To Mauvissiere the queen wrote that her health and the pain in her side worsen day by day, and she has been ill for the last three or four months. Three days previously, on removing to the manor, being in the air caused a 'catarrh on her face' and she is now abed. She has provided him with a list of requests: gain permission for her to visit the baths; obtain a passport for her treasurer, Sieur Dolu, who lingers in London; get Hannibal to bring 1,000 crowns so she can pay her servants; and find out Queen Elizabeth's thoughts on a petticoat and a rich pair of sleeves that she had sent her in February.

April 1576: News

The earl and countess are grief-stricken at news that their daughter Katherine Talbot, Countess of Pembroke has died; she had been sent by Queen Elizabeth in one of her own ships to Spa to seek a cure for her illness. In other sad news, nineteen-year-old Charles, Earl of Lennox has died from consumption.

M. Dolu arrived at Sheffield to go through the dowry accounts with the queen; he greatly pleased her with the news that Don John of Austria has been appointed governor-general in the Low Countries.

30 July 1576: Thanks

Back at Sheffield Castle, Queen Mary has written to thank Queen Elizabeth for allowing her a six-week sojourn at Buxton, saying her physician is in greater hope of her recovery, as he can tell her in person. She is sending with him 'a casket and light coiffure', offering to make more beautiful ones if the English queen is pleased, and asked for a pattern of one of her 'bodies with a high collar' so as not to leave her hands idle.

20 January 1577: Marriage

Andrew Beaton is in love with Mary Seton, although she is coy at his marriage proposal. He is off to visit his brother for his consent to the marriage and to visit the theologians of Paris to relieve his beloved of the vow she says she took in her mind not to marry. When Mary Seton pointed out to her mistress their disparity in rank, Queen Mary said she would ennoble her suitor; then, saying she preferred the single life, the queen coaxed her to the contrary.

February 1577: Will

In melancholy mood, the queen wrote her will: she affirms she will die a Catholic and requests her body be taken to France to be buried in St-Denis near her first husband. All she owns, her rights to the crowns of Scotland and England, she leaves to her son, on condition he is a Catholic; if he is not, she transmits those rights to the King of Spain. In among other bequests, she revoked the grant of Orkney to her natural brother Robert and the earldom is to revert to the crown, along with that of the earldom of Moray, disinheriting his daughters. She has sent copies to King Philip and the Pope.

18 March 1577: Portrait

Aware some of her correspondence has gone astray, Queen Mary wrote to warn the archbishop that Queen Elizabeth suspects she has secret agreement with the kings of France and Spain and Don John to disturb the peace of this kingdom; the 'false rumours' had led to restrictions on her liberty. Referring to the letter in which he had written Don John intends to land in England, she asked him to 'keep your eyes open and write to me the particulars of the enterprise', assuring him she is no further participant, keeping even the archbishop in ignorance that among her several missives sent overseas was one to Don John's mother, Madame Barbara Blomberg, with a portrait of herself which she asked to be sent on to her son at his request.

April 1577: Accounts

As soon as M. Vergier stops occupying the queen with daily reckonings and departs, the earl intends moving to Chatsworth. The earl, to his displeasure, has discovered that he and his household had been given mocking nicknames by Andrew Beaton, so her servants can talk freely and not be understood.

June 1577: Serving Her Turn

Gilbert Talbot has been left in charge while Lord and Lady Shrewsbury entertain the Earl of Leicester and his brother, the Earl of Warwick, at the baths. The weather has been foul.

The queen has written to the archbishop saying Don John minds to catch 'two strings in his bow' but she is loath to lose any advantage she might have of him serving her turn 'as he minds to do his of me'.

3 August 1577: Liking

Hearing Don John captured Namur in July, Queen Mary wrote to the archbishop that he had not yet 'provoked' directly to have her in marriage; nor has she been 'forced to utter her liking', which is contrary to what she has previously written to the Spanish ambassador.

11 August 1577: Death

Little George, the son of Gilbert, died suddenly a little before supper at Chatsworth; the earl is distraught that his only grandchild, his 'sweet babe' and 'dearest jewel', should be so suddenly taken ill and is awaiting permission to go to Chatsworth to comfort his wife, who is making herself ill with continual weeping.

27–31 August 1577: Turbulent Imaginations

Amused, Queen Mary wrote to Andrew Beaton that she hears everyone suspects he is in France to deal with the marriage between herself and Don John; she also reminds him not to forget the various articles which have been ordered. In her letter to his brother the archbishop, who had gone to Spa, she reminded him not to let his brother carry any ciphers on his return and wrote, 'Walsingham with all his artifice and subtlety, he has not known how to seize any opportunity sufficient to give faith and proof to his turbulent imaginations, which I am sure hold him well in play, and he will not leave any stone unturned to surprise me if I leave anything for him to bite at.' Though Dolu has sent the confectionery, lemons and a chess set purchased in London which the queen ordered, she has instructed he is to be sacked for he does nothing she asks him; Nau added a PS that the painter had not perfected her portrait before the bearer left so it will come with the next despatch. The box of various silks from France have arrived. She also relates her displeasure at the marriage of Magdalen Livingston to Sir James Scrimgeour, who is to no longer receive gifts from her.

The earl, busy with preparations for the remove, has offered some hunting to the queen along the way to Chatsworth.

5–7 November 1577: Spycraft

A new safe and secret way being found for correspondence, the queen has been busy reading and replying to several letters. To the archbishop she sent condolences on the death of Andrew Beaton and her discontent at the little care and affection she receives from the Pope, who is to be informed her dower is insufficient to maintain her own servants and assist banished English and Scottish Catholics; if she receives no help, she says she will make no further entreaty. She asks him to pass to her cousin 'q' (Duc de Guise) her thanks for speaking of helping her to regain her liberty but, besides the little appearance of bringing such a thing to pass, 'I shall be with difficulty persuaded to change the state in which I have lived since my widowhood'. She relays notice that the English 'forward preparations for an army, commanded by Leicester, to sail for Flanders'.

To enable the archbishop to write freely and fully with his advice, the queen has given him a lesson in espionage: he can send her any book and 'write in white in the interlines' using alum or nut-gall, or 'make use of linen or white taffeta'. She had told him he is not to send the Agnus Dei and the chaplets from Rome and to distribute the money from the sale of offices, bar £1,000, to the poor. The bed he sent had arrived but she has not pressed the earl to accept it but retained it for her own use; perhaps he could procure a bed of finer stuff and half a dozen great hall candlesticks, the 'largest, finest, richest and best made that you can', and send them carefully packed via Mauvissiere to Nau and she will reimburse him. She also received news King Philip had been informed by Don John he means to make war upon England to set her at liberty.

March–April 1578: Devoted

At Hackney, on 7 March, sixty-two-year-old Margaret, Countess of Lennox died of colic. She left all her jewels to Arbella and to her grandson, King James, her new field bed of black velvet embroidered with flowers, its curtains, quilt and bedstead. Queen Mary told her ladies she was happy that she had reconciled with Lady Lennox, who had only done injury to her originally at the express orders of Queen Elizabeth.

Rumour has reached the earl that people are saying he is 'too much at the devotion of Queen Mary' and should be removed from his charge. He is greatly upset, saying he has served his queen faithfully for ten years and has 'stood sword in hand to stop her liberty'.

News from Scotland delighted Mary: Morton has resigned the regency for James has taken the reins of government. She has told the archbishop to tell Queen Mother Catherine she approves her proposal of marrying her son to a princess of Lorraine, though she believes it a ploy to stop Prince James marrying the Infanta. He is to tell Catherine that James is entirely devoted to his mother. He is to write to Morton to compromise him with Queen Elizabeth and assures him Walsingham, despite his boasts, has no idea how she gains her intelligence.

Then to the Bishop of Ross she wrote that now she has the great love and regard of her son, she 'shall be able to dispose not only of him but of all the rest according to the judgment of my mind ... considering his grave and imminent danger' and 'the daily plots taken in hand by Queen Elizabeth with the aid of most corrupt traitors' to get him into her hands or to kill him. He is to arrange for James to be sent to her Guise relatives.

May 1578: 'To my advantage'

Two letters have been sent to Mauvissiere: the first instructs him to tell Walsingham that if he preserves the rights of Mary and her son to the English throne, she will agree to stay in captivity. Secondly, in cipher, she says she wishes Shrewsbury to remain in charge of her for she would not be in danger from him were Queen Elizabeth to die; she hears his mistress has different diseases which 'waste her from day-to-day' and is expected to die soon and 'it would be 'greatly to our advantage to have an army so near this place ... tell the Duke of Guise he may freely use and employ Don John'. They could then demand her liberation and declare her right to the succession.

The countess, readying Chatsworth for the household, has reminded her husband he needs to bring five tapestries and carpets with him. She sends him lettuces every second day because the earl loves them and shares them with the queen.

22 July 1578: Requests

Wishing new servants to replace those wanting to retire, Queen Mary wrote for passports for her physician, Sieur de Castil, now eighty years old and feeble, and her woman Mme de Raulet, now seventy years old, who has been ill in bed since Easter; for replacement she requests the fourteen-year-old daughter of the Laird of Fernihurst. She has informed the queen she requires a new officer for the kitchen and a chambermaid to replace the wife and daughter of her current squire of the kitchen.

2 August 1578: Denied Right

Consternation in the house as news came Arbella was denied her right to the earldom of Lennox and lordship of Darnley, for James had granted it to the Bishop of Caithness, a sick old man whose heir is thirty-five-year-old Esme Stewart, Lord d'Aubigny.

15 September 1578: Instructions

Aside from her usual complaints, Queen Mary wrote to the archbishop the earl is sending his people to Rouen to fetch a bed and other furniture for her – he is to ensure money and letters are secretly hidden in the bottom of coffers and in one of the mattresses.

October 1578: Melancholy

News came from court that Don John had died of the plague at Namur on 1 October, five months after news had come to Queen Mary of the death of Bothwell. Although Chatsworth usually cheers the queen, she has stayed in melancholic mood, saying she is abandoned by everyone.

December 1578–January 1579: Intrigues Revealed

Countess Elizabeth returned from court on Christmas Eve, having first taken Arbella to Chatsworth. She brought with her questions from Walsingham regarding Guaras. She told the earl in annoyance he was not to write her answers in case he added more than she said, which offended him. She said she would write what was needful regarding any marriage between herself and Don John. She then took to her bed and stayed there except for Christmas Day.

On 2 January, Queen Mary wrote to Walsingham that she has always desired to make her behaviour in England agreeable to her good sister, and now her enemies wish to charge her with 'divers intrigues with foreign princes' imagined from letters they pretend to have been written in her name, which she 'absolutely denies', nor has she 'carried on any intrigue of consequence'. If the queen is pleased 'to show her the original' letter, she will be able to convince her of its falseness.

7 June 1579: Scotland

The queen has sent Nau to visit her son with a letter which she entitled 'to our loving son James Prince of Scotland', accompanied by some valuable jewels and a vest embroidered with her own hand. She sends him mainly to pass her instructions to Lords Ogilvy and Seton and gain exact knowledge of Scottish affairs.

24 June 1579: Physician

The queen has not received her summer purging for du Val has not arrived. Recently, after she began suffering from a hard, dry cough, the earl prepared to remove the households to Chatsworth for the fresher air and in July aims to take her to Buxton Baths after the visit by her treasurer. Today she wrote to the archbishop to 'put the irons in the fire again' to find her another physician.

4 July 1579: Return

When Nau returned from Scotland, he told Queen Mary he was refused admittance into James's presence because she had not entitled him king, though James had asked for him to be admitted. He told her the council had begun to waver when Morton arrived at Stirling two hours after dinner. The queen sent a ciphered letter to the archbishop that she had foreseen Nau would not be received but he had exactly fulfilled his mission. She was assured her son was dedicated to her but 'the poor child dare not show it'.

August 1579: Motley

The queen's valet Jacques de Senlis has brought over from du Vergier in France a motley of items: inventories of accounts, papers and rolls, bound in parchment; two engraved watches and a gilt alarm clock, garnitures of lace, a packet of requests and supplications from her officers, instructions to her officers, papers of a lawsuit and two pounds of starch.

19 September 1579: Order

The queen gave a written order to Thomas Fowler, sole executor of the Countess of Lennox, to deliver to Elizabeth, Countess of Shrewsbury all jewels bequeathed to Arbella with an extra instruction that if Arbella dies before she attains fourteen years, they revert to the use of her 'dear son'.

October 1579: Scottish News

News arrived that the queen's thirteen-year-old son made a state entry into Edinburgh at the end of September, along the usual processional route under a canopy of purple velvet through streets lined with tapestries and the buildings limewashed. Various pageants were put on and celebrations hosted by former regent Morton at Dalkeith for him. He is much taken with his cousin, an older man named Esme Stewart d'Aubigny, and has prepared an apartment for him next to his own.

6 January 1580: Spain

Through Mauvissiere's offices, Queen Mary secretly informed the archbishop she is 'determined to place herself, her son and her realm in the hands and under the protection of his catholic Majesty King Philip unreservedly', and if it his majesty's pleasure, to send her son to him and have him married there. She also told him that means had been offered her to escape but she has refused them for she was resolved only to 'leave her prison Queen of England and not otherwise, even though it cost her life'. The queen is considering the idea of marrying Alexander, Prince of Parma, the new governor of the Netherlands.

20 January 1580: 'Break his designs'

In an open letter Queen Mary has asked Mauvissiere to apologise to Francois, Duke of Anjou and Alencon when he arrives for not having written to him, telling him she neither wished to put him under suspicion nor harm his marriage negotiations with Queen Elizabeth. In a secret letter she asked the archbishop to sound him out as to whether he would support her right to England, 'the maintenance of which I hope that the greatest and best part of England will hazard their lives' and if the duke would do nothing for her, not even to gain her better treatment, she will 'break his designs'. She also instructed him to 'execute diligently' her last instructions regarding Spain and request an 'express reply' for, with the state of affairs in England and Scotland, it would be easy 'to form great intrigues'. Her enemies are attempting to persuade her son that she means to disinherit him and dispossess him of Scotland and she wishes him to inform him it is untrue. Lastly, when Mauvissiere sends 'the preserves', she wishes for 'Spanish ones'.

20 February 1580: Necessaries

In a spate of letters, the queen has told Mauvissiere that the earl is so sick she fears he will soon die; he is to ensure her safety by influencing the choice of her new guardian. To the archbishop, enclosed in the ambassador's letter, she sent two memos. The first is for necessaries and apparel she requires for the summer, being ill provided with clothes; as John le Compiegne has died, she requires Jacques de Senlis to make them as at his last visit he took measure of all her dresses. The other memo is for 'gold articles' for tokens and New Year gifts, for she did not have enough to give out last time. He needs not worry regarding the linen, silk, lace and other small items as du Vergier's wife will obtain them for him. She also sent him an annual order for 10,000 livres, reserved for her use, which he is to keep and send if she needs it. She believes the proposed match between Queen Elizabeth and Anjou is growing stale and he is to let the king know Leicester, their enemy, is restored to her favour.

2 May 1580: Ill Health

The new physician, M. Dominique Bourgoing, has requested Mauvissiere to tell Queen Elizabeth that his patient's health is bad; that he has done as much as he can for her whole body and the pain in her side which 'permanently vexes her' and wishes to recommend she be allowed to visit the baths. The hardening of her side, the rising up of her blood with increasing age and her diminishing bodily strength, not to mention the rigour and severity of her narrow prison, would be 'enough to render for ever weak and sickly the strongest body in the world'.

On this affirmation of ill health, the queen wrote to Queen Elizabeth that she often asked her to reconsider 'the unworthy and harsh treatment' she receives, despite giving proof of her entire and sincere affection towards her, and humbly begged to be delivered from captivity which would release her 'from the continual suspicions, distrusts, and impressions with which they trouble you daily against me' and would consider any just and reasonable condition, reminding her she came of her 'good and free will and put ourself in your hands' for the support she had promised her against her traitorous subjects; that she is her nearest relation and 'most just heir'; what reputation will she have if she allows her to 'languish so many years in such a miserable state', too young and strong for death to deliver her? She pleads to be allowed a journey to Buxton, having not found 'any remedy better for the complaint in my side, with which I am extremely tormented', this in the '12th year of my prison'.

20 May 1580: Assurances

Hearing the earl's servant Jailheur had been arrested and accused of delivering letters for her, the queen quickly sent to the archbishop saying he was not to worry for his letters of 27 February and 26 March were safely delivered. She instructed him to hastily conclude the Spanish overture or get her son removed to France; either will prevent Huntingdon from 'endeavouring daily to persuade this queen to remove my son here', which in her opinion (though not her friends') was ever more necessary for the safety of both of them and for maintaining the right of succession to the crown. Importantly, if he is out of power, she could say she had comported herself circumspectly. His final instructions are that Balfour 'should labour ... for the ruin of Morton and continue the good offices to the Earl of Northumberland's son, but as secretly as you can; and, if you are requested by his tutor to provide him with any money, supply him with it promptly'.

12 June 1580: Godmother

Having been secretly 'invited to gossip' at the baptism of Mary, daughter of Gilbert and Mary, the queen has asked the archbishop, 'not having anything here to serve as a present', to promptly send her a double marten with gold head, collar and feet enriched with gems; failing that, if it cannot be done so soon, a barrette, necklace and chain and gold bracelets enriched with gems will suffice.

25 June 1580: Entreaties

Complaining that 'no proof has yet been found for us to deserve the treatment we receive', Queen Mary has written again to Queen Elizabeth begging her not to remove from her heart one so nearly related to her, particularly entreating that her enemies provide proof of the intelligence and financial succour with which she is supposed to maintain English rebels. To Mauvissiere, she affirmed she has 'no practice or secret negotiation ... with any other whatsoever against or to the prejudice' of Queen Elizabeth or her realm and could not 'however I might have the will ... her dower having been diminished by the loss of several great rights ('the cause of which I only impute to my captivity)'; that the earl had seen her accounts when they were audited and said he found it strange a Queen of France had only 50,000 livres as dower. She entreats him to get permission for her to visit the baths, 'where I can say, I have always had less liberty than any other place in England'.

24 July 1580: Enterprises

While preparations went ahead for the move from the manor, with Nau being ill, the queen wrote with her own hand to the archbishop that she is content with the negotiations for James's marriage in Spain. Lord Ogilvy is to make secret preparations for her son to be immediately taken to Spain, or better still to Ireland if the Spanish expedition had arrived there.

26 July–24 August 1580: Buxton

The queen's horse jerked aside as Queen Mary was being helped to mount, which made her fall back onto the steps. For a few days, her back hurt her so much, she could not hold herself upright, but although complaining of the pain for two weeks, she had managed to take the bath once or twice a day. But she has only taken the air in the close once, of an evening.

Everyone except the queen and the earl's immediate family have fallen sick of the 'new disease' as it is called, which comes with a headache and a stitch over the stomach for a few days.

The earl confirmed by letter to Burghley that as usual there is not 'as much as a beggar in the town' and they must wish her gone so they can come to the well. Not one of the queen's attendants has been allowed any further than the wall, and even then guarded by soldiers in line with his orders for the last seven years.

27 September 1580: Messenger

One of the queen's messengers for seven or eight years, Singleton, told the queen he is being vigilantly sought and wishes to lie low overseas so Queen Mary has written to Morgan to procure him 500 crowns and a pension. She enclosed it in a letter to Mauvissiere in which she complained that the Earl of Huntingdon, supported by Leicester, is trying once more to become her keeper.

During the month the queen sent a 'beautiful and rare gelding' to her cousin the Duc de Guise; the other to make the pair will have to be sent later for it was not well.

5 January 1581: Powers

Henri, Duc de Guise has been given powers by Queen Mary to advise, confirm and treat with her son in her name as if she was present in person and appoints him her lieutenant-general in Scotland.

12 January 1581: Exultation

To the queen's exultation she has heard the Earl of Morton was surprised in his chamber at Holyrood on New Year's Day, arrested, charged with eleven counts of treason including being principal author of the murder of King Henry and imprisoned in Edinburgh Castle. Informed Randolph and Hunsdon are on the way to Berwick, she wrote to the archbishop that the Earl of Huntingdon is taking 10,000 men into Scotland and he is to advise her son to go to Dumbarton Castle for his safety. In fact, Queen Elizabeth has commanded 2,000 footmen and 500 horse be laid on the borders.

February 1581: Better Use

The French ambassador has informed Queen Mary that the earl is no longer to receive as much money for her support; Queen Elizabeth had told him it would be better if she used her dowry to maintain herself instead of promoting plots and practices in Spain, Italy and Scotland to stir up war with England and maintaining servants and pensioners in all parts of the world; and that, for all her complaints, Queen Mary writes to whom she pleases and receives news from everywhere; further, that if she but knew it, she is happier and safer in her captivity for if she had more liberty her mind would not rest long before 'getting into mischief'.

23 April 1581: Play

The earl allowed a troupe of comedians to stage in one of the great halls of the castle a tragicomic play to celebrate the Feast of St George.

1 May 1581: 'Bad meat'

Shrewsbury was mortally offended by receiving a letter from the Earl of Leicester informing him the French ambassador had complained at court that Queen Mary had written she had been given few dishes on Easter Day, and those with bad meat. Further, that the earl had said with her allowance cut he could yield her no better. Accusing the queen of saying such to his dishonour, she instantly denied she had written any such thing, saying she would write to the ambassador to rebuke him. Instead, she complained to him that she was so weak she was unable to take 100 steps on foot, having since Easter been carried in a chair: 'You will also renew, if you please, the application previously made by you for the passports of my Lord Seton and Mistress Lethington, or others of their quality, to come and serve me here, and at the same time for two women and two valets de chambre; not being able in the invalid state in which I have been thrown by ill-treatment for some years to be helped and served by so few servants as I have near me.'

21 May 1581: James

Delighted at letters and tokens that came from her son, Queen Mary wrote to the archbishop that given time she will reduce him entirely to her devotion and her freedom would shortly follow, especially if she and her son can come to some 'good conclusion' and that she was happy her son has been educated in the 'dance of cruelty' committed on previous Kings of Scotland; it will teach him his subjects should depend on him, rather than him on them. If her son seeks to marry the Princess of Navarre, the archbishop is to 'cross the alliance' for it is most unpleasant to her.

June 1581: Executed

News arrived that the Earl of Morton was beheaded on 2 June by Maiden guillotine, condemned for having foreknowledge of the king's murder even if had no participation in the act. Two ministers had asked him why he had not revealed his knowledge. He asked them, 'To whom could I have revealed it? To the queen? She was the doer thereof.' His body was left on the scaffold for a day before being buried in an unmarked grave in Greyfriars; his head was spiked on the north gable of the Tolbooth. The queen was delighted he met a traitor's end.

IN FRIENDSHIP FALSE...

When Morton's execution was reported to Queen Elizabeth, she stood alone in a window recess, overheard by her ladies angrily saying to herself, 'That false Scots urchin, for whom I have done so much! To say to Morton the night before he arrested him, "Father, no-one else but you has reared me and I will defend you from your enemies" and then next day order his arrest and his head smitten off! What can be expected from such double dealing as this?'

In August, James made Esme Stewart Duke of Lennox and gave William, Lord Ruthven the earldom of Gowrie; this news displeased Mary as much as finding out her son had sent George Douglas to King Henri to be recognised as King of Scotland. Immediately the archbishop was instructed to prevent this, for she had a new scheme in mind to gain her liberty and restoration. She instructed the Duke of Lennox to convince her son he was a usurper but she would, for love of him, share the crown of Scotland with him, otherwise she would ensure he only bore his father's title.

Saturday evening, 11 November, Robert Beale arrived at Sheffield, sent by Queen Elizabeth to ascertain how Mary intended to associate her title with her son. The earl was ill in bed with gout and the queen was said to be lying sick in hers. At an audience after dinner on Sunday, Beale asked Mary if her son was aware of her intent. She replied that as she was not allowed to communicate with him, she could only assume he was a natural, dutiful child. She was greatly displeased when Beale informed her that Queen Elizabeth, not wishing to deal with Mary without James's knowledge, had sent an envoy to him. She said she had wanted to send her own envoy and wished only to 'make valid and perfect that which was not and so thought by other princes', ending with her litany of complaints and wishing she could prove her 'devotion and innocence to his queen'.

Over the next couple of days, Mary and her attendants did their best to convince Beale she was seriously ill and had been so for weeks. On 21 November, a dark and gloomy day, the queen summoned Beale to her bedchamber where, as he reached her door, he saw candles being extinguished and her ladies sobbing. In a faint voice, the queen told him she had not long to live. Discomposed, Beale commended her 'unto the Lord' and left. When the countess looked in, Mary was sleeping. The next day, Shrewsbury informed Beale his own physician had found Mary's pulse strong. A week later Beale informed Mary that (as Mary had primed James) Queen Elizabeth's envoy had been refused permission to enter Scotland and, after several protestations by Mary of her 'sincere friendship', he left on 3 December 1581.

The New Year saw Queen Mary busy as ever with letters: she arranged for Jesuits to be sent to her son; to Mendoza, the new Spanish ambassador, she was assured by her son's letters of his entire obedience to her and that once restored to her crown via the association with her son she would ask King Philip to aid her in claiming the English crown. She makes no mention of the countess being prostrate with grief at the death early in the morning of 21 January of her daughter Elizabeth, Countess of Lennox. Mary in April hired a new courier, Francis Throckmorton (codenamed La Tour). More letters were sent: to Mendoza that when needed she would provide information on harbours and fortresses and asking what forces and money she could expect; to Lennox to reiterate James was no lawful king and to hasten association with his mother; to Mauvissiere of her ill health and ill usage, complaining the two physicians she had seen recently were sent by Walsingham, one of whom had recommended she drink gold water, and that if they gave him medicine for her, on no account was he to send it. At Buxton in June, she received a letter from her son saying he had read her last three letters, recognised all the honour he had originated from her and asked for the articles of association so he could 'execute her will'.

Tension arose in Chatsworth when one of Mary's attendants said to one of the countess's ladies that Queen Mary should be Queen of England. Frances Battell had retorted, 'It were better that Queen Mary was hanged before that time should come to pass.' Soon after, the earl and his wife began drifting apart.

During August, diplomats Jean Champuon, Sieur du Ruisseau and Albert Fontenay came from France to Chatsworth, arriving on a day when Queen Mary was out hunting. Via their services she intended to send out yet more letters: to Mauvissiere saying she was too ill to survive the next winter; to King Henri to arrange for James to be taken to France to save his life from Elizabeth's endless wicked designs (referring to the kidnapping of her son by the Earl of Gowrie); to Guise to hasten his invasion, with directions on how easily she could escape the house. These remained unsent because Queen Elizabeth, made aware of Mary's double dealings, ordered the earl to keep her officers under house arrest. Queen Mary immediately wrote to Mauvissiere that she was 'astonished beyond measure at this proceeding knowing in my conscience how little occasion I have given for it'. Meanwhile, the earl buried his eldest son and heir, Francis, in the family vault at Sheffield; he had suddenly died while on a visit to Belvoir Castle.

The New Year of 1583 saw Secretary Davison escort Mothe-Fenelon into Scotland to visit James, taking with him Mary's Articles of Association. They met Lennox on his way to France via London having been exiled from Scotland by the Protestant lords. Mary wrote to Mauvissiere of her puzzlement that Mothe-Fenelon travelled to Scotland 'almost a prisoner' and instructed that regarding the mother refusing to support her illegitimate daughter by Kirkcaldy, would rather see her whipped while tied to the back of a carriage rather than assist such a man-chaser. When James read the articles, he found his mother had a number of expectations. He must agree he held the crown of Scotland unlawfully, beg her pardon for detaining the crown since he had come to the age of understanding, declare and vow he held it now only by virtue of associating with her, and promise to follow her advice, counsel and commandments and not treat without her with foreign princes in war, peace, alliances, leagues or his marriage.

Delighting in sowing discord, Mary in February instructed Mauvissiere to inform Queen Elizabeth that the Earl of Leicester intended to imitate his father and marry his son to Arbella and then kill her son to usurp the Scottish throne; further, he was to let slip to Burghley that the earl had sent portraits of his son to the countess. Rumours began trickling in that the Countess of Shrewsbury was accusing her husband of being in love with Queen Mary. In June the Duke of Lennox died in Paris, and the following month James escaped from the hands of Gowrie, Mar and Angus, and resumed exercising his royal authority.

In January 1584, Mauvissiere received further instructions from Queen Mary: he was to deny there had been any intimacy between herself and Shrewsbury (and said she could provide proof that would ruin the countess) and raise the issue of the treaty between her and

Queen Elizabeth remaining unresolved. Regarding the arrest of Francis Throckmorton, though she had not been involved in any plotting, she was resigned to charges being brought against her. However, the earl was informed differently. Throckmorton had been caught at his lodgings in the process of encoding a letter to Queen Mary and lists had been found of English Catholic supporters and also harbours with their depths. Mendoza, implicated in a plot to bring about a Spanish invasion led by the Duc de Guise and assassinate Queen Elizabeth to place Mary on the throne, was expelled from England. Queen Mary earnestly assured Shrewsbury it could not be proved she took part in 'any of these pretended plots'. She wrote to Mauvissiere to assure Throckmorton in her name that the suffering he endured on her account would never be 'effaced' from her heart.

When Queen Elizabeth was asked if she would resume the treaty negotiations, she instructed the earl to tell his charge that when her son changed his conduct and Mary stopped her plotting she might consider her just demands, but for now she believed the treaty had been used to lull her. At that Mary was much offended, calling upon God she 'did not know who was the luller and the lulled'. She took some amusement in drafting an epistle to Queen Elizabeth that the countess had told her Elizabeth was 'not as other women' and those desiring her to marry Anjou were foolish 'seeing it could never be consummated'; that she would not wish to lose 'making love and gratifying yourself with new lovers'. The English queen, she said, was very vain, having a lofty opinion of her beauty as if she was a 'heaven-born goddess', avowing people could not look her straight in the face 'as it shone like the sun'. The countess and the ladies of the court apparently flattered her in extravagant doses, not daring to look at one another in case they burst into laughter.

Mid-May, Beale arrived back at Sheffield to negotiate a treaty between the queens. Queen Mary refused to make any promise unless first assured she had Elizabeth's favour and promise that the treaty would be concluded. At the same time, Beale tried to amend matters between the countess and the earl, and the earl with his son Gilbert, who had supported his stepmother. The earl told Beale that his 'son is ruled by his wife who is directed by her mother from whom the late slanders emanated, whatever my son says'. Considering Beale's report, Queen Elizabeth said she found 'no disposition' in Queen Mary to proceed in the treaty and was 'content to forbear any further proceeding'.

On 19 June, Queen Elizabeth received news that Anjou had died on 10 June and went into mourning at losing a 'very good friend', telling Shrewsbury he could take Queen Mary to Buxton. In August, Queen Mary received a letter from Fontenay: he had presented her sword to James (although as agreed in the name of the Duc de Guise). James had laughed and told Fontenay to tell her he would be 'a good and loyal knight all his life' and within a few days Lord Lindsay and other of her enemies would 'prove how religiously he wished to keep the oath of knighthood'. When Fontenay questioned his reluctance to publicly admit the association and his affection for his mother, he declared he would go with horses himself and rescue her, and sent her a letter, using a heart to serve for his name.

Sir Ralph Sadler, now aged seventy-seven years, arrived in the evening of 25 August to take charge of Mary, while Shrewsbury attended court. On the journey to Wingfield on 2 September, Mary talked with John Somer, Sadler's son-in-law, who wrote to Burghley that the queen 'loudly professes such goodwill and love towards Queen Elizabeth, you would expect no more faithful servant, friend or younger sister; and never stops rehearsing the nearness of their blood'. She had asked Somer if he thought she would escape if she might. He answered that it was natural for her to seek liberty; she said he was deceived, that she 'would rather die in captivity with honour than run away with shame'. A few weeks later, Mary was told by Sir Ralph that Queen Elizabeth placed no confidence in her words: the Jesuit Creighton had been arrested and although he had torn up his papers and thrown them into the wind, enough were carried back and pieced together to reveal clearly a plot to invade England stopped by the death of Lennox. Indeed, the participation of herself and King James had been revealed, and his queen had taken it as an 'irreparable wrong' that Mary had told Guise to make haste to stop her killing James. Tearfully, Queen Mary protested she neither knew Creighton or any plot and had no way of contacting her son and desired only that Queen Elizabeth 'treat nobly with her'.

Mid-September 1584: Marriage

Letters arriving from Liggons and Father Parsons confirmed Queen Mary's letters and cipher had reached the Prince of Parma, who said he was 'ready to venture his life for her relief'. Parsons advised that Parma was keen on marrying her and that, though he said he was unworthy, she well knew 'every man, whatsoever he pretends, seeks his own interest'. He advised her to find her own means of escape: if caught in this way the punishment would only be stricter arrangements, whereas if an invading force were involved it could put her life in peril. He suggested she wait for a long winter night, pretend to be ill, disguise herself and be outside the house around midnight – if he knew the time, place and number of horses, he would get her to the coast and a waiting ship.

1 October 1584: Instructions

Four letters arrived from Patrick, Master of Gray. He is being sent by James to the English court. Queen Mary directed a letter to reach him when in London with her further instructions: he was to declare to Queen Elizabeth that James acknowledged he owed everything he has to her and for the treaty to be concluded between the two of them and Queen Elizabeth – the key conditions to facilitate her liberation and restoration.

7–9 October 1584: Vigilance

Finding out from Sir Ralph that the Earl of Shrewsbury is asking to be released from his charge of her, Queen Mary frets at not being able to stay in a house she knows well. She was mulling over the question of her new keeper until Sir Ralph told her he suspected her of having something in hand. Tetchily she told him her left foot was too swollen and she too ill with a rheum to undertake anything. The comment did not stop Sir Ralph increasing the watch day and night, putting four guards under her windows, two at the door of her lodgings and two on patrol. He has also alerted the villages to watch out for strangers. Mocking his vigilance, Queen Mary smuggled out a letter to Sir Francis Englefield urging 'the great plot and design to go forward without respect to her own peril or danger', and for it to be executed next spring.

18 October 1584: Threat

Ruminating on stopping her removal, Queen Mary has instructed Mauvissiere to demand of Queen Elizabeth that the Countess of Shrewsbury make reparation for the lies she has spread about her or she will denounce the countess's unworthy conduct towards her to all Christian princes, article by article, with places, times and people; and she cannot be removed from the earl's care until her name is publicly cleared for it would be to both their dishonours.

31 October 1584: Reconciliation?

A letter arrived from Walsingham giving consent to Nau to come to London, so long as he was accompanied by someone to oversee all his doings. Nau asked if he would be allowed to buy some things in London, to which Sir Ralph said no, that he will lodge a few miles outside to make it an easier ride to Kingston. Sir Ralph asked the queen why she thought his mistress would have no care for her safety and he was instructed to tell her, 'Touching her desire to have jealousy and mistrust removed ... you may let her know we wish she had been as careful in time past ... for she herself knows, wherein we appeal to her own conscience, how great contentment and liking we had for a time of her friendship ... so are we now as much grieved to behold the alteration and interruption thereof, taking no pleasure in looking back on causes that have bred so unpleasant effects – which we wish had never been, or at least we could never remember, and that she were as innocent therein as she labours greatly to bear us and the world in hand she is.' His queen hoped that Nau might bring from her 'such sufficient matter as might work upon good ground a thorough reconciliation between us, which, as she seems greatly to desire, so should we also be most glad of'.

7–15 November 1584: 'Stand as fast'

As soon as the dark nights of November arrived, Queen Mary began retiring to her bed complaining of pain in her right arm.

In audience, Sir Ralph enquired of the queen whether she knew Master Gray. She replied she neither had knowledge of him nor what state or credit he has in Scotland. Informing her that English nobles and gentlemen had made an association to punish any conspiring against Queen Elizabeth and those in whose favour such plots may be framed, the queen said she would sign it and 'stand as fast as any English subject'.

Nau, using his own horses, set off for court on 10 November after being told that unless he finds good appearance of a treaty for her liberty he is not to deliver her mind in all things. He is also instructed to request she be allowed to exercise within ten or twelve miles around her abode, six horses for her attendants when she exercises outdoors, five other attendants and a lady in place of Mary Seton who, to Mary's grief, had retired months ago to the Convent of St-Pierre at Reims accompanied by Marie Courcelles. Nor should he allow her removal from Wingfield but relay her 'hard conceit' for Tutbury. This statement Sir Ralph wondered at, for he said she often complains of her lodgings, though she has the best in the house, albeit her occasional dining room is assailed with smoke and the scent of meat cooking from one of the kitchens below. He also wrote to Walsingham that despite Queen Mary saying she is unable to walk and has to be carried, there is no reason why she cannot be moved by coach with her foot laid on a pillow. Regarding her service, he only knows what he sees: that she has daily carried to her four or five dainty dishes for her own eating such as capon, rabbit, partridge, woodcock and, in season, venison, but her usual meat is mutton, which she particularly likes, and partridge. She would like seafood such as plaice, turbot, sole and lobster, which is seldom brought.

2 December 1584: Silver

Understanding Queen Mary has scant household stuffs, Sir Ralph arranged for John Somer to confer with Andrew Melville, master of her household. He found the household had for some years used the earl's silver but it had been removed and replaced by pewter when it was evilly used. (Somer noted that the pewter, as her folk handle it, is not meet to be set before mean persons.)

Personally, Queen Mary still owns a small silver posnet and chafing dish. She asked if Queen Elizabeth would honour her with the use of between thirty-six and forty pieces of silver, great and small – she would receive them very thankfully – and also for herself two gilt basins, a gilt ewer, a covered gilt cup, four livery pots, a lesser pot for wine at night in her chamber, three silver flagons and a gilt salt cellar, a silver basin and ewer for Melville and for her household two salt cellars and three bowls, eighteen silver plates, a dozen silver spoons and six silver candlesticks.

The queen has sent a letter to Nau to tell Walsingham she was upset his three despatches came together. Her illness and pain in her side is worse and he is to pursue more quickly her liberty, for Tutbury will end her captivity by death – especially as, she says, 'the best has been appointed for her guardians'.

8 December 1584: Bitter Birthday

It being her birthday, Queen Mary wrote in bitterness to Queen Elizabeth that though having the honour of being 'descended from blood so royal as yours, and sincerely resolved to give you every proof of an obedient and affectionate relative … submitting to you, as they say in our country, as to the chief of our house', yet still she was treated with severity despite placing herself absolutely in her hands. 'In short, I entreat you, remove me from the distress in which I am … May God give you, madam my good sister, as many happy years as I have had of sorrows these last twenty years! Wingfield, this day, the forty-second of my age, and eighteenth of my imprisonment.'

21 December 1584: Tutbury

When Sir Ralph was informed by Walsingham that Curle had complained Tutbury had unglazed windows and was in such need of repair it was uninhabitable, he rode to the house to look over it for himself. He told Walsingham, and Mary, that the windows broken in the great tower had already been amended and the lodgings appointed for her were the best of the house, 'flanking all along a fair large green court, the prospect to the east very fair, but not so far to the west because of some partitions and making of a chimney. The dining chamber is fair, about 36' long, with a private cabinet, with a chimney. Her bedchamber is about 27' long and has two beds and a pallet and private closet. There are other good rooms for those of her gentlewomen who do not lie in her chamber and for her grooms, and a convenient place for her people's table, and a handsome room for a close-stool. Everything is on one floor under one roof, and a private stair from the coal-place to an entry that leads to the rooms underneath which are in number eight chambers, four with chimneys. There is a tower standing at the south end of these lodgings with fair chambers with chimneys and necessaries.' She also has her own fair kitchen 'with all offices belonging, a buttery and pantry private to herself, and good water in a large, deep well at hand'.

5 January 1585: Association

The association made for the defence of Elizabeth by the English Estates was signed by Queen Mary.

14 January 1585: Arrival

When Queen Mary arrived at Tutbury Castle, Sir Ralph had already arranged hangings for her chambers, 300–400 weight of feathers for amending thin beds and bolsters, blankets, linen, Turkey carpets, window curtains, plate and other items had also arrived but not in nature and number as requested. Her cloth of estate had already been set up in the great chamber.

The queen has heard her new keeper is to be Lord St John.

6 February 1585: Service

Sir Ralph asked for audience to tell the queen his mistress gave apologies that so little care was had by those appointed to furnish Tutbury and her majesty was ashamed she 'was constrained to complain of the want thereof by her letters' and promised to amend all that was amiss. Sir Ralph grumbled to Walsingham that though there had been some initial wants, such as window curtains, they had soon been provided and her household well furnished while his own servants 'bore things patiently'.

It is agreed that on flesh days, Queen Mary will be served (dependent on the season) beef, veal, mutton, pig, capons, coney, lamb or kid along with wildfowl such as lark, partridge, woodcock, snipe, pheasant and, if wildfowl is not available, pigeons and chickens; on nones beef tongue, calves' feet and tripe; on fish days ling and cod, and every day twelve dishes at the seasonal discretion of the cook of a mix of seafood such as sole, skate, plaice, lobster, crab, gournard, haddock and whiting (and when in season mussels and oysters) and freshwater fish such as salmon, pike, carp, tench, bream, perch, barbel, and eels. Daily items are to include bread, eggs, butter, milk, cream, lard, suet, vinegar and wine for boiling of fish as well as wine, ale and beer for table and kitchen. In Lent there will be salt salmon, salt and red herring, stockfish, pease, barley, onions and herbs as used in pottages, and on nones there will be almonds, prunes, rice, oil and figs. Spices are to include sugar (as need shall require), pepper, ginger, mace, nutmeg, saffron, cloves, raisins, dates, capers, olives and so on. Other items include wood and coal, wax lights and white lights.

Having not heard from Mauvissiere for a long time, Queen Mary wrote for him to request her to have two chamber ladies, two gentlemen and two valets de chambre and to establish a stud of twelve horses besides her coach, she being unable to walk fifty paces together.

Sir Ralph having brought his hawks and falconers allowed the queen, to her delight, with two of her gentlewomen, to see his hawks fly a few miles along the rivers nearby. They were well guarded there, and he does not forget to set up watch and guard in about the castle day and night. He informed her that Sir Amias Paulet is to take charge of her.

18 February 1585: Dissatisfaction

Aching in her side and hips, Queen Mary took to her bed on 12 February but arose when she heard old Mistress Raulet, who is around seventy-four years old and had served her since she was a girl in France, was dying and went to comfort her.

She told Sir Ralph she knew Sir Amias Paulet had been ambassador in France and fears what she has heard of him and is dissatisfied his queen would appoint someone who is of no higher quality than a knight.

2 March 1585: Comforts

The queen's gentlewomen requested Sir Ralph to send for six pairs of large fine sheets and a dozen pillowcases along with more feathers, curtain rings, coverlets lined with canvas and twelve pairs of blankets. Turkey carpets have been placed around her bed, under her seat in her dining chamber and under the table in her bedchamber where she eats when she is unwell. Old long carpets are used for her to walk on in her chamber.

12 March 1585: Ingrate

With pleasure, Queen Mary received the headdresses that Mauvissiere's wife had sent her. The next moment, shocked and looking up from the ambassador's letter, she stated that until she heard it from the lips of her own son she would not believe he means not to associate with her. The next letter she came to was from her son but she said it could not be from him. Instantly, she sent to Queen Elizabeth 'to give the lie to the ruffian, Gray', and then wrote to instruct Mauvissiere to 'immediately and for the future take from James the name of king since he will not hold it of me and can never claim it from his father's head; that her son has sent the reason he cannot join with her is because she is 'held captive in a desert'. In her own hand she added a postscript that she was 'grievously wounded and cut to the heart by the impiety and ingratitude' her son shows to her and if he persists 'will invoke the malediction of God on him ... disinherit him and deprive him as an unnatural son, who is ingrate, perfidious and disobedient ... and will give my right to the greatest enemy he may have'.

23 March 1585: Grief

In another letter asking Queen Elizabeth to conclude the treaty for her liberty, Queen Mary offered to 'give up without any reserve, save honour and conscience' to entirely satisfy her to be removed out of her slavery, or 'desert captivity' as her son had called it by renouncing forever all rights she or hers could have in England after her, removing all motives of distrust. She also asked her to believe that she had not been mixed up with the one called Parry who she was informed had planned to shoot Queen Elizabeth when she went abroad to take the air in the fields, saying she abhors such detestable practices and horrible acts for 'to speak freely madam, I believe that those who attempt your life would do as much on mine … you will find that I bear a heart far enough from any such wicked intention … in tears and oppressed with grief'.

29 March 1585: Motion

To the queen's further devastation, Queen Elizabeth wrote to her affirming James had freely avowed he had read the Articles of Association but never signed or did any act that might conclude them. As for Master Gray, she had no reason to be his advocate, but can affirm on his behalf that he had 'dutifully performed' the instructions given him by his master. Further, Parry had confessed his assassination attempt was 'to advance you to this crown' and found it hard to believe she was ignorant of his plotting. Parliament had made a motion with 'general applause of the whole house, to revive the former judicial proceedings against you, proposed thirteen years past'. She had stayed them then and has stayed them now but asks: 'Does she think the time apt for a treaty for her liberty?'

As for Paulet, she reputes him 'faithful and honourable' and, in respect of the antiquity of his house, most noble. 'If you still profess to love and esteem best those who serve us most faithfully you have more cause to like him than dislike him, for he would never do anything unworthy'.

6–11 April 1585: Unlucky

Within ten paces of the queen's chamber, almost in full view of her windows, a poor young Catholic man was found hanged. Queen Mary complained the castle needed not to have been used like some common jail, refusing to believe the man had committed suicide, saying she had seen him forcibly dragged into the chapel and declaiming that she awaits some attack to be made upon her by Puritans and if she was attacked for her religion 'she is perfectly ready to lay down her neck under the axe'. She grumbles the place is unlucky after a poor man was found tumbled into the well.

A letter arrived from Morgan informing her that Paulet is a gentleman of an honourable family, Puritan in religion but courteous and his wife a plain gentlewoman, daughter and heiress of a Mr Anthony Harvy, a Catholic gentleman of the West Country.

18 April 1585: New Keeper

Queen Mary, granting Paulet his first audience, told him she had heard he was ill affected towards her. He responded she should judge him by his actions. After listening courteously to her complaints and protestations, he asked for her servants, and his own, to come before him and charged each to give no injury in word or deed to another.

27 April 1585: Restrictions

Paulet upset Queen Mary by having her cloth of estate in the great chamber removed, telling her it was sufficient she has one in her own dining room; that as he and his household eat in the great chamber, it makes it in effect Queen Elizabeth's room. As well as this, her coachman, Sharpe, has been blocked from going abroad without consent. After complaining on behalf of his mistress, Nau took the opportunity to ask if Paulet had any other restriction and was told that Paulet greatly misliked the queen's servants walking on the walls overlooking the gate, viewing all comers and goers, when they had no need to take the air there, having freedom to walk in convenient sort when they required it.

11 May 1585: Alms

Finding Sir Amias Paulet had stopped her priest, du Preau, going house to house giving alms to the village poor, Queen Mary stormed at him that she was sure no Christian could disapprove; that she only looked to be afforded some consolation amid her sickness and affliction.

6–9 June 1585: Diet

Summoned to attend Queen Mary on 6 June, Paulet and his wife came after dinner to her bedchamber where she lay abed. She told them her six-week diet was over and she wished to take the air in her coach at the end of the week. After chatting a while, she told them she found it strange and unkind that in her six weeks of dieting she had no letters or messages from Queen Elizabeth. Paulet said that as she had been hunting and hawking sundry times and walked in the gardens, he had not informed Queen Elizabeth; that 'her diet' was not considered in England a sickness but 'rather a means to prevent it'.

10–16 July 1585: Discontent

In another complaining letter to Mauvissiere, the queen wrote she fears for her health in the coming winter; that Bourgoing says he will give up all hope of a cure without her having better lodging, her bedchamber being exceedingly cold, notwithstanding the stoves and continual fire. And if such be the case in the warmth of this season, she leaves him to judge what it would be like in the middle of winter. The house is of timber and situated upon a hill in the middle of a plain and the wind enters her chamber on all sides. There are 100 peasants in the village at the foot of the castle who are better housed than she for she 'only has two small, wretched rooms and some closets not fit for anything except water closets. I have no place for recreations and no covered walk to take the air in daytime.'

Wishing to see her new greyhound run at a deer, Paulet was asked, via Curle, if she might go hunting. Assent was given with the proviso du Preau did not ride with them as they were going to Stockley Park, which meant going first through the town. On their return, she summoned him to say she disliked 'her servants should be forbidden to attend on her'. He answered that all her gentlemen had attended on her, and du Preau was not of that number. 'I must be attended by others than gentlemen,' she replied. 'So you have, madam', Paulet replied. 'You have one to carry your cloak; if you will have more, I will not let it.' She said she disliked being 'commanded'. He replied he 'but prayed leave to direct her servants; that he took no pleasure in offending her and if she gave him leave to be an honest man he would not offend'; that du Preau was free to attend her when she walks in the meadow but is not allowed in the town. Turning away, she said she would complain to her sister.

19 August 1585: Requests

In several letters to everyone she could think of, passed to Paulet for sending, she asks for them to make on her behalf the following requests: different lodgings while Tutbury is repaired and enlarged so she can have a hall for her meals and a gallery or large room to walk in; permission to ride further and without foot soldiers, being constrained to their pace; when riding abroad that she may take such of her servants as she thinks fitting; permission to give alms to the poor; the attendance of the Countess of Atholl, her daughter and Thomas Livingston; and for her embroiderer and all his family to be allowed to retire to France. Expressly she told Mauvissiere she is 'kept prisoner more vigorously and inconveniently than ever', is fallen ill again from chills, and fears sciatica forming in one thigh through the draughts, damp and coldness 'to which my chamber is exposed'. She urges him to press her son to execute the association so she could 'render him rightful possessor of all the greatness that belongs to me'. She enjoyed the dry comfits he sent during Lent – and wishes he 'cause those of which the note was last addressed to you to be as well-chosen'.

2–5 September 1585: Wretched Chambers

When Paulet came to Queen Mary during the evening of 2 September, he informed her, apart from persons leaving or arriving, all her requests had been granted. Weeping, she complained 'the deeds did not fulfil the fair words'. Faced with her dissatisfaction with her chambers, Paulet offered to give up his own apartments to her but she said they were too cold. Before he left, he reminded her she had failed to tell Queen Elizabeth she had been taken at least three times into a greater park in which she had coursed and hunted, and had not been constrained to the park only half a mile from the castle.

Over the next few days, the queen compiled a joint letter to Mauvissiere and incoming ambassador, Chateauneuf. She told them she believed her lodgings are not accurately reported to them or Queen Elizabeth, for she is 'in a walled enclosure on the top of a hill, exposed to all the winds and blasts of heaven … in a very old hunting lodge, built of timber and plaster, cracked in all parts, the plaster adhering nowhere to the woodwork and broken in numberless places, the lodge distant three fathoms or thereabouts from the wall and situated so low, the rampart of earth behind the wall is on a level with the highest point of the building so the sun never shines on that side, nor any fresh air come to it, making it damp and you cannot put any piece of furniture in that part without it being in four days completely covered with mould. I leave you to think how this must act upon the human body and in short, the greater part of it is rather holes for base and abject criminals than a habitation fit for a person of my quality, or even of a much lower … The only apartments I have for my own person consist of two little wretched chambers, so extremely cold, especially at night, that but for the ramparts and defences of curtains and tapestries which I have had made, it would not be possible for me to stay in them and no-one staying up with me at night during my illnesses have escaped without cold or catarrh …. I have no gallery or cabinet to retire to be occasionally alone, excepting two paltry holes, with windows in the shadow of the wall … for taking the air abroad, on foot or in my chair I have only about a quarter of acre of ground at the entrance to the stables, which Somer had dug up last winter and enclosed with a fence of dry wood, a place, to look at, fitter to keep pigs in than to bear the name of garden; there is not a sheep-pen amidst the fields but makes a better appearance.'

It is impossible to take exercise on horseback for snowfalls, she writes, and rains break up the roads and there is no place to walk a mile, even with her coach. She is ashamed to be compelled to say that, with the house filled with so many common people, it cannot be kept 'long clean, whatever decent people may be put therein, so this lodging lacking pits for private easements is subject to such a continual foulness that each one overflows, one is compelled to avoid them and such is beneath my windows from which I receive a perfume not the most agreeable'. If her life is cut short it will be due to the deficiency of her dwelling. She had more servants when with the Earl of Shrewsbury but needs them more now, and has no lady companion worthy of her rank or age, seeing as the company of the Countess of Atholl is denied her; further, she is debarred from hearing about her son and his health and pleads they intercede for her.

23 September 1585: Response

Walsingham informed Paulet that Queen Elizabeth, receiving a passionate letter of complaints from Queen Mary, was considering moving her to Chartley, the Earl of Essex's house 12 miles away, but fears she might view it having a moat with disfavour. Paulet rode out to view the place and told Queen Mary it was large enough for both households.

When Paulet told Queen Mary that he had been instructed that her packets for France were no longer to go via the French ambassador but through Walsingham, she was incensed: 'We can see plainly our destruction is sought and our life taken from us one of these days.' He told her he could see no reason for her anger, as they would be easier conveyed than before. He thought it 'a foul and wicked slander' that she feared she would be destroyed and asserted that she should understand 'if any other prince had received the wrong which his queen had received at her hands' she would not have been in case to complain.

10 October 1585: 'No niggard'

When Paulet offered to give up his large dining chamber to Queen Mary, she declined, telling him 'she would remain and die in her own bad lodging' with several other bitter words to which Paulet was heard to say to his wife, 'Whereof she is no niggard.' She also inveighed against her son for accepting six pairs of bloodhounds sent by Queen Elizabeth.

23 October 1585: Marriage

Gilbert Curle and Barbara Mowbray, daughter of the laird of Barnbougle and granted a passport by Queen Elizabeth though she arrived without warning, were married today in the castle.

12 December 1585: Scotland

Paulet informed Queen Mary that, despite her ill-informed letter to Chateauneuf that her son was in prison and peril, she might be pleased to know King James had assembled Parliament in Linlithgow's great hall; that the young Duke of Lennox carried the crown, the Earl of Huntly the sceptre and the Earl of Atholl the sword. Her son had made a speech which ended with him restoring the honours and offices of the noblemen, lately distressed, after they declared their affection and obedience to him. Nau answered for the queen that the king had dissembled with his lords before. Paulet said Queen Mary should be satisfied to hear that her son had been hunting and hawking without guard.

He told Nau the move to Chartley will take place on the Tuesday before Christmas; Nau said the queen will require four carts for her books and apparel.

15 January 1586: Impending

Paulet has written to Walsingham that Bastian's wife is near term and Curle's wife likely to follow shortly; that Queen Mary, now based at Chartley, boldly uses her mass priest, Camille du Preau, seeing Queen Elizabeth has allowed it so long as it moves not beyond her household, so there will be no question as to how the children will be baptised but he would ask direction on providing a midwife and nurse.

31 January 1586: Espionage

The queen has been ill in bed for nigh a week with pains in her limbs. She complained to Paulet that she finds the feathers in the mattress hard and coming through the ticking, and prays to be provided with one of down.

Not confident that her earlier ciphered letter had reached Chateauneuf, Queen Mary sent him a duplicate, desperate to know why Baron d'Esnaval had travelled into Scotland, the not knowing leaving her troubled, 'sleeping little and eating less'. Although previously warning him not to use alum as it is easily suspected and discovered, she additionally advised that if he has to use it to do so between the lines of new books, on the fourth, eighth, twelfth and sixteenth leaf, continuing four to four and attaching green ribbons to them; in like manner, delicate cloth like white taffeta or lawn can be written upon and sent half a yard longer than ordered. She also suggested sending packets in high slippers in place of the cork used in the sole over the heel, or spread out between the wood of trunks and boxes with a padlock attached to the fold of the lock.

2 March 1586: Laundresses

The queen has told Paulet that Sharpe, her coachman, desired to leave her service along with his wife, sister and sister-in-law, the laundresses, who say their legs are swollen from continual washing and they could no longer endure it. Paulet is sending for instruction on the matter.

24 March 1586: Warnings

A flurry of letters arrived secretly today: Chateauneuf thanked Queen Mary for her good counsel but says he cannot send letters inside the cork of slippers, not wishing to confide in a shoemaker; otherwise, he will do the best he can. He sent news: John Maxwell, Earl of Morton caused mass to be publicly said and has been imprisoned in Edinburgh Castle; the Duke of Mayenne is with King Henri fighting in Guienne against the King of Navarre and awaits the arrival of mercenaries sent by Queen Elizabeth; and Cordaillot was bringing a box of sweetmeats with twenty letters and packets. In her reply, she sent him warning that if the new gentleman he was using is named Phelippes, as she suspects, then he is Walsingham's servant who about Christmas resided in her house above three weeks and to beware, for if he 'has promised to do me service, I know he plays a double game'.

21–22 April 1586: Bed

Summoned to her presence, Paulet found the queen sitting on the side of her bed, saying she was unable to walk and wished to complain she is receiving no replies to her letters. She also requested Bessie Pierrepont be sent back to her family, having been with her since she was four years old and, though she looked younger, now seventeen and of an age to be looking for a husband. Paulet said the kind thought was to her honour but doubted the girl would want to leave her.

The bed and linen for Queen Mary arrived and was well accepted by her.

30 April 1586: Her Sufferings

The queen wrote to M. d'Esneval in reply to his letter that she would find it an especial pleasure if he would inform her, from time to time, of the health and state of her son, her maternal affection having never failed, although 'his bad ministers' make him forget her sufferings.

18–20 May 1586: Cascade

A veritable cascade of letters arrived. From the archbishop the queen learned the Duke of Savoy's expedition against Geneva had gone off in smoke, and that Mendoza had informed him the Spanish army grows rapidly and will be the finest by sea ever seen when it attacks England. She wrote to ask him to keep her informed of any enterprise 'in this country, especially if it counteracts Leicester in Flanders and Drake in the Indies'. She told him that when Nau went to court he said he had broken a design of the Puritans to have her barred from succession to the crown and stopped her leaving the hands of the earl by showing 'the proof against his wicked wife who was made to contradict her lies in the presence of the queen and beg pardon'. She instructed him that he is to do his best to break the treaty made between her son and Queen Elizabeth, to stop all traffic with Scotland in France and to lay all Scottish ships under embargo – and bring them all back to a sense of their duty.

Six letters arrived from Charles Paget, to which the queen sent answer on principal points. First, he must find out if King Philip intends to 'set on England', which would be the surest way to rid himself altogether of the Queen of England's malice against him and lead him 'to the same remedies as in Don John's time were propounded' – that is, for King Philip to assure dominion of the Low Countries with a prince who is his friend on the English throne; if she could not persuade her son to enter the enterprise, he must arrange to have him delivered into the hands of King Philip or the Pope, with promise for him to be set at liberty whenever she desires or if, after she dies, he is Catholic he will be allowed to return to succeed to this crown. 'There shall remain in my heart a thousand regrets if I should die to leave behind me a tyrant and persecutor of the Catholic church.'

To Mendoza's two letters she replied, 'In case my said son should not embrace, before my death, the Catholic religion (of which I must confess to you I see little hope so long as he remains in Scotland), to cede and give by will my right to the succession to this crown to King Philip', which he is to keep secret otherwise she could lose her dowry, complete the rupture with her son and face total ruin and destruction.

When not reading, dictating or writing letters, the queen has been going out in her coach or carried in her chair to the ponds to watch the hunting of ducks.

31 May 1586: Removal

Instructing Chateauneuf to ask again for Elizabeth Pierrepoint to be returned to her father and mother, Queen Mary revealed her real reason: Nau wishes to marry her, but the girl has too much of her grandmother the countess's nature in her behaviour and she would not bestow her on any man that she would wish good to.

25 June 1586: Letters

Told Anthony Babington inadvertently holds some of her letters from France and Scotland, Queen Mary wrote to ask him to give them to the bearer.

8 July 1586: Despatch

By safe means a letter arrived from Anthony Babington who tells Queen Mary his service to her was interrupted by her removal from her last abode into the custody of a wicked puritan, and he had determined to go overseas when Ballard told him of the great preparations that Christian princes – her allies – are making to deliver England from its miserable state. And, although it might cost them their lives, he and his friends considered what they might do in her service and considered what things were necessary: invaders to arrive in sufficient strength, ports for their arrival and military support to join with them, her deliverance and the 'despatch of the usurping competitor'. He vowed that all 'shall be performed or all our lives haply lost in the execution' and asks her 'to direct us by your princely authority to enable such as may advance the affair'. He would be able to recommend some men fit to be lieutenants. For her rescue: 'Myself with ten gentlemen and a hundred followers will undertake the delivery of your royal person ... For the despatch of the usurper ... there be six noble gentlemen all my private friends who for the zeal they bear to the Catholic cause and Your Majesty's service will undertake that tragical execution.' By her wisdom they hope to reduce all into method; her happy deliverance first, 'for thereupon depends the only good, and that all the other circumstances concur so untimely beginning of one end does not overthrow the rest'. All of them will think their lives happily spent if they obtain such an end; he will be at Lichfield from 12 July to await her answer.

12–16 July 1586: Greatest Enemy

In letters to the Archbishop of Glasgow, Queen Mary complained that her keeper could not watch her more rigorously were he the greatest enemy she had in England; the archbishop is to inform her relatives she would be in danger in Paulet's hands if the English queen dies and wishes to be entrusted into the care of someone of higher quality.

After an outing in her coach, the queen wrote to Chateauneuf to tell him Paulet is being 'more overbearing and rigorous than normal' and she would not be 'sorry to change my host, for he is one of the most whimsical and austere persons whom I have ever known ... fitter for a jail of criminals than custody of one of my rank and birth', and if the English queen died her life would be very insecure in his hands, he being of little rank, credit, influence and power; perhaps the ambassador could speak to Burghley in conversation without giving him suspicion that 'the wind blows from this quarter'.

17 July 1586: Plot

After much consideration, Queen Mary replied to Mr Babington's overture wanting to ensure the enterprise was well grounded. She enquired as to how many foot and horse they could raise by themselves; who would be captains if a general in chief cannot be had; what towns, ports and havens would offer succour north, west and south from the Low Countries, Spain and France; the fittest place to assemble the principal company of their forces and which way to march; what munitions and foreign forces, horse and foot, he required and how long paid from the foreign princes and the forts fittest for their landing; whether he needs provision of armour and money; and 'by what means do the six gentlemen deliberate to proceed and the manner of my getting away from this house'. Once resolutions are taken on these points among the principal authors, they should keep themselves few in number and impart the same to Mendoza by one faithful person to keep things more secret.

She said once the messenger had returned with 'sure promise and sufficient assurance of the succour requested', then secretly they should make provision of armour, horse and ready money and hold themselves in readiness to march as soon as they are signified by the principals in every shire, using as their excuse that provisions are made only for fortifications in case of need against the Puritans of the realm; perhaps they should let the bruit go that Catholics are to be overthrown when forces return from the Low Countries.

'The affair thus prepared, forces in readiness without and within the realm, then it will be fit to set the six gentlemen to work, taking order upon the accomplishment of their designs, I may be suddenly transported out of this place, and that all your forces at the same time be in the field to meet me.' As no certain day can be appointed for accomplishing the said gentlemen's designs and so that others may be ready to remove her, she advised they have about them, or at least at court, 'four stout men furnished with good and speedy horses' to set off 'divers ways' and 'cut off the post's ordinary ways', to arrive with all diligence to alert those waiting to transport her from her abode 'before my keeper can be advised of the execution of the said design, or at least before he can fortify himself within the house or carry me away'.

She reiterates that they need to be assured of sufficient foreign force or for her to be set in the midst of a good army which can keep her safe to await the foreign forces, for if insufficient the queen could recapture her and enclose her forever in some hole from which she would never escape. They must also consider whether or not they would pursue transporting her and executing the rest of the enterprise if their designs fail to take hold.

For her part Queen Mary said she would do her utmost to make Scottish Catholics rise, get her son in their hands and perhaps arrange some stirring in Ireland as a distraction. She has heard she might be moved to Dudley Castle in the summer and they may have to see about how she could escape from there. Otherwise, from Chartley, there are three means: first, on a day appointed in her 'walking' abroad on horseback on the moors between this and Stafford, fifty or sixty men well horsed and armed could take her away, her keeper usually only having eighteen to twenty horsemen with daggers only; second is to 'come at midnight and set fire to the barns and stables' which are near to the house and 'while my guardian's servants shall run to the fire', they might 'surprise the house'; equally they might prepare some carts, which usually come early in the morning, so they fall down in the middle of the great gate and they and their followers come suddenly to makes themselves master of the house and thereby carry her away, which would be easily achieved as the soldiers lodge in sundry places, some a half and some a whole mile off before they could bring any relief. 'Whatsoever issue the matter takes, I do and will think myself obliged towards you as long as I live for the offers you make to hazard yourself as you do for my delivery ... fail not to burn this letter quickly.'

27 July 1586: Design

To provide intelligence of the latest enterprise, Queen Mary wrote to several: to Mendoza that, hearing anew King Philip's good intentions in this direction, she had advised on every point of a new design, bidding the principals to confer with him on their needs, having already informed them how she can escape; to Charles Paget, much as he had written, she has been told of the intentions of the principal of the Catholics and 'they, having asked my direction for executing the whole, made an ample letter giving point-by-point my advice' and told them to confer with Mendoza and Ballard so the requisite support of horsemen, footmen, armour, munitions and money can be pursued hotly. She has told the Catholics to stir nothing on this side until they have sufficient promise and assurance, having doubts the Prince of Parma can spare as many as necessary for the enterprise, nor King Philip before the recovery of Cuba and Domingo and the arrival of the fleet from the Indies.

Assuring Sir Francis Englefield that she had received his last letters, she thanked him for gaining the grant of 12,000 crowns which shall be 'employed to no other use than to accomplishing my escape from hence' as she has lately designed. She then wrote to the archbishop to send the money quickly either with her new servants or in the two secret hiding places in the trunk of the boxes of comfits from Italy and Spain, saying she will write for them in the open way.

In her letter to Chateauneuf, she asked him to find out the purpose of Phelippes' month-long visit at Chartley with Paulet and requested he ensure any new guardian will be such that in the event 'either of the death of the Queen of England or an uprising in the country' her life will be safe.

11–12 August 1586: Stag Hunt

Sending Curle to Paulet, Queen Mary let him know she desired to walk after dinner. He replied she could go if she wished; and if she was well enough the next day he could offer her a little pastime, as Sir Walter Aston, who lived 3 miles away, would give her the pleasure of a stag hunt, with the desire she might kill the stag by her own hand as she has done before. The queen was delighted though she hesitated at first, the next day being Friday, but accepted rather than lose an opportunity. In the end she need not have worried; the weather was too bad for hunting and it was deferred until the 16th, so she spent Friday fasting as normal.

16 August 1586: All Merry

Attired for the hunt, the queen was followed by Nau (who as always dressed himself well), Curle, Melville, Dr Bourgoing and Hannibal who carried her bows and arrows. Mounting, all were merry. Queen Mary galloped for a mile but, seeing Paulet had fallen behind, stopped to let him catch up. A little way on, Paulet approached the queen and said, 'Madam, there is a message for you', pointing to Mr Gorge, a groom of the privy chamber, dressed in green-braided serge. He dismounted and came to the queen, who remained on her horse. 'Madam,' he began, 'the queen my mistress finds it very strange that you have undertaken against her and her estate what she never would have thought of if she had not seen it with her own eyes.'

Queen Mary replied, 'Very far from having conspired against the queen, we have not even had such a thought; she has been wrongly informed; nor is it the first time she has been misinformed and done us injustice.' As she called Nau to her, Gorge stopped him by stepping between them. Resisting, Nau insisted excitedly he had to speak to her. Gorge told him he was fulfilling the orders of his queen. The same was said to Curle when he said he would take leave of his mistress. Both were set apart. All her gentlemen were disarmed of their swords and daggers and, apart from the doctor, who was allowed to remain, each one was guarded and conducted away. Seeing her servants being taken away, she demanded Paulet tell her where she was being taken.

'Not far,' came the answer.

She told him she would ride no further and, dismounting, sat on the ground weeping, leaning against Gilbert's sister Elspeth, who joined her. She again asked where she was being taken.

Paulet replied, 'A good place, more beautiful than this.'

She told him she would rather die.

He told her he would send for his carriage and put her into it.

She said that 'no carriage horses are available for Nau has one and Bastian the other'; that it was 'infamous to be treated in such a manner, being a Queen … We ought not to be treated in such fashion as to please our enemies, who seek our ruin and why we have such things done to us we do not know having done nothing to deserve them.' Blaming Paulet for taking such action against her, she said he 'had better take care what you do for this act might cause bloodshed and the death of many as foreign princes would take vengeance on England'.

Becoming impatient, Paulet said she should 'quiet herself and not vex herself for no harm was intended to her and the longer she remained there, the more harm it would do her', this being reiterated by her doctor, who said she could not remain there all night.

She complained she had need of her people, her clothes and night gear. He said she would have her maids, necessary servants and effects waiting for her at Tixall Manor.

Finally, she rose. Supported under each arm, she retired under a tree to pray loudly that God would have pity on her and her people; that perhaps England wished to place her person in safety or in surer custody because the Queen of England was ill or dead.

25 August 1586: Return

When Queen Mary was leaving Tixall to return to Chartley, seeing some poor folks assembled around the gates, she began weeping and loudly declaimed, 'I have nothing for you, I am a beggar as well as you, all is taken from me.' To the gentlemen assembled to escort her, she said, still weeping, 'Good gentlemen, I am not witting or privy to anything intended against the Queen.'

When she entered Chartley, she first visited Curle's wife who had given birth to a daughter early on Tuesday 23 August. When she and her household rejoined, tears flowed abundantly on all sides. After tears were passed away, Queen Mary was silent except for remarking that all her papers had been taken away 'but two things could not be taken from her, her English blood and her Catholic religion'. She was angry when she was shown a promise of marriage on a torn parchment between Nau and Elizabeth Pierrepoint which had been found in the young lady's coffers and which she had signed and kept secret; she was also furious with Nau, who had made her a solemn promise he would not propose marriage to the lady. Paulet informed her that the secretaries had been sent to London.

Later she asked, as her priest had been removed, whether Paulet's minister would baptise the little girl. When he refused, she shocked him by going into Curle's chamber, laying the baby on her knees and, taking water out of a basin, casting it in the child's face, saying she baptised her Mary in the name of the Father, Son and Holy Ghost.

13 September 1586: Money

Paulet asked the doctor if he could see the queen; she sent back reply that she was ill in bed and begged to be left alone. He was insistent and ordered her ladies and servants out of her room. She was then asked to give what money she held into his hands, for which he would give her receipt. She refused. He said she had done much harm and suborned many people with it; she refused this by saying if asked for help she could not refuse it. He again asked her to voluntarily give up her money or he would have to take it by force. She refused to hand him her cabinet keys. When he called for bars to break the door, she gave up the key with many bitter words against him including that his queen 'might have her body but never her heart'. He accounted for five rolls of canvas containing 5,000 French crowns and two leather bags with gold and silver, the latter left with her. In Nau's chamber were various bags of money which were sealed. Paulet reserved £500 for use by the household and left the queen personally with 10 crowns for necessities, although Paulet said he knew well she had a good store of money kept in the French ambassador's hands.

15 September 1586: Reduced Household

For the move on the morrow to an unnamed house, the queen's attendants were reduced to Jane Kennedy, Renee de Rallay (usually called Beauregard), Gillis Mowbray (Barbara's sister) and Elspeth Curle as her maids of honour, her surgeon Jacques Gervais, her apothecary Pierre Gourgon, Didier the butler, Martin Huet her master cook, Jean Lauder the baker, (the latter three having been with her since she came to England), Nicholas de la Mare, Hannibal, the doctor and the master of her household, Andrew Melville. The rest of her household are to stay behind, except for those who have already been discharged.

Paulet came to the queen asking if she would listen quietly and not abuse him. He revealed Babington's plot was known, including the six men who intended to kill Queen Elizabeth and the means she had provided to make her escape. She denied all knowledge of Babington or of any plot.

Asking if he could distribute wages to her servants, she refused flatly, saying she would not make him her treasurer. Paulet said he would give each what she wished with a receipt and so she made a memorandum in her own hand as to who was to be paid and what amount.

21–26 September 1586: Last Journey

All the doors of the rooms which housed those servants who were to stay at Chartley were shut, stopping anyone communicating with Queen Mary before she left. They travelled with an escort of 200 horse, half in front and half behind. They stopped that night at Burton. Before their journey resumed, Mr Gorge came with a message for her: that his queen thought it strange she would be 'accessory against her, being a relation and the same rank; that she knew well if she had been sent into Scotland, she would not have been safe and to send her to France, she would have been thought a fool'. Her answer was that she had neither thought of nor undertaken anything against her good sister, 'nor had she so little prudence as to conspire against her or put her hands upon a consecrated queen', ending with all her accustomed complaints. They set off at eleven o'clock that morning and arrived at Hill Hall Castle in Abbots Bromley, a house belonging to the Earl of Huntingdon. The two following days the cavalcade set off at ten o'clock, first lodging in Leicester at The Angel and then at a house in Rutland.

On 25 September they entered Fotheringhay Castle. Immediately, Queen Mary complained there was a lack of proper accommodation for herself and her servants. The next day she complained that there were many beautiful rooms which were uninhabited. She was told the lords of the council were coming to occupy them.

5 October 1586: False Reports

Queen Mary managed to smuggle out a letter for the Duc de Guise, telling him all is over if he does not find means to succour her: 'They intend to accuse me of laying plots against the queen and troubling her estate.' She says they claim to have seized letters belonging to her which prove it, acknowledged by Nau and Curle, who must have been tortured. 'Whatever you hear, these are false reports ... I expect to be despatched with poison or some secret death. I am nearly maimed by their bad treatment, my right hand swollen and painful I can scarcely hold the pen or assist myself to eat but my courage shall not fail me. If my son does not concur now in avenging his mother, then I give him wholly up; and I beg that you and all my relations will do the same.'

11–15 October 1586: Examination

The peers, privy councillors and officers who had arrived at Fotheringhay on 11 October assembled in the castle chapel the following morning to attend preaching and prayers. Afterwards, Sir Walter Mildmay, Sir Amias Paulet and public notary Edward Barker came to her to present her with a letter from Queen Elizabeth in which she was asked to answer those present as if she herself was present; that as she lived under her protection, so she was subject to the laws of the realm. Immediately Queen Mary bridled that she was written to as if she was a subject, 'but we are a queen and a born daughter of a queen, nearest relation to Queen Elizabeth ... a prisoner for 18 years ... ill-treated, afflicted and troubled by continued persecution'. Alone, without counsel, her servants removed; no criminal was ever so destitute of all aid, she said.

On Thursday, around ten o'clock in the morning, after Queen Mary assented to hearing the commissioner, they entered her chamber with great ceremony. The Lord Chancellor spoke first, saying he had been given authority to examine her on certain charges against Queen Elizabeth's person, and after taking advice of the doctors of law they would proceed in their commission with or without her. She protested she had never plotted to injure or kill the queen, despite being offended at the wrongs and indignities done to her. When she fell silent, they asked her to say plainly if she would make answer before the commissioners. She said their commission was founded on a law meant to ensnare her; that she would not wrong her ancestors by owning herself a subject of the English crown, and would rather die a thousand times than to answer as if a criminal.

Vice Chamberlain Hatton spoke then, explaining that Queen Elizabeth had been greatly grieved to hear that Queen Mary was procurer of her death and that nothing would be more joyful and acceptable to her than to hear the report to be untrue and she innocent.

On Friday, Queen Mary sent for some of the commissioners and repeated her protestation: she was an anointed queen, subject to neither their laws nor their queen; she would consent to answer, but only to one allegation: that of plotting her sister queen's death. The commissioners assembled in the great chamber, where a chair of estate and canopy had been set in the upper part. Further off, a crimson velvet cushioned chair was placed on a foot carpet for Queen Mary. On either side of the room, benches were placed to seat the earls, lords and privy councillors. In front of them sat the chief justices and doctors of law. In the middle, at a little table, sat attorney Popham and solicitor Egerton and their clerks.

Queen Mary entered. She wore a white lawn veil over a black gown with a long train carried by Beauregard. She was supported on either side by Melville and Bourgoing and attended by her gentlewomen Jane Kennedy and Elspeth Curle. When she had taken her seat, Lord Chancellor Bromley, hatless, stood up and spoke into the silence: having been told, to her great grief and anguish of mind, that Mary had plotted the destruction of her, of England and religion, Queen Elizabeth has appointed these commissioners to hear the matters which 'shall be objected against you and to clear yourself from the crimes laid against you and show your innocence'.

The accused rose up, protesting that she arrived in England to request aid which was promised her yet had been detained in prison. She said that she was no subject of the queen but a free and absolute queen, not to be judged by any but God alone. She would show by her answers she was not guilty of the crime against Queen Elizabeth with which she was charged and only on this point would she answer. They ordered her protestation to be recorded.

After Gaudy, the queen's serjeant at law, had given account of Babington's conspiracy, he concluded she knew of it, approved and assented to it, promised her assistance and showed ways and means for effecting it. Queen Mary denied she had communicated with Babington and claimed that not one person could truthfully assert she had ever done anything to harm the Queen of England. Copies of her letters were read out. She thereupon accused Walsingham of tampering with the evidence, insisting upon seeing the originals. Walsingham said he called God to witness that he had done nothing unbeseeming an honest man or anything unworthy as a public man. Then she began to weep, saying if she had ever planned or consented to such, may God never grant her mercy.

When questioning resumed after a break, she was told Nau and Curle had owned to answering certain letters by her order and that after they had written them, she read them, shut them and sealed them in her cabinet. She replied that she could not answer for Nau and Curle or what they might have written about this enterprise of themselves and not communicated with her; she entirely repudiated their evidence and wanted them brought to face her – not that she wished to accuse them, but sure they must have been under fear of death or promise of saving their lives to so accuse her, thinking she could save herself better. Burghley told her Nau had made his deposition of his own free will. She said she disbelieved that, and proceedings were adjourned.

On 15 October Queen Mary repeated all her former protestations and complaints, adding that had Queen Elizabeth been under the new Act in earlier times she would have been drawn into question for the conspiracy of Thomas Wyatt, which sought to remove Mary I in favour of Elizabeth, then a princess. Weeping, she asked for a lawyer and a different assembly, appealing to God and to her allies and friends. As more letters were read out, she made objection, saying it was not their business to speak of the affairs of princes. Burghley countered with a question: if the number of soldiers discussed had come into the country on behalf of the King of Spain, the Pope and M. Guise, would she have been willing to answer for the life of Queen Elizabeth and the state of the country?

She said she did not know their intentions; all she had wished for was her deliverance.

Burghley recapped, referring to her communications with Charles Paget and Mendoza, which revealed the plot to invade England and on the death of Queen Elizabeth for Queen Mary to be put in her place; that she had also written separately to Mendoza of her determination to send her son into Spain and to assign to King Philip her right to the throne of England.

She told him she had 'read a book which proved King Philip's right'.

Burghley replied that the Kingdom of England could not be transferred but descended only by right of succession according to the law. He then asked her if she wished to say anything else. She charged that they had condemned her before they arrived and wished to be heard in a full parliament or to speak with the queen and her council in person.

The examination was adjourned until 25 October and moved to the Star Chamber at Westminster.

23 October 1586: Quietness

Paulet came to visit the queen for she had been troubled with a pain in her shoulder. Seeing her quietness, he tarried with her for an hour and a half, during which time she talked as she pleased with him, the Countess of Shrewsbury and Lord Abergavenny.

20 November 1586: Death

After dinner, Paulet and Sir Drew Drury came to ask permission to bring Lord Buckhurst and Mr Beale to see her. Queen Mary was informed that the whole Parliament of England had assembled and affirmed the sentence of death against her.

16–23 December 1586: Priest

Queen Mary's priest, Camille du Preau, was allowed to see her. The queen gave him letters to safeguard and smuggle out: the letter to Mendoza dated 23 November she made her adieu, denying she had done any act or deed against Queen Elizabeth except assert her right to the crown as acknowledged by all Catholics; she went on to say that the bearer would relate how rigorously she had been treated and described the scaffold being erected in her hall. He was to know she was content at having made over all her rights to King Philip and, as she expects her request for a priest not to be granted, asked him to order a mass for her and sent him a diamond held very dear, 'having been given to me by the late Duke of Norfolk as a pledge of his troth, and I have always worn it as such: keep it for my sake'; to the Duc de Guise she sent rings as tokens and bade him farewell, 'being on the point of being put to death by an unjust judgement'. Lastly, she wrote to the Pope that if her son persisted in his errors, she transmits to King Philip all the rights she has to the throne of England.

Queen Mary sent for Paulet and Drury on 19 December to give them a letter she had written to Queen Elizabeth, showing it to them open before shutting it with white silk and sealing it with Spanish wax.

23–24 January 1587: Murder

Paulet forbade the porter to carry the rod before Queen Mary's dinner. He said when Melville was removed from her presence, he thought the practice would stop.

The next day, Queen Mary sent Dr Bourgoing to Paulet, instructed to say she believed she was about to be murdered considering that all her state and dignity was removed; she was astonished that a thing of so little consequence was forbidden which neither hurt nor profited anyone.

Paulet said it was a great wrong to suppose Queen Elizabeth would undertake anything so unworthy and outrageous as to kill her, either by night or day, secretly or suddenly; further, he was offended she thought he could commit an act of butchery or permit it to be done, and as a woman of reason wondered why she so tormented herself.

Bourgoing said she had read in the chronicles they had done the same to King Richard, degraded from all honour and dignity, and put to death suddenly, murdered in a moment.

4 February 1587: Herbs

Dr Bourgoing was sent to Paulet by Queen Mary to ask if he could gather herbs from the garden to help her while she was ill. Delayed consent was given and Bourgoing, with the apothecary, gathered the herbs necessary for Queen Mary to begin her cure next day.

7 February 1587: Shed Her Blood

After dinner on 7 February, the Earls of Kent and Shrewsbury sent to ask for an audience with Queen Mary. She sent back reply that she was readying herself for bed; however, if it was urgent, they could come to see her. They, with Beale, Paulet and Drury, entered her chamber and stood at the foot of her bed. Shrewsbury, head uncovered, told her that Queen Elizabeth had sent them so she might hear her sentence. Beale then read aloud from a parchment bearing the Great Seal of England.

When he finished Queen Mary thanked them for such welcome news, saying that having been imprisoned eighteen years she was ready and willing to shed her blood in the cause of God and the Catholic Church.

She swore on her Bible she had neither sought nor attempted the death of the queen and asked when she was to die.

'Tomorrow, eight o'clock in the morning.'

At that she wept bitterly, and fell silent.

Her servants, crying, said the time was too short in which to arrange her affairs, entreating the execution be deferred.

Queen Mary asked where she was to be buried. They replied they had no orders but doubted it would be in France. She asked after her servants; then after Nau, asking if she was to die and he be saved; that she would die for the life of him who accused her, who caused her death to save himself.

During the afternoon she wrote to du Preau, who had been prevented from attending her, that as she was denied him hearing her last confession and receiving the sacrament, she would have his advice for the right prayers to speak, confess grief for her sins in general, and ask him to pray for her.

After supper she sent for all her servants, begging them to live in friendship among themselves and give over all past enmity and ill will. She distributed her clothes among them. After resting for half an hour, she wrote her will: she requested a complete service performed for her soul in St-Denis and St-Peter in Reims, with her servants attending; an annual obit to be founded for prayers for her soul in perpetuity, funded by selling her houses at Fontainebleau; her Trespagny estate to be kept as a marriage gift for one of the daughters of the Duc de Guise; and her debts to be discharged, including the 2,000 crowns given to Curle for his marriage portion. Her accounts were audited and she was granted various bequests of wages and gifts of money, for a hospital at Reims to be founded, her scholars supported and money given to four mendicants as her executors – Guise, Glasgow, Ross and du Ruisseau – saw fit.

Two hours after midnight she wrote her last letter to King Henri: 'This day, after dinner, I received notice of my sentence, that I should be executed tomorrow like a criminal.' She protested that she was innocent of any crime now and ever since she had been in England, her Catholicism being the sole reason for her condemnation. She asked for her servants to be given wages and pensions, and for the king to take Dr Bourgoing into his service and give du Preau a benefice.

8 February 1587: Delivered

In the morning Queen Mary remained in prayer until Dr Bourgoing begged her to break and take a little bread and wine. The sheriff arrived about nine o'clock. At the stairfoot leading into the hall, a kneeling, tearful Melville waited for her. Bidding him rise, she kissed him and asked that he pray for her. At her earnest request, Bourgoing, Gervais, Gourgon, Nicolas de la Mare and old Didier were allowed in; Jane Kennedy and Elspeth Curle were sent for and allowed to attend their mistress, while Melville himself carried her train.

She entered the hall wearing a French-embroidered black satin gown, set with acorn buttons in jet, and trimmed with pearl. The gown had a train and long sleeves, with a pair of purple velvet sleeves underneath. A veil of white lawn covered her head and gown. Her kirtle was figured black satin over a crimson velvet petticoat. About her neck she had a pomander chain and an Agnus Dei, a crucifix in her hand, and at her girdle hung rosary beads with a silver cross.

In the hall, steps led to the raised platform which was 2 feet high and 12 feet square, two sides railed and hung with black material. On one side seats had been placed for the Earls of

Shrewsbury and Kent. The headsman's block was about a foot in height and covered in black. Before it was a little black cushioned stool where Queen Mary could sit while her apparel was removed.

She refused flatly to hear the minister, who insisted on praying; she prayed louder and more zealously in Latin. Giving her servants her blessing, her maids, with the two executioners, disrobed her into her petticoat. She said, 'Never before have we been undressed before so many nor by such grooms.' As her maids removed her veil, mantle and train and her stomacher, she begged them to stay their weeping.

She knelt before the block and held her hands up to heaven, still clutching the crucifix. Taking a cambric kerchief with gold embroidery, Jane bandaged her eyes. The queen then placed her head in position, extending her neck, which she kept still, awaiting the blow. All the time she prayed: *'In manus tuus domine commendo* (Into Thy hands, O Lord, I commend my spirit).'

'And immediately her spirit passed away,' observed Bourgoing, 'and the Queen of Scots was delivered from all her cares.'

AFTER...

Body and head were placed together and covered with black cloth. When servants came to carry the corpse, movement revealed between her torso and head her little blood-covered terrier, who must have crept in with her under her skirts. He refused to move but was eventually carried away and washed. Everything touched by her blood was burnt or washed. The queen's body was opened and embalmed by a Stamford physician assisted by two surgeons. It was then encased in lead and coffined in wood.

On 25 February, Sir Amias Paulet brought the servants left at Chartley to Fotheringhay – M du Preau, Balthasar, Bastian with his wife and daughter, Curle's wife Barbara with Susanne, Hannibal, Symon the page, Robin Hamilton and Laurens – for none of these were to be discharged until after her funeral. Certain items were committed into the custody of Andrew Melville, Dr Bourgoing and Jane Kennedy for later distribution. Melville had charge of bed furniture with needlework of silver and gold silk, along with unfinished devices and arms, a piece of unicorn horn with a little pendant of gold, jewels, a cloth of estate and pictures of the late queen's ancestors – all to be delivered to King James.

On Sunday 30 July 1587, Garter King of Arms and five heralds came to Fotheringhay Castle. They laid the queen's body reverently into a royal coach at ten o'clock that night. Drawn by four horses covered with black velvet and the arms of Scotland, the corpse was conveyed by torchlight to Peterborough Cathedral, arriving around two o'clock in the morning, accompanied by seven of her officers: Andrew Melville as master of her household, Dr Bourgoing, Pierre Gourgon, Hannibal, Nicolas de la Mare, Jean Lauder and Jacques Gervais.

The bishop, dean and chapter, with Clarenceux King of Arms, received the coffin which, because the weather was very hot and the leaded coffin very heavy, causing fears the solder would part, was laid directly in a vault prepared in the choir opposite the tomb of Queen Katharine of Aragon. Workmen immediately set about making an arch of brick over the grave, leaving only an aperture to allow admittance the next day for the broken staves of office and the flags. In the middle of the choir of the black-hung cathedral was erected a hearse 26 feet square and 27 feet high, like a French *chapelle ardente* except covered with gold-fringed black velvet garnished with the arms of Scotland.

On Monday, her ladies were brought to the bishop's palace. The heralds asked if they wished anything amending or changing. They replied coldly it was not for them to find fault, for the whole was dependent on their mistress's pleasure.

On Tuesday 1 August the Countess of Bedford, acting as chief mourner, was placed under a cloth of estate of purple velvet. Around ten o'clock that morning the whole company was marshalled, led by two conductors in black carrying black staves, followed by fifty pairs of poor women mourners, the Standard of Scotland, Queen Mary's male servitors in cloaks followed by English gentlemen in cloaks and gowns, Mary's doctor, priest and master of the wardrobe, the Bishops of Peterborough and Lincoln, then the great banner and finally the master of her household Andrew Melville. The late queen's helm and crest was borne by Portcullis Herald; her target by York; her sword by Rouge-dragon and her coat by Somerset; all were followed by Clarenceux.

Six men bore the 'corpse', represented by a bier covered with black velvet with a crimson velvet pillow housing a jewelled crown, followed by eight bannerolles; the canopy of black velvet fringed with gold was borne by four knights, followed by Garter King of Arms. The bier was set within the royal hearse. The Countess of Bedford followed, supported by the Earls of Rutland and Lincoln, the English ladies and Mary's eight Scottish gentlewomen – Barbara Mowbray, Christily Hog, Gillis Mowbray, Elspeth Curle, Renee de Rallay, Marie Pagez, Jane Kennedy and Susanne Kirkcaldy – followed by 166 yeomen wearing black.

Before the Bishop of Lincoln began his sermon, all the Scottish queen's servants departed except for Melville. Afterwards, the chief mourner and her ladies made the offering, followed by the queen's achievements; then came the standard and great banner borne by the Earls of Rutland and Lincoln. After the service a dole was given to the poor, while those attending departed after their degrees to the bishop's palace for dinner.

Bibliography

Anderson, James, *Collections Relating to the History of Mary Queen of Scotland* (Edinburgh: 1727 and 1728)

Arnot, Hugo, *The History of Edinburgh* (Edinburgh and London: W Creech and J Murray, 1779)

Bain, Joseph (ed.), *Calendar of the State Papers Relating to Scotland and Mary Queen of Scots 1547 to 1603* (Edinburgh: H M General Register House, 1898-1900)

Bain, Joseph (ed.), *The Hamilton Papers: Letters and Papers Illustrating the Political Relations of England and Scotland* (Edinburgh: H M General Register House, 1890-1892)

Bagot, Lord, *Letters Relating to Mary Queen of Scots* (Birmingham: 1895)

Bannatyne Club from 16C MS of Sir John Maxwell of Pollock, *A Diurnal of Remarkable Occurrents that have passed within the Country of Scotland* (Edinburgh: 1833)

Barbe, Louis A., *In Byways of Scottish History* (London and Glasgow: Blackie and Son Limited, 1912)

Bell, Clara, *About Catherine de' Medici* (London: Macmillan and Co Ltd, 1897)

Bingham, Caroline, *Darnley: A Life of Henry Stuart, Lord Darnley Consort of Mary Queen of Scots* (London: Constable, 1995)

Birch, W de G, *Original Documents Relating to Sheffield, Principally in Connection with Mary Queen of Scots* (London: Journal of the British Archaeological Association, 1874)

Blakeway, Amy, *Religious Reform, the House of Guise and the Council of Fontainebleau: The French Memorial Service for Marie de Guise, August 1560,* (Études Épistémè [En ligne], 37 | 2020, mis en ligne le 01 octobre 2020, consulté le 13 mars 2023)

Bonner, Dr Elizabeth Ann, *The French Reactions to the Rough Wooings of Mary Queen of Scots,* (from Journal of the Sydney Society for Scottish History, vol 6 1998, pp. 9-161)

Boyd, William K, (ed.), *Calendar of State Papers relating to Scotland and Mary, Queen of Scots 1547-1603 Volumes III-IX* (Edinburgh: 1903-1915) (also accessed online: www.british-history.ac.uk/cal-state-papers/scotland – June 2023)

Brewer, J. S., Gairdner J. and R. H. Brodie, *Letters and Papers, Foreign and Domestic of the Reign of Henry VIII, 1509-1547, 21 Volumes and Addenda* (London, 1862-1932)

Brown, K. M., *The Records of the Parliaments of Scotland to 1707* (St Andrews: 2007-2022) (accessed online www.rps.ac.uk – May 2022)

Burns-Begg, Robert, *History of Lochleven Castle* (Kinross: George Barnet, 1887)

Burns-Begg, Robert, *The Secrets of my Prison House* (Kinross: George Barnet, 1901)

Burton, John Hill, (ed.), *The Register of the Privy Council of Scotland Vol I 1545-1569* (Edinburgh: H M General Register House, 1877)

Castelnau, Michael de, *Memoirs of the Reigns of Francis II and Charles IX of France* (London: 1724)

Chambers, R., *The Book of Days* (London & Edinburgh: W & R Chambers, 1864)

Chartrou, Josephe, *Les Entrees Solennelles et Triomphales a la Renaissance (1484-1551)* (Paris: 1928)

Cockburn, Henry and Thomas Maitland (eds), *Les Affaires du Conte de Boduel l'An 1568* (Edinburgh: 1829)

Cowan, Samuel, *The Last Days of Mary Stuart and the Journal of Bourgoyne her Physician* (London: Eveleigh Nash, 1907)

Crosby, Allan James (ed.), *Calendar of State Papers, Foreign Series of the Reign of Elizabeth 1566 to 1574* (London: Longman & Co., and Trubner & Co., 1871-1876)

Dallier, Jean, *C'est L'ordre & Forme qui a este tenue au Sacre & Couronnement de treshaulte & tresillustre Dame Madame Catharine de Medicis, Royne de France, faict en l'Eglise M. St Denys en France le x jour de Juin 1549* (Paris: 1549)

Dallier, Jean, *C'est L'ordre qui a este tenu à la nouvelle et joyeuse entrée, que treshault, tresexcellent, & trespuissant Prince, le Roy treschrestien Henry deuxiesme de ce nom, a faicte en sa bonne ville & cité de Paris, capitale de son royaume, le seziesme jour de Juin 1549* (Paris: 1549).

Dickinson, Gladys (ed.), *Two Missions of Jacques de la Brosse* (Edinburgh: Scottish History Society, 1942)

Donaldson, Gordon, *Mary, Queen of Scots* (London: The English Universities Press Ltd, 1974)

Drummond, William, *The History of Scotland from the Year 1423 to the Year 1542* (Glasgow: R Urie, 1749)

Ellis, Henry, *Original Letters, Illustrative of English History Vol II* (London: Harding, Triphook and Lepard, 1825)

Fleming, David Hay, *Mary Queen of Scots from her Birth to her Flight into England* (London: Hodder and Stoughton, 1897)

Forbes-Leith, William, *Narratives of Scottish Catholics under Mary Stuart and James VI* (London: Thomas Baker, 1889)

Fraser, William, *The Book of Carlaverock: Memoirs of the Maxwells, Earls of Nithsdale, Lords Maxwell and Herries, Vol. I* (Edinburgh: 1873)

Fraser, William, *The Douglas Book Vol. II Angus Memoirs* (Edinburgh: 1885)

Fraser, William, *The Lennox* (Edinburgh: 1874)

Gibb, Sir George Duncan, *The Life and Times of Robert Gib* (London: Longmans, Green, And Co., 1874)

Grant, James, *Memoirs and Adventures of Sir William Kirkaldy* (Edinburgh and London: William Blackwood and Sons, 1849)

Green, Mary Anne Everett, *Calendar of State Papers, Domestic Series, of the Reign of Elizabeth, Addenda 1566-1579* (London: Longman & Co., and Trubner & Co., 1871)

Guizot M and Madame Guizot de Witt, *France Vol III* (New York: Peter Fenelon Collier & Son, 1900)

Hardwicke, Philip Yorke, Earl of, *Miscellaneous State Papers from 1501 to 1726 Vol I* (London: W Strahan & T Cadell, 1778

Haynes, Samuel, *A Collection of State Papers* (London: William Bowyer, 1740)

Hearn, Thomas (ed.), *De Rebus Britannicis Collectanea of Joannis Lelandi Vol IV* (London: Benjamin White, 1774)

Herries, Lord, *Historical Memoirs for the Reign of Mary Queen of Scots* (Edinburgh: 1836)

HMSO, *Calendar of the Manuscripts of the Hon. The Marquis of Salisbury* (London, Eyre and Spottiswoode, 1883 to 1889) (also accessed online: *Calendar of the Cecil Papers in Hatfield House*: www.british-history.ac.uk/cal-cecil-papers – July 2023)

Hume, Martin A. S., (ed.), *Calendar of Letters and State Papers relating to English Affairs preserved principally in the Archives of Simancas, 1568-1586* (London: Eure and Spottiswoode, 1894-1896 (also accessed online www.british-history.ac.uk/cal-state-papers/Simancas/ – October 2023)

Irving, Joseph, *The Book of Dumbartonshire* (Edinburgh and London: W and A K Johnston, 1879)

Jackson, Richard A., *Vive le Roi! A History of the French Coronation* (USA: University of North Carolina Press, 1984)

Knights, Jan-Marie, *The Tudor Socialite* (Stroud: Amberley Publishing, 2021)

Labanoff, Prince Alexandre, *Lettres, Instructions et Memoires de Marie Stuart* (Londres: Charles Dolman, 1844)

Lang, Andrew, *John Knox and the Reformation* (London: Longmans, Green and Co., 1905)

Lasry, George, Norbert Biermann & Satoshi Tomokiyo (2023): *Deciphering Mary Stuart's lost letters from 1578-1584,* (From Cryptologia, https://doi.org/10.1080/01611194.2022.2160677 – Accessed February 2023)

Lawson, John Parker, *Historical Tales of the Wars of Scotland* (Edinburgh, London and Dublin: A Fullarton & Co., 1849)

Leader, John Daniel, *Mary Queen of Scots in Captivity* (Sheffield: Leader & Sons, 1880)

Lemon, Robert (ed.) *Calendar of State Papers Domestic: Edward VI, Mary and Elizabeth* (London: 1855 to 1872) (also accessed online: www.british-history.ac.uk/cal-state-papers/domestic/edw-eliz – June 2023)

Lesley, John, *The History of Scotland by John Lesley Bishop of Ross* (Edinburgh: 1830)

Lodge, Edmund, *Illustrations of British History, Biography, and Manners Volume II Second edition*, (London: John Chidley, 1838)

Lovell, Mary S., *Bess of Hardwick* (London: Abacus, 2006)

MacGeorge, Andrew, *Miscellaneous Papers, Principally Illustrative of Events in the Reigns of Queen Mary and King James VI* (Glasgow: 1834)

Mackay, A. E. J. G., (ed.), *The Historie and Cronicles of Scotland by Robert Lindesay of Pitscottie* (Edinburgh and London: William Blackwood and Sons, 1899)

Maidment, James, *The Chronicle of Perth: A Register of Remarkable Occurrences* (Edinburgh: 1831)

Marjoreybanks, George, *Annals of Scotland from the Yeir 1514 to the Yeir 1591* (Edinburgh: 1814)

Marles, Jean de, *The Life of Mary Stuart, queen of Scots* (Boston: P Donahoe, 1857)

Massellin, Robert, *L'entrée du Roy nostre Sire faicte en sa ville de Rouen le mecredy premier de ce moys d'Octobre, pareillement celle de la Royne qui fut le jour ensuyant.* (Paris: 1550)

Maxwell, Sir Herbert, *A History of the House of Douglas* (London: Freemantle & Co., 1902)

Melville, Sir James, *Memoirs of his Own Life* (Edinburgh: 1827)

Mignet, F. A., *The History of Mary, Queen of Scots* (London: MacMillan and Co Ltd, 1899)

Morris, John, *The Letter-Books of Sir Amias Poulet* (London: Burns and Oates, 1874)

Mourey, Gabriel, *Le Livre des Fetes Francaises* (Paris: 1930)

Mumby, Frank Arthur, *The Fall of Mary Stuart: A Narrative in Contemporary Letters* (London: Constable & Company Ltd, 1921)

Murdin, William, *A Collection of State Papers Relating to Affairs in the Reign of Queen Elizabeth from the Year 1571 to 1596* (London: William Bowyer, 1759)

Noble, Alexandre le, *Histoire du Sacre et du Couronnement des Rois et Reines de France* (Paris: 1825)

Paul, Sir James Balfour (ed), *Accounts of the Lord High Treasurer of Scotland Vol III and Vol IV 1506-1507 and 1507-1513* (Edinburgh: H M General Register House, 1901 and 1902)

Pollen, John Hungerford, *Mary Queen of Scots and the Babington Plot* (Edinburgh: Scottish History Society, 1922)

Prescott-Innes, R., *The Funeral of Mary Queen of Scots* (1890)

Rait, Robert S. (ed.), *Mary Queen of Scots 1542-1587* (London: David Nutt, 1900)

Raumer, Frederick von, *Contributions to Modern History from the British Museum and the State Paper Office: Queen Elizabeth and Mary Queen of Scots* (London: Charles Knight & Co., 1836)

Rawdon Brown and G Cavendish Bentinck (ed.), *Calendar of State Papers Relating to English Affairs in the Archives of Venice* (London: 1890)

Rigg, J. J. (ed.) *Calendar of State Papers Relating to English Affairs in the Vatican Archives, Volume I, 1558-1571* (London: 1916)

Robertson, Joseph (ed.), *Inventaires de la Royne Descosse Douairiere de France* (Edinburgh: 1863)

Robertson, William, *History of Scotland Vol II* (London: Whitmore and Fenn, 1824)

Roeder, Ralph, *Catherine de' Medici and the Lost Revolution* (New York: The Viking Press, 1937)

Rubay, Le Baron Alphonse de, *Premiere Jeunesse de Marie Stuart* (Paris: 1891)

Ruthen, Lord, *Miscellanea Antiqua Anglicana Vol I: Some Particulars of the Life of David Riccio Chief Favourite of Mary, Queen of Scots to which is Added the Relation of his Death written by the Lord Ruthven, one of the principals concerned in that action* (London: Robert Triphook, 1816)

Sauval, Henri, *Histoire et Recherches des Antiquites de la Ville de Paris, Tome Second* (Paris: Charles Moette, 1724)

Sceve, Maurice, *The Entry of Henri II into Lyon September 1548* (Arizona: 1997)

Schiern, Frederik, *Life of James Hepburn Earl of Bothwell (translated from the Danish by Rev. David Berry)* (Edinburgh: David Douglas, 1880)

Scott, Alexander Malcolm, *The Battle of Langside* (Glasgow: Hugh Hopkins, 1885)

Secombe, Thomas, (ed.), *Tudor Tracts 1532-1588* (Westminster: Archibald Constable and Co Ltd., 1903)

Seton, George, *A History of the Family of Seton* (Edinburgh: T and A Constable, 1896)

Small, John, The Poetical Works of Gavin Douglas, Bishop of Dunkeld, Volume First (Edinburgh: William Paterson, 1874)

Smeaton, Oliphant, *William Dunbar* (New York: Charles Scribner's Sons, 1898)

Smith, G. Gregory (ed.), *Scottish History by Contemporary Writers: The Days of James iiii 1488-1513* (London: David Nutt, 1890)

Stair-Kerr, Eric, *Stirling Castle: Its Place in Scottish* History (Glasgow: James Maclehose and sons, 1913)

Stevenson, Rev. Joseph (ed.), *The History of Mary Stewart by Claude Nau, her Secretary* (Edinburgh: William Paterson, 1883)

Stevenson, Rev. Joseph (ed.), *Calendar of State Papers, Foreign Series, of the Reign of Elizabeth 1558-1559* (London: Longman Green, Longman, Roberts & Green, 1863)

Stevenson, Rev. Joseph (ed.), *Calendar of State Papers, Foreign Series of the Reign of Elizabeth 1560-1561 and 1562* (London: Longman, Green, Reader and Dyer, 1865 and 1867)

Stevenson, Rev. Joseph (ed.), *Calendar of State Papers, Foreign Series of the Reign of Elizabeth 1564-1565* (London: Longman & Co and Trubner & Co., 1870 and 1871)

Storer, J. & H. S., *Views in Edinburgh and its Vicinity Vol. II* (Edinburgh: A Constable & Co, 1820)

Strickland, Agnes, *Letters of Mary, Queen of Scots* (London: Henry Colburn, 1842)

Strickland, Agnes, *Lives of the Queens of Scotland and English Princesses Vols. I to VII* (Edinburgh and London: William Blackwood and Sons, 1850-1858)

Stoddart, Jane T., *The Girlhood of Mary Queen of Scots* (London: Hodder and Stoughton, 1908)

Stuart, Marie W., *The Scot Who Was a Frenchman* (London, Edinburgh & Glasgow: William Hodge and Company Limited, 1940)

Taylor, James, *The Pictorial History of Scotland* (London: James S Virtue, 1859)

Taylor, John, *The Illustrated Guide to Sheffield* (Sheffield: Pawson and Brailsford, 1879)

Taylor, Rev. J. W., *Historical Antiquities of Fife* (Edinburgh: Johnstone, Hunter, & Co., 1875)

Teulet, A, *Lettres de Marie Stuart* (Paris: Librairie de Firmin Didot Freres, 1859)

Thomson, Thomas, *A Collection of Inventories and other records of the royal wardrobe and jewelhouse, and of the artillery and munition in some of the royal castles* (Edinburgh: 1815)

Trollope, T. A., *The Girlhood of Catherine de' Medici* (London: Chapman and Hall, 1856)

Turnbull, William B, *Calendar of State Papers Foreign: Edward VI 1547-1553* (London: HMSO, 1861)

Turnbull, William, *Letters of Mary Stuart, Queen of Scotland* (London: Charles Dolman, 1845)

Udall, William, *The Historie of the Life and Death of Mary Stuart Queene of* Scotland (London: John Haviland, 1636)

Warnicke, Retha M., *Mary Queen of Scots* (London and New York: Routledge, 2006)

Williams, Neville, *Thomas Howard Fourth Duke of Norfolk* (New York: R P Dutton & Co Inc, 1965)

Williams, H. Noel, *Henri II: His Court and Times* (New York: Charles Scribner's Sons, 1910)

Williams, H. Noel, *The Brood of False Lorraine: The History of the Ducs de Guise* (1496-1588) (London: Hutchinson and Co., 1918)

Wood, Marguerite (ed.), *Foreign Correspondence with Marie de Lorraine Queen of Scotland* (Edinburgh: Scottish History Society, 1928)

Wood, Mary Anne Everett, *Letters of Royal and Illustrious Ladies of Great Britain Volume* I (London: Henry Colburn, 1846)